Mass Communication
Research

edited by
W. Phillips Davison
Frederick T. C. Yu

The Praeger Special Studies program—utilizing the most modern and efficient book production techniques and a selective worldwide distribution network—makes available to the academic, government, and business communities significant, timely research in U.S. and international economic, social, and political development.

Mass Communication Research

Major Issues and Future Directions

PRAEGER SPECIAL STUDIES IN INTERNATIONAL POLITICS AND GOVERNMENT

Praeger Publishers   New York   Washington   London

Library of Congress Cataloging in Publication Data

Davison, Walter Phillips, 1918-
    Mass communication research.

    (Praeger special studies in international politics
and government)
    Bibliography: p.
    1. Mass media—Research.   I. Yu, Te-chi,
1921-   joint author.   II. Title.
P91.D37   301.16'1'072   74-5576
ISBN 0-275-09320-4
ISBN 0-275-88870-3 (pbk.)

PRAEGER PUBLISHERS
111 Fourth Avenue, New York, N.Y. 10003, U.S.A.
5, Cromwell Place, London SW7 2JL, England

Published in the United States of America in 1974
by Praeger Publishers, Inc.

Printed in the United States of America

PREFACE AND ACKNOWLEDGMENTS

Preparation of this volume started in the summer of 1972. The editors, assisted by a small advisory group, reviewed the available literature on directions in mass communication research and drew up a list of areas into which they felt the field could be subdivided. The advisory group consisted of Professors Allen Barton, Herbert Gans, and Paul F. Lazarsfeld of Columbia University; Professor Gladys Engel Lang of the State University of New York at Stony Brook; Professor Walter Weiss of the City University of New York; and Professor Elihu Katz of the Hebrew University of Jerusalem, who was then teaching at the Columbia summer session.

A set of guidelines and suggestions regarding the treatment of individual areas was then prepared, and topics were assigned to a number of communication researchers, each of whom was requested to write a paper dealing with a designated area. Authors of individual papers were free to follow or ignore the guidelines and accept or reject any suggestions made by the editors. Each, therefore, followed a slightly different approach, conditioned by individual interests. In general, however, all the prepared papers deal with two broad questions: What is the current state of knowledge with respect to the area in question? And what might be the most fruitful directions for future research?

In May 1973, a two-day conference was held at Arden House in Harriman, New York, to discuss the papers. This conference was attended by the authors and editors of this volume, and also by the following, who kindly consented to provide their advice: Elie Abel, Forrest P. Chisman, Marc Glassman, Gladys Engel Lang, Kurt Lang, William J. McGuire, Ithiel de Sola Pool, John P. Robinson, Bernard Roshco, Eli A. Rubinstein, Walter Weiss, and Charles R. Wright. The conference, at least for the undersigned editors, proved to be a stimulating and exciting occasion, and would have been so even without a violent thunderstorm, which punctuated one of the evening sessions.

Based in part on the discussion at the Arden House conference, the authors revised and extended their papers. These revised versions are presented to the reader in this volume, together with an introduction and a concluding chapter, both of which also benefited from the conference discussions. Any deficiencies in the individual chapters must be laid at the door of the authors and editors jointly; flaws in the volume as a whole are the responsibility of the editors alone.

We should like to express our deep appreciation to all those who cooperated in the preparation of this survey—to our advisory group, to the authors of the individual chapters, to those who attended the Arden House conference, to Judith Devons, who edited the chapters for publication, and especially to the John and Mary R. Markle Foundation, which, through a generous grant to the Graduate School of Journalism, Columbia University, made the whole undertaking possible.

W. Phillips Davison
Frederick T. C. Yu

CONTENTS

Mass Communication
Research

AN ATTEMPT
TO STRUCTURE THE FIELD
W. Phillips Davison
Frederick T. C. Yu

During the past two decades the amount of attention devoted to communication research has increased enormously. Programs leading to advanced degrees in communication have been established at dozens of universities; new research centers devoted to the study of the mass media have proliferated; journals specializing in research on communication have grown in circulation, and new journals have been started. Technological developments, such as communication satellites and cable television, have stimulated public interest in research on the problems and possibilities they conjure up.

Yet, during the same period, one could frequently encounter statements to the effect that communication research was without direction, sterile, or "running out of steam." One authority wrote in 1959: "My theme is that, as for communication research, the state is withering away" (Berelson, 1959). Another, writing more recently, entitled his article, "The Famine in Mass Communications Research" (Gans, 1972).

Why is a field, so obviously alive, so often buried? Part of the answer may be that communication research has grown to such a size and expanded in so many directions that a single scholar has difficulty in perceiving its outlines and keeping track of developments in it. Probably of greater significance is the fact that so much communication research does lack direction: it neither contributes to basic theory nor is it helpful in solving practical problems. On the one hand, researchers appear to be swimming in circles around small islands of theory established in the 1940s and 1950s; on the other, they are dashing off in all directions to describe widely disparate aspects of the communication process in varied contexts. A meeting of UNESCO consultants in 1971 referred to "the many discrete piles of unintegrated data which litter the communication research field," and criticized the lack of continuity in research which, they felt, was not making the best use of scarce resources (UNESCO, September 1971, p. 5).

This lack of continuity is emphasized by the extent to which many questions posed by communication researchers in the past have not been attacked and many promising areas of inquiry have not been followed up. More than ten years ago, in an afterword to Steiner's *People Look at Television*, Lazarsfeld (1963) outlined a number of areas in which significant research was missing. Most of it is still missing. Breed's landmark study of social control in the newsroom (1955) has been replicated only recently, but our understanding of the phenomena involved has scarcely been advanced. The work of H. A. Innis (1950) on the relationship between characteristics of communication channels and types of political structures remains as fresh as the day it was published. Some other lines of inquiry have been pursued more systematically, but the record of discontinuity is impressive.

Direction and relatedness can be given to the efforts of students in a given field by an overarching theory to which the work of all contributes, or by a common recognition of certain major problems, or, preferably, by both. Yet communication research enjoys neither of these unifying elements. One can document this lack of consensus by examining chapter titles and section headings in texts and "readers" on mass communication, works in which conceptual integration and identification of major problems would presumably be pushed as far as possible. There is some overlap in major categories, much of which can probably be traced to Lasswell's (1948) seminal description of communication research as the study of who says what, to whom, through what channel, with what effect; or to the somewhat more complicated model suggested by Westley and MacLean (1957). But beyond sharing a few terms— such as "audience," "content," "effect," and "feedback"—each work tends to reflect idiosyncratic conceptions and interests.

Unfortunately, these criticisms apply also to the present volume. We have not been able to provide an integrative theory; neither can we be assured that the research problems we have identified are the most significant ones. We have, however, sought to structure the field in such a manner that the interrelatedness of its parts is more apparent. And we have tried to suggest directions for future research that will fill some of the existing gaps in knowledge. If the exercise stimulates further efforts along these lines, then it will have served its purpose.

COMMUNICATIONS AS BUILDING BLOCKS FOR PERSONALITY AND CULTURE

In order to structure an area, one must step back until the whole area is in view. The realm of communication is so large that to see it as a whole one must include nearly all aspects of social life and culture, leading almost to the point of professional solipsism, where nothing but communication seems to exist or have reality: the human personality is a product of communication; human culture and all social institutions are products of communication.

Instead of rejecting this conception, which at first sight would appear to be so broad as to be unmanageable, let us accept it at least for heuristic purposes and see where it leads. There is considerable authority for it, even though as far as we know it has never been expressed so baldly. Observation of a small number of unfortunate beings who have been kept in almost complete isolation since infancy has shown that they lack most of those characteristics that we define as human. As a result of greatly attenuated communication, the personality has not developed (Davis, 1940; Wassermann, 1924). Their behavior is close to that associated with animals, whose opportunities for communication are limited more by biological than by social factors. The part played by communication in the formation of personality was also stressed by George Herbert Mead, among others, who saw the conception of the self as emerging from interaction between the individual and the social environment (Strauss, 1956). Similar notions are expressed fairly frequently in more recent writings of social psychologists and sociologists.

Specialists in communication, also, have hinted at the fundamental role of interaction among individuals in the formation of personality, although without spelling out the implications of this view for the development of the self. There is, for example, the conception of person-to-person communication as an adaptive process analogous to biological evolution (Ivey and Hurst, 1971). And communication has been defined as the study of ways in thich people affect each other (Darnell, 1971), a view that could be stretched into an explanation of the formation of personality. The most explicit statement along these lines that we have encountered is that of Montagu (1967, p. 450), who writes: "The most important agency through which the child learns to be human is communication, verbal and also non-verbal."

Anthropologists and others sometimes refer to communication as a building block of culture. Indeed, one of the chapter titles in Hall's (1959) *Silent Language* is "Culture Is Communication." Kroeber and Kluckhohn (1952, p. 181), as a part of their definition of culture, note that it consists of "patterns, explicit and implicit, of and for behavior acquired and transmitted by symbols. . . ." Matson and Montagu (1967), in their *Human Dialogue*, include a section entitled "Culture as Communication."

If we are willing to accept, at least for heuristic purposes, that culture is a product of communication and is transmitted by communication, it is a short and easy jump to the view that all social organization results from the interchange of ideas among people. This view is supportable on the level of personal experience and common sense. If you want to form an organization you get on the telephone, or you personally invite a number of people to meet in your living room. And what is any organization beyond a complex of conferences, telephone calls, memoranda, reports, and instructions! There may be in addition a building and physical equipment, but these do not constitute organization. It is communication that makes possible decision making, coordination of effort, and the exercise of power.

When we study communication, we are dealing with life itself: human life (as distinct from biological life) and social life. The newborn infant is, for our purposes, a biological mechanism that has potentialities as a sender and receiver of messages. It acquires humanity as a result of the process of interacting with other individuals. The human personality is a nexus of communication. Human life, as distinguished from animal or vegetable life, begins when communication starts; it ends when there is no more communication, even though a heartbeat may still be detected. The tiny baby becomes a human being as we talk to it and care for it, and as it expresses its feelings and needs to us through contented or unhappy noises, wiggles, and kicks—and we react to these. With amazing speed, a personality begins to emerge from this interactive process, but it is never fully formed. Although a personality is more and more difficult to modify as the years go by, it continues to develop as long as the individual communicates with other human beings, and they with him.

The real person, as distinguished from the physical organism, is invisible. He or she is a complex of sentiments and ideas expressed to others and by others. Thus, we are totally interdependent. Each person is the product of all the contacts ever experienced with other people, directly or indirectly. Our voices, gestures, and nervous systems reflect and refract the stimuli to which we have been exposed.

This does not mean that the physical organism is unimportant in the development of personality; it is of enormous importance. Even though the personality itself is a nexus of communications, the organism initially determines which communications are sent or received, and it continues to exert an influence on communication in both directions through life. We recognize this crudely when we accept that a person who is hard of hearing receives fewer communications than one who has sharp ears, or that a child who is tired learns less in the classroom than one who is wide awake, or that some infants are able to express their feelings and needs more loudly than others. But what about those physical and chemical differences among human organisms that are so minute as to be almost undetectable? It is logical to assume that these, also, affect the sending and receiving abilities of the individual. Neurophysiologists attending a conference on media research in 1973 stressed that the biological aspects of communication, the central nervous system and the frequency of its malfunctioning, should not be excluded from the attention of those studying the future of the mass media (*Information or Noise?* 1974).

The importance of the physical organism in the development of personality is one reason parents can take only limited credit or blame for the personalities of the children they foster. They may be able to control most of the communications that reach the infant, but the organism that processes these communications and reacts to them is a composite of many generations extending back to times unknown.

Interaction between the organism and communications that are sent and received rapidly produces a variety of psychological constructs, which we refer to by such terms as attitudes, values, images, and beliefs. These constructs then take on a life of their own and help to determine what further communications are received and what happens to them—how they are interpreted and whether they are remembered or forgotten. The same constructs help to determine more complex needs and their mode of expression.

Thus, there seem to be three principal elements involved in forming the individual's personality: communication, which serves as a link with the family and with society as a whole; the organism; and the psychological constructs to which interaction between the first two elements give rise.

It is much the same with social organizations, whether large or small, formal or informal. They are products of intercommunication among people, mediated by physical surroundings and technologies which, initially at least, determine who can communicate with whom, and how frequently or easily.

The environment also conditions needs. It is reasonable that people who live in valleys and fish in streams should communicate among themselves differently and form different types of social organization from those who live on plains and subsist by hunting. But organizations, like individuals, soon develop constructs for filtering incoming and outgoing communications. These include customs and behavior patterns, norms and goals. Such constructs, once established, influence the course of an organization's development long after the needs that led to their initial formation may have been forgotten. Or, if the constructs change, then the organization's structure itself will change. If communication is cut off, the organization dies.

The communications that enable personalities and social organizations to form and function are made possible by a variety of mechanisms for sending and receiving messages. These mechanisms include physiological components (eye, ear, nose, throat, nerve endings, organs used in gesturing) as well as systems of signs and symbols (primarily languages), social organizations (intelligence networks, news networks, rumor chains, mass meetings), and complicated products of modern technology (computer composition and television satellites). Some of these mechanisms play a part in shaping messages that are sent; others affect the way in which messages are received or perceived. The mechanisms, in turn, are affected by the physical and social environments of those who use them. Some environments offer materials for making drums of papyrus; others offer skills for constructing transistor radios. Some cultures emphasize keenness of hearing and sharpness of eye; others place more stress on loudness of voice.

If there is insufficient need for a communication mechanism, it will not be used. This might seem like a self-evident statement, but it has not been taken into account by those who assume that a mechanism will be adopted just because it is technologically possible. Whether two-way cable television will actually lead to some phenomenon resembling an electronic town meeting, as often predicted by futurists, will depend on the political and economic forces affecting the needs of broadcasters and on the number and characteristics of individuals who might be motivated to participate (Parker, 1970b). Conversely, the existence of a channel may create needs for the receiver, the sender, or both—as has been the case with advertising. Those who become literate, thus gaining access to new channels of communication, also develop new needs and these in turn affect the needs of other communicators and receivers (Sagasti, 1972).

The content of any message sent or perceived can be explained by examining the sender, receiver, and channel, and the relationships among them. Commercial television fare, for instance, is shaped in part by the fact that many people view television in family groups, especially at certain hours. Broadcasters, aware of this, try to select programs that will appeal to people of different ages. Those who create plots and dialogue shape them in such a way that they are redundant and predictable, so that they can easily be followed by people who may be distracted by each other or miss segments of a program while in the kitchen or bathroom. Commercial breaks serve the same function. Print, on the other hand, is consumed individually; redundancy and interruptions are non-functional to the needs of the sender or receiver. The relationship among the three primary elements in the communication process is quite different (Chaffee, 1972, p. 114). The same three variables can be used to explain the content of a face-to-face conversation, a telephone call, or a cable sent by an ambassador to the foreign office of his government.

Students of communication are thus concerned with the ways in which messages of all types affect the formation and functioning of the human personality and social organizations, and with the mechanisms by which these messages are sent and received. Three principal elements are involved: the individual, the collectivity, and the channel. These can serve as basic categories for communication studies, and are so used in this book.

SENDERS AND RECEIVERS OF MESSAGES

A further breakdown is suggested by the fact that each individual and each collectivity is both a sender and a receiver of messages, and must be considered in both roles. What is the significance for the individual of what he says, or writes, as well as what he hears and sees? How do outgoing as well as incoming communications affect the functioning of an organization?

If we use lines to indicate two-way communication channels, the simplest model of communication in society consists of double lines linking individuals with individuals, collectivities with collectivities, and individuals with collectivities, as shown in Figure 1.

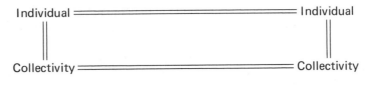

FIGURE 1

But the mass media introduce new dimensions into this model. They are themselves social organizations within which individual personalities play a strong role. Like other organizations, they serve as senders and receivers of messages, but they are distinguished from other organizations in that they more often serve as selective relay stations for messages originated elsewhere. One of the principal tasks of mass communication research is to explain why some messages are relayed and others are not; why some information is modified in the relay process, and how this occurs. To construct a simple model of communication processes in which the mass media are involved, we must link them with individuals and collectivities, as shown in Figure 2.

With the addition of the mass media to the model, ten kinds of basic communication processes are indicated. These are listed below, together with examples of each:

1. From an individual to one or more others (remark made by a speaker in a conversation).
2. To an individual from another (remark heard by a listener in a conversation).
3. From an individual to a collectivity (complaint to the gas company).
4. From a collectivity to an individual (bill from the gas company).
5. From one collectivity to another (a diplomatic note that is sent).
6. To one collectivity from another (a diplomatic note that is received).
7. From a mass medium to an individual (news satisfying an individual need).
8. To a mass medium from an individual (a letter to the editor).
9. From a mass medium to a collectivity (news satisfying an organizational need).
10. To a mass medium from a collectivity (a public relations release).

Communication processes of greater complexity consist of various combinations of these basic units. A converstaion involves the first two: a speaker and a listener. If the speaker is a prominent figure, and a reporter is taking part in the conversation, the message may be relayed in whole or in part to other individuals and organizations by a mass medium. And one mass medium may communicate with another. Communication research is concerned with all of these processes and combinations of them.

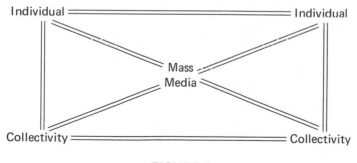

FIGURE 2

THE TASK OF MASS COMMUNICATION RESEARCH

Mass communication researchers are particularly concerned with processes in which the mass media are involved. In common with all students of communication, they study the ways in which the interchange of messages affects the behavior of individuals and organizations and the mechanisms by which these messages are sent and received. But their attention is focused primarily on messages that are rapidly transmitted and accessible to large numbers of receivers.

The mass media are of particular interest to those concerned with applied social research, not only because of the large numbers of individuals and collectivities affected by them but also because they are relatively more manipulable than other communication mechanisms. The role they play in society can be influenced by conscious decisions, even though these decisions are not always made. Social engineers can design media systems to serve particular needs of senders and receivers in huge areas, as has been done in the Soviet Union and China in recent times. A publisher or broadcaster can, within a short period, meet specialized needs as they arise—whether the needs are shared by an esoteric group, such as operations researchers, or are of a less recondite nature, such as those of rock music fans. Abuses in the mass media, once identified, can sometimes be corrected by pressure of public opinion, industry codes, or various forms of regulation. Other forms of communication may change, too, but ordinarily more slowly and with more difficulty. Patterns of interpersonal communication are culturally defined and change only as cultures change. Languages are only slightly more manipulable. The human voice and the human ear seem to have retained substantially the same characteristics for thousands of years; they cannot easily be restructured on demand. Decision-makers and public opinion have more control over the mass media.

Mass communication research cannot, however, exclude attention to other categories of communication and the mechanisms they involve. In order to deal with its central questions, communication research must include study of the interfaces between the media and person-to-person or organization-to-organization channels. How do modern systems affect older, oral systems, and vice versa? How can the two systems function most fruitfully in concert to satisfy individual and social needs? These interfaces have received some attention from students of developing countries, from those concerned with news and information diffusion, and from those examining patterns of opinion leadership, but much more attention is desirable. There are many ways in which the mass media affect the basic communication processes in which they are not directly involved, (those numbered one through six above). Perhaps they can serve some of the expressive needs of individuals more effectively. Perhaps they can do more to help people communicate with the leadership of large organizations to which they belong, thus promoting organizational democracy.

Research on the central questions involved in mass communication also requires familiarity with as much as possible of the work of specialists in all those fields that impinge in some way on the communication process: the psychologist studying perception, the anthropologist analyzing linguistic patterns, the sociologist investigating the structure of large organizations, the economist examining entrepreneurship, and many others. Since each question has a historical dimension, the work of historians is also relevant. Ethical dimensions, comparative dimensions, and artistic dimensions involve other fields of study. The physiologist who dissects the ear and the engineer who constructs an information retrieval system also have something to offer. The mass communication researcher thus functions as a bridge between the media and all bodies of knowledge that can help answer the central questions regarding them. All specialists have the right and the obligation to borrow any ideas that will be useful to them, but the communication researcher must be a particularly compulsive kleptomaniac.

THE ORGANIZATION OF THIS VOLUME

One could section the field of mass communication research into numerous subdivisions of varying types, depending on the criteria used. If the above conceptual scheme is followed, three principal areas for research emerge: (1) relationships between the individual and the mass media, (2) relationships between social organizations and the mass media, and (3) the way these relationships interact with communication mechanisms and technologies to result in the formation of particular types of message content.

Each of these areas could be subdivided further, depending on the degree of detail in which they were explored and the particular aspects of each area that were emphasized.

In this volume, the relationship between the individual and the mass media is examined from two standpoints: First, how does the individual experience the mass media, and what uses does he make of them (Katz, Blumler, and Gurevitch)? Second, how do the media contribute to the formation of the individual personality and to socialization of the individual in general (Hyman)? The first approach is concerned primarily with relatively short-term and consciously experienced uses and gratifications; the second with longer-term and mainly extra-conscious results of individual exposure. For the sake of completeness, it would have been desirable to add a third approach: How do the media serve the expressive needs of the individual? In what ways do they, directly or indirectly, enable him to communicate with others?

Relationships between social organizations and the mass media are considered in the three following chapters. One consists of a general survey of these relationships (Davison). A second focuses mainly on national states (Lerner). The third examines relationships between the media and government (Bobrow). This last set of relationships was singled out for special attention in view of the continuing debate in democratic states over the proper roles of government with respect to the mass media, and of the media with respect to government.

Mass media mechanisms are likewise treated in three chapters. The first examines the internal structure and functioning of the media themselves, with emphasis on the role of the journalist (Bagdikian). The second explores some of the ways in which management decisions may affect media content (Bogart). The third deals with questions raised by new communication technologies (Parker).

This scheme for subdividing the field omits a number of categories that have traditionally served as chapter and section headings in volumes on mass communication research. Perhaps most noticeable is the absence of any section labeled "effect." This is because we felt that all aspects of communication involve effects. The term is so broad as to be unhelpful when it comes to specifying particular questions for study. Similarly, "content" is involved in all communication processes. It is not a useful category for our purposes, since efforts to explain content must invariably lead back to the characteristics of senders, receivers, and the mechanisms used. We omitted "audience" as a major heading on the grounds that all individuals and groups are both senders and receivers of messages. To consider the "receivership" role by itself would be less enlightening than trying to think about the total relationship between mass communication mechanisms and those who use them. No chapters on perception, attention, and other psychological concepts were included since these concepts enter into many aspects of the communication process; they are used in the study of numerous questions relating to the mass media. We did not include "political communication," "advertising," or "international communication" as separate headings since we hoped that propositions could be developed that would apply to many kinds of individuals, collectivities, and situations, rather than specifically to politics, business, or international relations. The level of generality we are seeking is indicated by a remark applying to the study of international communication: "We should move more rapidly toward treating phenomena that cross national lines as instances of phenomena that occur in several types of social units" (Bobrow, 1972, p. 55). The same observation could be made with regard to the study of political or business communication.

Our aim was to subdivide mass communication research in such a way that the categories established could collectively include all questions of present or potential interest to mass communication researchers and at the same time would be discrete and overlap each other as little as possible. We are under no illusions that the scheme described satisfies these criteria completely. Nevertheless, it has proved to be a useful one for our purposes, and we hope that it can be refined further.

Regardless of whether the taxonomy we have adopted here proves to be fruitful for future research, we feel that development of the best possible way of subdividing the field deserves more emphasis than it has received so far. A systematic scheme for classifying communication research is not the same thing as an overarching theory, and cannot take the place of a theory, but it may help to identify areas that have received insufficient attention and to enhance the degree to which each research advance can be related to other research findings. A coherent taxonomy is necessary if communication research is to lead to a systematic body of knowledge rather than to a collection of discrete insights and data.

2

USES OF MASS COMMUNICATION
BY THE INDIVIDUAL

Elihu Katz
Jay G. Blumler
Michael Gurevitch

Suppose that we were studying not broadcasting and society in mid-twentieth century America but opera and society in mid-nineteenth century Italy. After all, opera in Italy during that period was a "mass" medium. What would we be studying? It seems likely, for one thing, that we would be interested in the attributes of the medium—what might today be called its "grammar"—for example, the curious convention that makes it possible to sing contradictory emotions simultaneously. We would also be interested in the functions of the medium for the individual and society; the perceptions of expressed and underlying values; the phenomena of stardom, fanship, and connoisseurship; the festive ambience that the medium created; and so on. It seems quite unlikely that we would be studying the effects of a particular opera on opinions and attitudes, even though some operas were written with explicit political, social, and moral aims in mind. The study of short-term effects, in other words, would not have had a high priority, although it might have had a place. The emphasis, by and large, would have been on the medium as a cultural institution with its own social and psychological functions and, perhaps, long-term effects.

We have all been over the reasons why mass communication research took a different turn, preferring to look at specific programs as specific messages with, possibly, specific effects: we were social psychologists interested in persuasion and attitude change; we were political scientists interested in new forms of social control; we were commissioned to measure message effectiveness for marketing organizations, public health agencies, churches, political organizations, or the broadcasting organizations themselves; and we were asked whether the media were not causes of violent and criminal behavior. If we had been asked whether one specific opera incites to violence or whether another incites to revolution, it is doubtful that we would have attempted an answer without reference to the over-all place of the opera in the lives of its audience. With a theory of the uses of the medium one has a better chance of understanding its effects.

But the case for uses and gratifications research should not be stated only in terms of its capacity to enhance and refine the study of mass communication effects. The uses and gratifications approach has proposed concepts and presented evidence that are likely to explain the media behavior of individuals more powerfully than the more remote sociological, demographic, and personality variables (Weiss, 1971). Compared with classical effects studies, the uses and gratifications approach takes the media consumer rather than the media message as its starting point, and explores his communication behavior in terms of his direct experience with the media. It views members of the audience as actively utilizing media contents, rather than being passively acted upon by the media. Thus, it does not assume a direct relationship between messages and effects, but postulates instead that members of the audience put messages to use, and that such usages act as intervening variables in the process of effect.

Furthermore, the uses and gratifications approach provides a broader perspective for the exploration of individual media behavior by tying it to the continuous search for the ways in which humans create and gratify needs. While many of the needs studied up to now might be described as media-related, others are not necessarily dependent on media use and thus may be gratified through either media or non-media sources. Thus, exposure to the media constitutes one set of "functional alternatives" for the satisfaction of needs, which should be compared, in the first instance, with the function of other leisure pursuits. The approach postulates that gratifications can be derived not only from media content, but also from the very act of exposure to a given medium, as well as from the social context in which it is consumed. This facilitates a dynamic view of the totality of factors involved in media consumption, suggesting ways in which a division of labor may be said to obtain among the different media, and offering insights into the constant shifting and transformation of media roles by media users. Consequently, the approach facilitates comparisons among different media and types of content in audience-related terms rather than in technological, aesthetic, ideological, or other more or less "elitist" terms. Finally, by looking at the social origins and differential life experiences of media users, it connects mass communication with social roles and psychological dispositions and, through them, ultimately with other social institutions.

ORIGINS AND DEVELOPMENT OF USES AND GRATIFICATIONS RESEARCH

Interest in the gratifications that media provide their audiences goes back to the beginning of empirical mass communication research. Such studies were well represented in the Lazarsfeld-Stanton collections (1942, 1944, 1949): Herzog (1941) on quiz programs and the gratifications derived from listening to soap operas, Suchman (1942) on the motives for getting interested in serious music on radio, Wolfe and Fiske (1949) on the development of children's interest in comics, Berelson (1949) on the functions of newspaper reading, and so on. Each of these investigations came up with a list of functions served either by some specific contents or by the medium in question: to match one's wits against others, to get information or advice for daily living, to provide a framework for one's day, to prepare oneself culturally for the demands of upward mobility, or to be reassured about the dignity and usefulness of one's role.

What these early studies had in common was, first, a basically similar methodological approach whereby statements about media functions were elicited from the respondents in an essentially open-ended way. Second, they shared a qualitative approach in their attempt to group gratification statements into labelled categories, largely ignoring the distribution of their frequency in the population. Third, they did not attempt to explore the links between the gratifications thus detected and the psychological or sociological origins of the needs that were so satisfied. Fourth, they failed to search for the interrelationships among the various media functions, either quantitatively or conceptually, in a manner that might have led to the detection of the latent structure of media gratifications. Consequently, these studies did not result in a cumulatively more detailed picture of media gratifications conducive to the eventual formulation of theoretical statements.

Hints that the issues explored in these studies could be examined from other angles were provided by studies that derived from other traditions: Erich Fromm (1941) wrote about the psychological functions of cat-and-mouse movies and the larger social meaning of why the mice win, Warner and Henry (1948) performed a "symbolic analysis" of the status-giving functions of soap operas, and "motivation research" listed the social and psychological gratifications involved in consuming various products and reading various advertisements. These approaches, too, yielded primarily simple and discrete lists of functions, but they alert us to the fact that a functional view of media consumption can also be found outside the media research fraternity.

Then there was quiet on this front, as studies of persuasion and influence took over; the voting studies at Columbia and Michigan seem to have monopolized the limelight for some years. This preoccupation with attitude and opinion change, and with the informational content of the media as triggering these psychological processes, is, perhaps, partly responsible for the relative neglect of the entertainment content of the media and the variety of "escape" and other functions related to it. Ironically, the concept of entertainment and its functions seems to have had no place in empirical media research and was relegated to the critics and analysts of popular culture.

Nevertheless, during this period, several new links were forged in the chain of gratifications research. One of these was the study by the Rileys (1951), which demonstrated that children who were well integrated with their peers used adventure stories differently from children who were socially isolated. Freidson (1953), and later Johnstone (1961), suggested that the relative strength of attachment to parents and peers could lead to differential patterns of media preferences. Maccoby (1954), Schramm, Lyle, and Parker (1961), and Himmelweit, Oppenheim, and Vince (1958) tried to determine whether a child's acceptance in family and school resulted in different patterns of media exposure, different diets of fantasy and reality, and thus different uses of the media in accordance with underlying needs.

This strand of studies is essentially different from the pioneering work in that it focuses primarily on the link between different patterns of exposure, conceived as indicators of patterns of media use, and certain individual attributes, particularly those having to do with psychological and social integration and isolation. In these studies the gratifications associated with various media behaviors are inferred, rather than explicitly explored (Weiss, 1969). But while they were not conceived and designed primarily to study gratifications, they nevertheless contributed to, and advanced the methodology of, future gratification research by highlighting the importance of the relationship between media use, on the one hand, and psychological disposition and social location, on the other. The implicit logic moves from differences in social integration to resultant differences in psychological need, and from there to differences in patterns of selection, exposure, and, implicitly, gratifications secured.

Links to this line of analysis are evident in the work of Horton and Wohl (1956), who explored the para-social functions of the media for isolated people; and even in the opinion-leader studies (Katz and Lazarsfeld, 1955), which explained the opinion leaders' greater attentiveness to the media partly in terms of the expectations of their followers. These studies were paralleled by yet other work that implied that persons with different value orientations might use the media differently. Lowenthal (1944), for example, speculated at an early stage on the relationship between chance of mobility and symbolic identification with "heroes," a theme that has reemerged over the years in various psychological studies of the "stars." Alberoni (1972) offers the latest example of work in this tradition.

Thus, the ground was prepared for attempts at some theoretical integration of this area. Two prominent examples of such attempts were provided by Wright (1960) and Klapper (1963), who demonstrated the applicability of the functional paradigms of Merton (1957) and Lasswell (1948) to the analysis of mass media behavior. Wright's formulation, in particular, showed how statements concerning explicitly defined functions of the media could be applied to both micro- and macro-sociological entities. Subsequently, Stephenson (1967) also offered a functional-theoretical approach to the analysis of communication behavior, proposing that much media use centers around the concept of "play."

The last few years have witnessed something of a revival of direct empirical investigations of audience uses and gratifications, not only in the United States but also in Britain, Sweden, Finland, Japan, and Israel. These more recent studies have a number of differing starting points, but each attempts to press toward a greater systematization of what is involved in conducting research in this field. Taken together, they make operational many of the logical steps that were only implicit in the earlier work. They are concerned with: (1) the social and psychological origins of (2) needs, which generate (3) expectations of (4) the mass media or other sources, which lead to (5) differential patterns of media exposure (or engagement in other activities), resulting in (6) need gratifications and (7) other consequences, perhaps mostly unintended ones.* Some of these investigations begin by specifying needs and

---

*Rosengren (1974) has proposed a refined formulation of such a paradigm for studies of uses and gratifications.

then attempt to trace the extent to which they are gratified by the media or other sources. Others take observed gratifications as a starting point and attempt to reconstruct the needs that are being gratified. Yet others focus on the social origins of audience expectations and gratifications. But however varied their individual points of departure, the convergence of their foci, as well as of their findings, indicate that there is a clear agenda here—part methodological and part theoretical—for a discussion of the future directions of this approach.

SOME BASIC ASSUMPTIONS OF THEORY, METHOD, AND VALUE

Perhaps the place of "theory" and "method" in the study of audience uses and gratifications is not immediately apparent. The common tendency to attach the label "uses and gratifications approach" to work in this field appears to virtually disclaim any theoretical pretensions or methodological commitment. From this point of view the approach simply represents an attempt to explain something of the way in which individuals use communications, among other resources in their environment, to satisfy their needs and to achieve their goals, and to do so by simply asking them. Nevertheless, this effort does rest on a body of assumptions, explicit or implicit, that have some degree of internal coherence and that are arguable in the sense that not everyone contemplating them would find them self-evident. Lundberg and Hulten (1968) refer to them as jointly comprising a "uses and gratifications model." Five elements of this model in particular may be singled out for comment:

1. The audience is conceived of as active, i.e., an important part of mass media use is assumed to be goal directed (McQuail, Blumler, and Brown, 1972). This assumption may be contrasted with Bogart's (1965) thesis to the effect that "most mass media experiences represent pastime rather than purposeful activity, very often [reflecting] chance circumstances within the range of availabilities rather than the expression of psychological motivation or need." Of course, it cannot be denied that media exposure often has a casual origin; the issue is whether, in addition, patterns of media use are shaped by more or less definite expectations of what certain kinds of content have to offer the audience member.

Although these rival assumptions have rarely been tested against each other in the same study, it may be relevant to note Blumler and McQuail's (1968) finding that the number of election broadcasts seen by a sample of British voters during the 1964 election campaign was independently predicted, both by the respondents' customary viewing habits and by an index of their strength of prior motivation to secure political information from television.

Thus, much mass media consumption may be interpreted as a response to needs felt by the audience member: given psychological dispositions and social roles, the individual viewer, listener, or reader experiences or expects to experience some form of need-satisfaction through his media use behaviors

(Lundberg and Hulten, 1968). Different contributors to the field have outlined different views of the connection between audience needs and mass media use. Edelstein (1973), for example, conceives of an actor becoming aware of problems in his environment and turning to communication to help him to understand or solve them. Katz, Gurevitch, and Haas (1973) deal with a wide range of "media-related needs," which, however, may be served equally well by recourse to such non-media sources of satisfaction as family, friends, sleep, and other "functional alternatives." McQuail, Blumler, and Brown (1972) refer to media use as an "interactive process, relating media content, individual needs, perceptions, roles and values, and the social context in which a person is situated." Rosengren (1972) has pried some of these elements apart to form a hierarchy of concepts, originating in basic human needs, proceeding through "differential combinations of values on individual and environmental variables," and terminating in attempts at gratification-seeking in media and other sources. Despite their differences, however, all the current forms of systematic audience gratifications research are based on some explicitly stated notion of how individual needs are channelled into motivated media use.

2. In the mass communication process much initiative in linking need gratification and media choice lies with the audience member. This places a strong limitation on theorizing about any form of straight-line effect of media content on attitudes and behavior. As Schramm, Lyle, and Parker (1961) said:

> In a sense the term "effect" is misleading because it suggests that television "does something" to children. . . . Nothing can be further from the fact. It is the children who are most active in this relationship. It is they who use television rather than television that uses them.

Or, in the words of Katz, Gurevitch, and Haas (1973), the uses and gratifications approach "argues that people bend the media to their needs more readily than the media overpower them." Lundberg and Hulten (1968) said, "It is the receiver who primarily determines whether or not a communications process will occur."

Emphasis on audience initiative accounts for the tendency of investigators of uses and gratifications to regard this line of research as a promising route of entry into the study of other mass communication phenomena. The notion of the audience member as someone actively involved in selecting what he wants leads more or less directly to the supposition that audience expectations may: govern differential patterns of exposure, intimate demands on communicators that they must satisfy in order to realize their own goals, and mediate the impact of short- and long-term effects. In other words, individual and public opinions have power vis-à-vis the seemingly all-powerful media.

3. The media compete with other sources of need satisfaction. The needs served by mass communication constitute but a segment of the wider range of human needs, and the degree to which they can be adequately met through mass media consumption certainly varies. Consequently, a proper view of the role of the media in need satisfaction should take into account other functional alternatives —including different, more conventional, and "older" ways of fulfilling needs.

This perspective has already influenced the design of several major pieces of research, the outcomes of which have all strongly emphasized the importance of non-media sources. Lundberg and Hulten (1968), for example, found that:

> Mass media occupied a dominant place in Swedish respondents' consciousness only with respect to information-seeking and pure entertainment or amusement. All other types of goals elicited mention of a number of alternative means . . . such as physical change of environment, work, hobbies, personal social contacts, etc.

Katz, Gurevitch, and Haas (1973) reported that, even in the case of their so-called media-related needs, non-media sources, taken together, regularly surpassed media sources, taken together, as means of satisfaction. Perhaps the most prominent of such non-media sources is face-to-face communication. Furu (1971) found that Japanese tenth-grade children endorsed "conversation" more often than any single mass medium when they were asked to consider the following statements: "It affords the most enjoyable time," "It releases my frustrations," "It is consoling," "It stimulates my feeble mind," and "It is useful for solving my problems."

But other non-media sources probably have their place as well: the integrative functions of religious and secular holidays have long been recognised in sociological literature; likewise, there is nothing new in appreciating the function of hobbies for relaxation, of sleep for escape, or of drug-taking for "heightening awareness." Future research into the relationship between media and non-media elements as sources of need satisfaction will surely shed further light on the balance between the two, and thus on the relative importance of mass communication in people's lives.

4. Methodologically speaking, many of the goals of mass media use can be derived from data supplied by individual audience members themselves—i.e., people are sufficiently self-aware to be able to report their interests and motives in particular cases, or at least to recognize them when confronted with them in an intelligible and familiar verbal formulation.

Of course, the investigator's dependence on audience accounts of media gratifications gives rise to validity problems and draws attention to the boundary line that may separate the manifest from the latent functions of mass media. It may well be a limitation of uses and gratifications research that it has so far worked firmly within the more straightforward world of the manifest. However, the manifest is not necessarily coterminous with the most obvious or superficial of audience requirements. British viewers, for example, have apparently been able to give expression to their use of television not only for such familiar purposes as diversion, surveillance, social utility, and substitute companionship, but also to relate program materials to a deeper exploration of their own personal identities (McQuail, Blumler, and Brown, 1972).

5. Value judgements about the cultural significance of mass communication should be suspended while audience orientations are explored on their own terms. It is from the perspective of this assumption that certain affinities

and contrasts between the uses and gratifications approach and much specula-
tive writing about popular culture may be considered.

On the one hand, both the uses and gratifications approach and popular
culture theories share a common interest in understanding the audience's
attachment to mass media fare. In fact much of the thinking about mass
communication propounded by the popular culture theorists can be translated
into the language of uses and gratifications and subjected to empirical test.
What has been claimed for the notion of escape in this connection (Katz and
Foulkes, 1962) is but one example. Popular culture writers have also seen the
media as offering: larger-than-life substitutes for interpersonal communication
contacts (Jarrell, 1960), reassurance in a troubled world (Baldwin, 1960),
opportunities to revel without personal threat in the woes of others (Wade,
1973), and the satisfaction of regularly exercising one's social conscience in
response to a range of only mildly discomfiting problems (Urwin, 1973). In a
similar vein, Herbert Gans (1957) has been providing suggestions about the
differential gratifications likely to be obtained by people situated differently in
the social structure—adults and adolescents, WASPs and ethnics, middle-class
and working-class audience members—as a result of seeing the same motion
picture films.*
On the other hand, commentators on popular culture often (a) suppose
that the character of audience appeals may be identified from a close and
sensitive reading of content alone, and/or (b) imply that media output gener-
ates a powerful demand for the very qualities that it then satisfies, and/or (c)
project an essentially unflattering view of the audience's dependence on mass
communication. In contrast to those assumptions, practitioners of the uses and
gratifications approach are more likely (a) to insist on mounting direct studies
of audience appeals, independent of or coterminous with content analysis; (b) to
look for the origins of audience needs in psychological dispositions and social
roles rather than in features of mass media organization or content; and (c) to
suspect that a full understanding of what lies behind audience behavior would
neutralize at least some part of the criticism that is typically directed against it

---

*Criticism of the popular (and not so popular) arts is an altogether unmined source of
empirically-testable hypotheses. Consider opera, the medium to which we alluded earlier:
"Think," invites Bayard Northcott (1973), "of what Gaetano Donizetti could take for
granted as he sat down to write Don Pasquale in the autumn of 1842—indeed, of what he
already had in the 67 earlier operas which he had produced since 1818. In every Italian town
and most of the larger cities of Europe the opera house served the functions of social,
cultural and even moral centre. Audiences expected not only to be entertained, stirred and
seen, but also to be reminded of the Dictates of Honour, of the Sanctity of the Family, to be
assured that persistent folly provokes comic retribution or more solemnly that the 'joys of
the iniquitous are but a puff of smoke.'"
The New Statesman's opera critic has thus listed five "uses," or expectations, of the
opera for their audiences. The audience came to be (1) entertained, (2) stirred, (3) seen, (4)
reminded, and (5) assured; and the composer "had" to know it. Going beyond the point at
which most gratifications studies have stopped, Northcott attempts to specify which attributes of the medium, i.e., elements of its grammar, gratify these expectations.
For examples from the visual arts see D. W. Gotschalk (1947).

from elite quarters. In other words, they are reluctant to portray the audience's involvement in mass communication as if it were symptomatic of an intrinsically pathological condition.

THEORETICAL ISSUES: NEEDS, GRATIFICATIONS, AND EFFECTS

From the few postulates outlined above, it is evident that further development of a theory of media gratifications depends, first, on the clarification of its relationship to the theoretical traditions on which it so obviously draws and, secondly, on systematic efforts toward conceptual integration of empirical findings. Given the present state of the art, the following are priority issues in the development of an adequate theoretical basis.

Typologies of Audience Gratifications

Each major piece of uses and gratifications research has yielded its own classification scheme of audience functions. When placed side by side, they reveal a mixture of shared gratification categories and notions peculiar to individual research teams. The differences are due in part to the fact that investigators have focused on different levels of study (e.g., medium or content) and different materials (e.g., different programs or program types on, say, television) in different cultures (e.g., Finland, Israel, Japan, Sweden, the United Kingdom, the United States, and Yugoslavia).

But some of the disparities have deeper roots. For example, although several of the recently developed classification schemes enjoy empirical support from one or another form of correlational analysis, they also rest on certain conceptual distinctions—the dimensions of which differ from one study to another. At one extreme, there are the uni-functional conceptions of audience interests which have been expressed in various forms. Popular culture writers have often criticized the media on the grounds that, in primarily serving escapist desires, the audience is deprived of the more beneficial uses that might be made of mass communication (MacDonald, 1957). Stephenson's (1967) analysis of mass communication in terms of "play" may be interpreted as an extension, albeit in a transformed and expanded expression, of this same notion. A more recent example has been provided by Nordenstreng (1970); while breaking away from conventional formulations, he still opts for a uni-functional view when he claims that, "It has often been documented [e.g., during television and newspaper strikes in Finland, 1966-1967] that perhaps the basic motivation for media use is just an unarticulated need for social contact."

The wide currency secured for a bi-functional view of audience concerns is reflected in Weiss' (1971) summary, which states that, "When . . . studies of uses and gratifications are carried out, the media or media content are usually viewed dichotomously as predominantly fantasist-escapist or informational-educational in significance." This dichotomy appears, for example, in

Schramm's (1949) work (adopted subsequently by Schramm, Lyle, and Parker, 1961; Pietila, 1969; and Furu, 1971), which distinguishes between sets of "immediate" and "deferred" gratifications, and in the distinction between informational and entertainment materials. In terms of audience gratifications specifically, it emerges in the distinction between surveillance and escape uses of the media.

The four-functional interpretation of the media was first proposed by Lasswell (1948) on a macro-sociological level and later developed by Wright (1960) on both the macro- and the micro-sociological levels. It postulated that the media served the functions of surveillance, correlation, entertainment, and cultural transmission (or socialization) for society as a whole, as well as for individuals and subgroups within society. An extension of the four-functional approach can also be found in Wright's suggestive exploration of the potential dysfunctional equivalents of Lasswell's typology.

None of these statements, however, adequately reflects the full range of functions, which has been disclosed by the more recent investigations. McQuail, Blumler, and Brown (1972) have put forward a typology consisting of the following categories: diversion (including escape from the constraints of routine, escape from the burdens of problems, and emotional release); personal relationships (including substitute companionship as well as social utility); personal identity (including personal reference, reality exploration, and value reinforcement); and surveillance.

An effort to encompass the large variety of specific functions that have been proposed is made in the elaborate scheme of Katz, Gurevitch, and Haas (1973). Their central notion is that mass communication is used by individuals to connect (or sometimes to disconnect) themselves—via instrumental, affective, or integrative relations—with (or from) different social entities (self, family, friends, nation, etc.). The scheme attempts to comprehend the whole range of individual gratifications of the many facets of the need "to be connected." And it finds empirical tendencies for certain media to be preferred for particular kinds of connections.

Of course, the search for an all-embracing typology can be overextended. Media consumption geared to a "sociability" function, for example, is not necessarily part of a single homogeneous activity. It may subsume such diverse orientations as: liking to be in the company of others at the moment of media use, being able to chat informally about media materials with other people afterwards, gathering information from the media more purposively in order to perform effectively in some specific social role, and exchanging media-based information with others as a means of testing one's competence and knowledge-ability in a field of shared interest with them.

Another danger of a highly general scheme is that of losing the distinctive meanings that belong to popular usage of particular bodies of content. For some purposes, for example, it may be more revealing to study, à la Blumler and McQuail (1968), the four main classes of reasons for following political broadcasts (surveillance, contest excitement, reinforcement seeking, and vote-guidance seeking) than to strip these expectations of their specifically political connotations. Nevertheless, continued attempts to frame gratification typologies of a potentially wide application are of central importance because only such paradigms permit one to compare and contrast the findings of different workers in the field and contribute to the further development of theoretical statements.

Gratifications and Needs

The study of mass media use suffers at present from the absence of a relevant theory of social and psychological needs. It is not so much a catalogue of needs that is missing as a clustering of groups of needs, a sorting out of different levels of need, and a specification of hypotheses linking particular needs with particular media gratifications. It is true that the work of Schramm, Lyle, and Parker (1961) draws on the distinction between the reality and pleasure principles in the socialization theories of Freud and others, but more recent studies suggest that those categories are too broad to be serviceable. Maslow's (1954) proposed heirarchy of human needs may hold more promise, but the relevance of his categories to expectations of communication has not yet been explored in detail. Lasswell's (1948) scheme to specify the needs that media satisfy has proven useful, and it may be helpful to examine Lasswell and Kaplan's (1950) broader classification of values as well.

Developmental theories of various kinds are also relevant. Phase theories of socialization indicating the informational, conceptual, and emotional requirements of the child or adult as he grows older are good examples (e.g. Parsons and Bales, 1955; Becker and Strauss, 1957). Indeed, Freidson's (1953) and Johnstone's (1961) studies of the media preferences of children of different ages have drawn implicitly on theories of this kind. Phase theories of decision making provide another sort of example, insofar as they specify the rational and emotional steps implicit in making decisions. Blumler and McQuail's (1968) typology of voters can be transformed into a decision-making sequence (awareness, interest, decision, reinforcement), much as has been done with the many studies of the adoption of innovation in which the media can be shown to be differently appropriate to the needs of each mental phase in the adoption process (Rogers, 1972).

Alternatively, students of uses and gratifications could try to work backwards, as it were, from gratifications to needs. In the informational field, for example, the surveillance function may be traced to a desire for security or the satisfaction of curiosity and the exploratory drive; seeking reinforcement of one's attitudes and values may derive from a need for reassurance that one is right; and attempts to correlate informational elements may stem from a more basic need to develop one's cognitive mastery of the environment. Similarly, the use of fictional (and other) media materials for "personal reference" may spring from a need for self-esteem; social utility functions may be traced to the need for affiliation; and escape functions may be related to the need to release tension and reduce anxiety. But whichever way one proceeds, it is inescapable that what is at issue here is the long-standing problem of social and psychological science: how to (and whether to bother to) systematize the long lists of human and societal needs. Thus far, gratifications research has stayed close to what we have been calling media-related needs (in the sense that the media have been observed to satisfy them, at least in part), but one wonders whether all this should not be put in the broader context of systematic studies of needs.

Sources of Media Gratifications

Studies have shown that audience gratifications can be derived from at least three distinct sources: media content, exposure to the media *per se*, and the social context that typifies the situation of exposure to different media. Although recognition of media content as a source of gratifications has provided the basis for research in this area from its inception, less attention has been paid to the other sources. Nevertheless, it is clear that the need to relax or to kill time can be satisfied by the act of watching television, that the need to feel that one is spending one's time in a worthwhile way may be associated with the act of reading (Waples, Berelson, and Bradshaw, 1940; Berelson, 1949), and that the need to structure one's day may be satisfied merely by having the radio "on" (Mendelsohn, 1964). Similarly, a wish to spend time with one's family or friends can be served by watching television at home with the family or by going to the cinema with one's friends.

Each medium seems to offer a unique combination of: (a) characteristic contents (at least stereotypically perceived in that way); (b) typical attributes (print vs. broadcasting modes of transmission, iconic vs. symbolic representation, reading vs. audio or audio-visual modes of reception); and (c) typical exposure situations (at home vs. out-of-home, alone vs. with others, control over the temporal aspects of exposure vs. absence of such control). The issue, then, is what combinations of attributes may render different media more or less adequate for the satisfaction of different needs (Katz, Gurevitch, and Haas, 1973).

Gratifications and Media Attributes

Much uses and gratifications research has still barely advanced beyond a sort of charting and profiling activity: findings are still typically presented to show that certain bodies of content serve certain functions or that one medium is deemed better at satisfying certain needs than another. The further step, which has hardly been ventured, is one of explanation. At issue here is the relationship between the unique "grammar" of different media—that is, their specific technological and aesthetic attributes—and the particular requirements of audience members that they are then capable, or incapable, of satisfying. Which, indeed, are the attributes that render some media more conducive than others to satisfying specific needs? And which elements of content help to attract the expectations for which they apparently cater?

Certain writers have made a beginning, at least speculatively, in associating media attributes with audience needs. Richard Crossman (1969), for example, suggests that print media are well suited to democracy for the McLuhanesque reason that they favor ideas over personalities and thus cultivate emotional neutrality. Blumler (1972), however, has argued that in Britain political-reinforcement seekers tend to rely on newspapers and vote-guidance seekers tend to rely on television because newspapers editorialize while broadcasting better serves the norm of political impartiality. Donald Bogue (1962) maintains that print is the best medium for transmitting family-planning messages because it is consumed in private. John Robinson (1972a) implies that the characteristics of television favor time killing (easy availability) and para-social interaction (the regular appearance of attractive and friendly personalities). And Cazeneuve (1972 and 1973), Alberoni (1972), and Bakewell and Garnham (1970) suggest that the authority of television, and its "new priesthood," enable it to fulfill some of the needs that people previously satisfied through religion—e.g., for a guiding hand, a sense of magical control, and the imposition of normative limits.

It is possible to postulate the operation of some kind of division of labor among the media for the satisfaction of audience needs. This may be elaborated in two ways: taking media attributes as the starting point, the suggestion is that those media that differ (or are similar) in their attributes are more likely to serve different (or similar) needs; or, utilizing the latent structure of needs as a point of departure, the implication is that needs that are psychologically related or conceptually similar will be equally well served by the same media (or by media with similar attributes).

To illustrate the first approach, John Robinson (1972a) has demonstrated the interchangeability of television and print media for learning purposes. In the Israeli study, Katz, Gurevitch, and Haas (1973) found five media ordered in a circumplex with respect to their functional similarities: books-newspapers-radio-television-cinema-books. In other words, books functioned most like newspapers, on the one hand, and like cinema, on the other. Radio was most similar in its usage to newspapers, on the one hand, and to television, on the other. The explanation would seem to lie not only with certain technological attributes that they have in common, but with similar aesthetic qualities as well. Thus, books share a technology and an informational function with newspapers, but are similar to films in their aesthetic function. Radio shares a technology, as well as informational and entertainment content, with television, but it is also very much like newspapers—providing a heavy dose of information and an orientation to reality.

An illustration of the second aspect of this division of labor may also be drawn from the same study. Here, the argument is that structurally related needs will tend to be serviced by certain media more often than by others. Thus, books and cinema have been found to cater to needs concerned with self-fulfillment and self-gratification: they help to "connect" individuals to themselves. Newspapers, radio, and television all seem to connect individuals to society. In fact, the function of newspapers for those interested in following what is going on in the world may have been grossly underestimated in the past (Edelstein, 1973; Lundberg and Hulten, 1968). Television, however, was found to be less frequently used as a medium of escape by Israeli respondents than were books and films. And a Swedish study of the "functional specialties of the respective media" reported that, "A retreat from the immediate environment and its demands—probably mainly by the act of reading itself—was characteristic of audience usage of weekly magazines" (Lundberg and Hulten, 1968).

Media Attributes as Perceived or Intrinsic

When people associate book-reading, for example, with a desire to know oneself, and newspapers with the need to feel connected to the larger society, it is difficult to disentangle perceptions of the media from their intrinsic qualities. Is there anything about the book as a medium that breeds intimacy? Is there something about newspapers that explains their centrality in socio-political integration? Or, is this "something" simply an accepted image of the medium and its characteristic content?

In this connection, Rosengren (1972) has suggested that uses and gratifications research may be profitably connected with the long-established tradition of inquiry into public perceptions of the various media and the dimensions according to which their respective images and qualities are differentiated (cf. especially Nilsson [1971] and Edelstein [1973] and the literature cited therein). A merger of the two lines of investigation may show how far the attributes of the media, as perceived by their consumers, and their intrinsic qualities are correlated with the pursuit of certain gratifications. So far, however, this connection has only been partially discussed in the work of Lundberg and Hulten (1968).

Social Origins of Audience Needs
and Their Gratifications

The social and environmental circumstances that lead people to turn to the mass media for the satisfaction of certain needs are also little understood as yet. For example, what needs, if any, are created by routine work on an assembly line, and which forms of media exposure will satisfy them? What motivates some people to seek political information from the mass media and others to actively avoid it? Here one may postulate that it is the combined product of psychological dispositions, sociological factors, and environmental conditions that determines the specific uses of the media by members of the audience.

At certain levels it should not prove unduly difficult to formulate discrete hypotheses about such relationships. For example, we might expect "substitute companionship" to be sought especially by individuals with limited opportunities for social contacts: invalids, the elderly, the single, the divorced or widowed living alone, the housewife who spends much time at home on her own, and so on.

At another level, however, it is more difficult to conceive of a general theory that might clarify the various processes that underlie any such specific relationships. A preliminary structuring of the possibilities suggests that social factors may be involved in the generation of media-related needs in any of the following five ways (each of which has attracted some comment in the literature):

1. Social situation produces tensions and conflicts, leading to pressure for their easement via mass media consumption (Katz and Foulkes, 1962).

2. Social situation creates an awareness of problems that demand attention, information about which may be sought in the media (Edelstein, 1973).

3. Social situation offers impoverished real-life opportunities to satisfy certain needs, which are then directed to the mass media for complementary, supplementary, or substitute servicing (Rosengren and Windahl, 1972).

4. Social situation gives rise to certain values, the affirmation and reinforcement of which is facilitated by the consumption of congruent media materials (Dembo, 1972).

5. Social situation provides a field of expectations among the individual's social contacts of familiarity with certain media materials, which must then be monitored in order to sustain membership in valued social groupings (Atkin, 1972).

Although research into these relationships is still in its infancy, a few connections have already been established (McQuail, Blumler, and Brown, 1972), and attempts have been made to formulate a range of provisional hypotheses. Some examples may be taken from a research project currently being conducted at the Centre for Television Research, the University of Leeds, England. This study hypothesizes, for example, that use of the media to isolate oneself from the external environment characterizes individuals with poor personal adjustment and low self-esteem, functioning in job or family circumstances that provide restrictive repetitive environments; or, individuals who favor solitude rather than the company of others, as well as those belonging to downwardly mobile groups who are alienated from their peers and from society.

Alternatively, individuals characterized by high gregariousness but restricted opportunities for contacts with friends and peers—e.g., people who have recently experienced geographical mobility—might seek in the media an opportunity for emotional release. Use of the media for social integration might be characteristic of people who have recently undergone changes in status or postion (e.g., newly arrived immigrants); while a need for value-reinforcing materials might be found especially among individuals functioning in environments that challenge their personal convictions (e.g., those in government and bureaucratic positions, law enforcement agencies, and educational institutions). These examples are not necessarily definitive or exhaustive, but they illustrate the richness and subtlety of the hypotheses that can be generated in this area.

The Versatility of Sources of Need Satisfaction

Before becoming too sanguine about the possibility of relating social situations and psychological needs to media/content gratifications, it is important to bear in mind that gratifications studies based on specific media contents have demonstrated that one and the same set of media materials is capable of serving a multiplicity of needs and audience functions. Presumably, that is why Rosengren and Windahl (1972) have drawn attention to "a growing consensus that almost any type of content may serve practically any type of function." For example, Blumler, Brown, and McQuail (1970) have found that the television serial, *The Saint*, serves functions of personal reference, identification with characters, and reality-exploration, in addition to its more obvious diversionary function. Similarly, their study of the gratifications involved in news viewing referred not only to the expected surveillance motive but also to functions of social utility, empathy, and even escape. In summarizing the implications of their evidence, McQuail, Blumler, and Brown (1972) point out that:

> ... the relationship between content categories and audience needs is far less tidy and more complex than most commentators have appreciated. ... One man's source of escape from the real world is a point of anchorage for another man's place in it. There is neither a one-to-one correspondence between communication content and audience motivation, nor any such correspondence between the place on a presumed scale of cultural worth to which programme material may be assigned and the depth of meanings that may be drawn from them by many of their most keen attenders.

While this present state of affairs is confusing, it may also be exaggerated. Although each source (media or not) may be multi-functional, the range of functions it serves may still be circumscribed. There are also unexplored possibilities of variation in the numbers of people to whom the different functions appeal and in the salience of such appeals. A better understanding of the regularities and limits of the relationship between needs and the sources of their gratifications will have to await a more comprehensive profiling of the various needs served by different forms of available content than any investigation in the field has thus far supplied.

Gratifications and Effects

Pioneers in the study of uses and gratifications were moved chiefly by two aspirations. The first, which has largely been fulfilled, was to redress an imbalance evident in previous research: audience needs, they said, deserved as much attention in their own right as the persuasive aims of communicators with which so many of the early "effects" studies had been preoccupied. The second major aim of uses and gratifications research, however, was to treat audience requirements as intervening variables in the study of traditional communication effects. Glaser's (1965) formulation offers a typical expression of the rationale behind this prospect:

> Since users approach the media with a variety of needs and predispositions ... any precise identification of the effects of television watching ... must identify the uses sought and made of television by the various types of viewers.

Despite this injunction, hardly any substantial empirical or theoretical effort has been devoted to connecting gratifications and effects. Some limited evidence from the political field suggests that combining functions and effects perspectives may be fruitful (Blumler and McQuail, 1968). But there are many other foci of traditional effects studies for which no detailed hypotheses about gratifications/effects interactions have yet been framed.

One obvious example is the field of media violence. Another might concern the impact on inhabitants of developing countries of exposure to television serials, films, and popular songs of foreign (predominantly American) origin. Yet another might relate to the wide range of materials, appearing especially in broadcast fiction, that purport simultaneously to entertain and to portray more or less faithfully some portion of social reality—e.g., the worlds of law enforcement, social work, hospital life, trade unionism, working-class neighborhoods; or ways of life at the executive level in business corporations and civil service departments.

Hypotheses about the cumulative effects of exposure to such materials on audience members' cognitive perceptions of these spheres of activity, and on the individuals engaged in them, might be formulated in awareness of the likely fact that some individuals will be viewing them primarily for purposes of escape, while others will be using them for reality-exploring gratifications. In these circumstances should we expect a readier acceptance of portrayed stereotypes by the escape seekers—the thesis of Festinger and Maccoby (1964) on persuasion via distraction might be relevant here—or by those viewers who are trusting enough to expect such programs to offer genuine insights into the nature of social reality?

A similar body of recently analyzed materials may be found in the television soap opera, with its postulated capacity to "establish or reinforce value systems" (Katzman, 1972). In fact one cluster of gratifications that emerged from a British study of listeners to a long-running daytime radio serial (*The Dales*) centered on the tendency of the program to uphold traditional family values (Blumler, Brown, and McQuail, 1970). This suggests that an answer to Katzman's "key question" ("To what degree do daytime serials change attitudes and norms and to what extent do they merely follow and reinforce their audience?") might initially be sought by distinguishing among the regular followers of such programs those individuals who are avowedly seeking a reinforcement of certain values from those who are not.

In addition, however, the literature refers to some consequences of audience functions that conventional effects designs may be unable to capture. First, there is what Katz and Foulkes (1962) have termed the "feedback" from media use to the individual's performance of his other social roles. Thus, Bailyn (1959) distinguished child uses of pictorial media that might "preclude more realistic and lasting solutions" to problems from those that, at one level, were "escapist" but that should more properly be categorized as "supplementation." Similarly, Schramm, Lyle, and Parker (1961) maintained that child uses of the mass media for fantasizing might either drain off discontent caused by the hard blows of socialization or lead a child into withdrawal from the real world. And Lundberg and Hulten (1968) have suggested that for some individuals the substitute companionship function may involve use of the media to replace real social ties, while for others it may facilitate an adjustment to reality.

Second, some authors have speculated on the connection between functions performed by the media for individuals and those functions (or dysfunctions) for other levels of society. This relationship is particularly crucial for its bearing on evaluative and ideological controversies about the role of mass communication in modern society. Thus, Enzenberger (1972) suggests that the

8 millimeter camera may satisfy the recreational and creative impulses of the individual and help to keep the family together while simultaneously atomizing and depoliticizing society. Or news viewing may gratify the individual's need for civic participation; but if the news, as presented, is a disjointed succession of staccato events, it may also leave him with the message that the world is a disconnected place. Similarly, many radical critics tend to regard television as part of a conspiracy to keep people content and politically quiescent—offering respite, para-social interaction with interesting and amusing people, and much food for gossip—while propagating a false social consciousness.

Audience Gratifications and Mass Media Communicators

Finally, a theory of mass communication must take account of the linkage between the ways audiences use the media and the constraints that bear upon producers. Among these constraints, of course, are audience needs and goals—at least as perceived by the producers (Weiss, 1969). Indeed if institutions—regarded sociologically—are arrangements for satisfying basic human needs, then the institutions of mass communication must be explained at least partly in terms of the requirements of their audiences.

Consequently, at least two issues arise for further consideration. First, how are needs communicated to producers? The explanatory power of a simple feedback model of this process is likely to be impaired by (a) the absence of institutionalized channels and mechanisms for the transmission of adequately comprehensive feedback from a mass audience characterized by a high degree of heterogeneity (McQuail, 1969); and (b) the multi-functionality for members of the audience of the materials they regularly consume. It is precisely the subtlety and complexity of the resulting picture that highlights the inadequacy of much conventional audience measurement carried out by the research departments of broadcasting organizations.

A second set of issues arises from the possible existence of discrepancies between producer intentions and audience expectations. How can we empirically explore what fraction of material disseminated by the media is relevant to audience needs and requirements? Is the gap ever wide enough to provoke definite feelings of dissatisfaction or frustration? And if so, what implications follow regarding the tendency of some investigators of uses and gratifications to suppose that for most audience members the act of media consumption is an intrinsically rewarding pursuit?

METHODOLOGICAL ISSUES

Many of the differences between current and past investigations of audience gratifications lie in the realm of methodology. We have come a long way from the days when the functions of a program or medium were reported in a simple list of discrete uses. At the present state of the art, there are a number of major problems that need attention if the methodological foundations of uses and gratifications research are to be further strengthened.

Quantitative and Qualitative Methods

One development that marks the progress that has been achieved is the increasingly successful integration of qualitative and quantitative materials. In the earlier work, many different media-content foci (e.g., newspapers, adventure comics, science fiction stories, radio serials, etc.) intimated the existence of complex functional relationships with the needs of their audiences; much of the qualitative evidence lacked quantitative confirmation, and the quantitative evidence that was generated often lacked a firm qualitative base.

For example, in his still much-cited study of the functions of the newspaper, Bernard Berelson (1949) stopped short at a subjective analysis of sixty intensive interviews with readers who had been temporarily deprived of their daily fare by a strike. Even in Herta Herzog's (1942) call for a three-pronged approach combining content analysis, gratification research, and quantitative research into audience members' positions in the social structure, lack of reference to the need for systematic quantification in the measurement of gratifications themselves is noticeable.

The danger of separating an intensive study of certain media users' gratifications from a quantitative investigation lies in the risk of concluding, without warrant, that large numbers of people, known to compose the audience, uniformly seek the gratifications inferred from a small-scale qualitative study.

At the other extreme, where quantification has been employed, there has been some tendency to feed respondents single-sentence descriptions of media functions for endorsement without first ensuring their fidelity to the language and range of experience of the population under study. Nowadays, however, more pains are customarily taken to advance toward the quantifiable from a substantial initial investment in sustained qualitative work. But the strategies of doing so still need considerable exploration.

The Point of Entry

A second distinctive feature of recent research has been the efforts made to base media gratification categories on statistical associations of respondents' endorsements of batteries of statements about their needs and expectations. Thus, the tasks of defining and distinguishing classes of gratifications no longer proceed by face meaning and intuition alone but are guided by cluster analysis, Q-sorts, and smallest space analysis.

Nevertheless, the main methodologies in vogue at present do differ from each other in terms of the points of departure from which investigations are launched. One starting point is needs as such (cf. Katz, Gurevitch, and Haas, 1973). The object is to rate needs in terms of their importance to the individual and then to locate the media (or media content) and/or other sources that satisfy these needs as indexed by stated preferences or patterns of exposure. The advantage of this approach is that it facilitates comparisons among media as well as between media and other functional alternatives. But perhaps the ability of people to recognize and grade the relative importance of their needs, and to rate abstractly the extent to which the different media fulfill them may still be questioned.

A related, but more open-ended, starting point is that of Edelstein (1973) and Clarke (1971). Their object is to relate media evaluations and uses to a set of concerns that are freely designated by respondents as their prime pre-occupations. The strength of this approach derives from its focus on matters that are spontaneously salient to people, but it probably favors an exploration of instrumental media uses at the expense of expressive ones.

Another starting point is content, or specific programs. (cf. McQuail, Blumler, and Brown, 1972). The object here is to infer media-related needs by applying gratifications statements to a range of materials that have actually been consumed by audience members. The strength of this method lies in its closeness to media experiences that people can readily recall and reflect upon; but it may neglect the gratifications associated with the act, or context, of media consumption as distinct from the expectations that are tied to familiar bodies of content.

The Validity Problem

No systematic way of testing the validity of endorsements of gratification statements has yet been proposed, although scattered *ad hoc* references to validation do appear in the literature. They chiefly refer to confirmation of expected associations between gratifications sought and other variables—e.g., of exposure patterns, social positions, or post-exposure responses to communications. For example, Blumler and McQuail (1968) found that voters with different informational requirements tended to use the media differently. And Blumler, Brown and McQuail (1970) reported that those who followed *The Dales* in order to strengthen their sense of family values consisted largely of women who had made the transition from large families of origin to relatively small families of their own.

But to use results of hypothesis-testing to validate one of the measures deployed in an analysis cannot be deemed an entirely satisfactory procedure. Perhaps a more acceptable approach to validation must await the design of studies that would relate measured gratifications to the positions of audience members on scales of other psychological dispositions and needs.

The Problem of Salience or Importance

There is also a need to clarify the intricate relationships involved in measuring the salience to people of their utilization of mass communications for various purposes. Some difficulties arise from the variety of dimensions that can be subsumed under the notion of salience or regarded as in some way related to it: (a) the relative awareness of needs; (b) the relative importance of different needs in different circumstances and at different moments in time; (c) the relative opportunities to fulfill needs through non-media outlets; (d) the relative involvement in media sources of need-satisfaction; (3) assessments of the relative capacities of different media, or contents, to serve needs; and (f) the relative amounts of time spent with the media. Since most published studies have worked on no more than two of these dimensions, we have so far formed only a limited impression of how they may be related to each other. It is true that in two Swedish surveys, Rosengren and Windahl (1972) found positive and statistically significant associations between dimensions (c), (d), and (f), but they were not entirely satisfied with the validity of their measures.

A second problem arises from the fact that some content-focused gratifications research is based on respondents for whom the materials were bound to be relatively salient. The work of McQuail, Blumler, and Brown (1972), for example, depends on endorsements of statements about programs secured from their fans—that is, from people who had either named these programs among their favorites or had watched them at prestated levels of frequency and regularity. But the likely impact on their findings of the dilution of the audience by possibly large numbers of less committed viewers remains unexplored.

Yet another problem, stemming from possible discrepancies between different dimensions of salience, may be illustrated in the work of Katz, Gurevitch, and Haas (1973). Their procedure ignored the very real possibility that some needs deemed insignificant in the abstract might well assume greater importance when considered in closer association with actual media use—as might be expected, for example, in the case of escape.

The Introspective Ability of Respondents

Despite its adoption of sophisticated methods of data analysis, the uses and gratifications approach still tends to rely on relatively simple and straightforward techniques for item construction and questionnaire design. All the work undertaken in the recent upsurge of activity has depended on audience members' direct formulations of what they are seeking or getting out of media content and has taken such statements at their face value. But even if there were no reason to doubt the validity of such endorsements, it would still be relevant to ask how far they tell the whole story. In fact, there are a number of assumptions and hypotheses in the mass communication literature that are probably not amenable to investigation by the rather bald approaches to data collection that have so far prevailed.

How, for example, would we test the proposition that Westerns help the film-goer to resolve his Oedipus complex (Emery, 1959), or that many television programs offer the gratification of involvement without commitment (Wiebe, 1969)? It may be that more effort should now be expended on the design of indirect ways of getting at functions such as these, but as we depart from the seeming security of reliance on literal evidence, it will become even more urgent to face and resolve the previously mentioned problem of validity.

Which Comes First: Supply or Demand?

Another neglected problem involves temporal and causal relationships between audience members' gratifications and their experience of media exposure. In principle, a distinction may be drawn between expectations formed in advance of exposure and satisfactions subsequently secured from consumption. In practice, however, research workers have indiscriminately approached these phenomena from both ends without considering whether or not the point of departure might matter and, if so, in what way.

Perhaps the distinction is most crucial for its bearing on the assumption, adopted by many investigators of uses and gratifications, of the actively selective audience member. As has already been emphasized, the model postulates an individual whose sampling of media output is guided by prior motives that in turn derive from relevant psychological dispositions and social roles. Such a paradigm not only explains media behavior; it also offers protection against manipulation by would-be persuaders (cf. Bauer's [1964] notion of "the obstinate audience"). But if people are functionally related to mass communications more through satisfactions experienced than through gratifications sought, some parts of this edifice may crumble. People may be attached to the media through needs created in the first place by characteristics of media supply; they may then prove vulnerable to exploitation through their dependence on such media-generated needs.

Individual vs. Societal Functions

Still another challenge arises from the commitment of many investigators of uses and gratifications to an individualist methodology—one that focuses central attention on what individual audience members derive from their media experiences. Yet, ever since the appearance of Wright's (1960) seminal article, it has been evident that statements about media functions at the individual level could be paralleled by equivalent statements at supra-individual levels (specific sub-groups, society, culture).

Thus, for Katz (1971), election campaigns, when regarded from the perspective of society, are "integrative" institutions—focusing "all eyes on the center of political power at a time when the political parties are attempting to divide society as best they can,"—as well as "socializing" institutions—educating "members of the society to the fundamental rights and obligations of the role, 'citizen,' at a time when the parties are simply trying to win."

For Carey (1969), the development since the nineteenth century of national media, cutting across existing boundaries of sub-group differentiations to draw their audiences from the members of a diverse set of subsidiary communities and sectors, has tended "to create a consensus or at least a center of value, attitude, emotion, and expressive style," involving a blocking out "of those values, attitudes, and groups which threaten the tenuous basis of social order" as well as "a ritual celebration of the basis of social order."

For McCombs and Shaw (1972), the media set political agendas that influence the issues with which the electorate expect their politicians to wrestle. And for Cazeneuve (1973), the media define and adjust hierarchies of values, which provide normative guidance to individuals and regulative mechanisms for the social order.

Perhaps the two-fold issue underlying all this is, first, how far uses and gratifications research should be concerned at all with functions postulated at the supraindividual level, and second, whether the cultivation of any such concern would require an abandonment of its individualist methodology.

It may transpire that satisfactory answers to these questions can be framed only after detailed attempts have been made to operationalize the specific requirements involved in testing various hypotheses about societal functions. For example, in some cases such an effort might show that the postulated societal function presupposes an individual function that is amenable to investigation in the manner of traditional audience gratifications research. Thus, the identification by McQuail, Blumler, and Brown (1972) of an audience interest in "value reinforcement" could be relevant to the theses of both Carey (1969) and Cazeneuve (1972). In other cases, however, confirmation of the societal function might require the implementation of something more like a conventional effects study—as in investigations of the agenda-setting function of the mass media.

IMPLICATIONS FOR RESEARCH POLICY AND
MEDIA POLICY

While we have focused here on the utilization of mass media by the individual, we wish to emphasize that our object, ultimately, is to link gratification research to a more inclusive theory of mass communication that has implications for both research and policy.

From the point of view of media research, we hope to have conveyed the impression that effective research into audience gratifications may illuminate the study of communication phenomena at other levels—particularly content analysis and effect analysis. We have argued that there is little point in studying content or effects independent of the study of uses and gratifications, but that there is much point in studying them together.

Moreover, we have tried to show that study of the uses and gratifications of mass communication relates to the social situations of individuals and groups, and to their psychological dispositions. Indeed, the study of audience gratifications links up with the very general problem of categorizing individual and societal needs and specifying the sources of their satisfaction (or frustration). The several recent attempts to cluster or factor analyze media-related needs and gratifications may perhaps hold wider implications for social science.

In reviewing the state of the art of gratifications research, we have focused on issues—theoretical, methodological, and ideological—rather than on systematized findings. We have also tried to make manifest our assumptions. Thus, we have confronted the image of the beery, house-slippered, casual viewer of television with the notion of a more "active" audience—knowing that both images are true. We have asked whether a methodology based on respondents' introspection can be adequate. We have indicated the absence of satisfactory bridging concepts between the constraints arising from social situations and the gratifications sought from the media; or between particular patterns of use and likely effects.

These issues bear not only on the direction of future research, but also, echoing Nordenstreng (1970), on the relationship between research policy and media policy. Thus, we have raised the question of the extent to which the media create the needs that they satisfy. Even more fundamentally, we ask whether the media do actually satisfy their consumers—an assumption that radical critics of the media take more for granted than do gratifications researchers (cf. Emmett, 1968-1969). To assert that mass communication is a latter-day opiate of the masses presupposes a media-output audience-satisfaction nexus that gratifications research treats as hypothesis rather than fact.

In other words, our position is that media researchers ought to be studying human needs to discover how much the media do or do not contribute to their creation and satisfaction. Moreover, we believe it is our job to clarify the extent to which certain kinds of media and content favor certain kinds of use—to thereby set boundaries to the over-generalization that any kind of content can be bent to any kind of need. We believe it is part of our job to explore the social and individual conditions under which audiences find need or use for media material aimed at changing their image of the status quo or "broadening their cultural horizons" (Emmett, 1968-1969).

From the point of view of media policy, then, we reject the view that an application of the uses and gratifications approach to policy questions must inevitably support the status quo or exonerate the producers of junk. That belief seems to require the acceptance of one or both of two other assumptions: that existing patterns of audience needs support the prevailing patterns of media provision and no other; and that audience concerns are in fact trivial and escapist. For reasons that should now be plain, we find both these propositions dubious.

Though audience oriented, the uses and gratifications approach is not necessarily conservative. While taking account of what people look for from the media, it breaks away from determinist assumptions about the dependence of content on audience propensities by bringing to light the great variety of needs and interests that are encompassed by the latter. As McQuail, Blumler, and Brown (1972) have argued, uses and gratifications data suggest that the mass media may not, after all, be as "constrained as the escapist theory makes out from performing a wider range of social functions than is generally assigned to them in western societies today." In other words, instead of depicting the media as severely circumscribed by audience expectations, the uses and gratifications approach highlights the audience as a source of challenge to producers to cater more richly to the multiplicity of requirements and roles that it has disclosed.

In conclusion, one example may be cited from the political communication field to suggest that audience attitudes might support some reform of mass media provision. In the absence of gratifications data, political communications had long been discussed chiefly in terms tied to the aims of would-be persuaders—individuals and groups wishing to influence people and change their attitudes.

Empirical investigation of what voters look for when following an election campaign, however, not only helped refreshingly to change the perspective; it also underlined the importance for many citizens of the surveillance function of political information flows (e.g., to see what some party will do if it comes to power, to keep up with the main issues of the day, and to judge what political leaders are like).

This finding in turn provided a basis for the formulation of proposals to restructure the pattern of election broadcasting in order to make campaign argument more meaningful to people and to counteract incipient feelings of frustration, skepticism, and alienation (Blumler and McQuail, 1968, ch. 14); and to enhance the effectiveness of election campaigns regarded as "the major learning experience of democratic politics" (Katz, 1971). It is also of interest to note in this connection that most of the objections to these proposals stemmed, in Britain at least, from the major political parties; professional journalists and reporters working in the political communication field gave them wholehearted support (Blumler, 1969).

Thus, the constraints confining producers to familiar routines and conventional forms of packaging may derive less often than is commonly assumed from audience expectations, and more often either from characteristics of the media organizations that employ them, or from the dependence of these organizations on the surrounding power structure.

3

MASS COMMUNICATION AND SOCIALIZATION

Herbert H. Hyman

"Three passions, simple but overwhelmingly strong, have governed my life," Bertrand Russell (1951) informs us in the opening sentence of his autobiography. Apart from "the longing for love" and "the search for knowledge," his third passion, which I stress now, was "unbearable pity for the suffering of mankind." He tells us, "echoes of cries of pain reverberate in my heart." His beginning makes a fine beginning for us.

My primary purpose here is to emphasize important and neglected problems in the study of mass communication and socialization and to suggest some new and needed lines of theorizing and research, rather than to review past work. Russell's remarks, however remote from the topic they may seem, will free our thoughts from their conventional moorings and start us on a new and fruitful course. A more traditional treatment of the topic can wait and will be presented later.

THE SOCIAL SENTIMENTS AND MASS COMMUNICATION

Ponder Russell's phrasing. He does not say cries of pain arouse his passion. The echoes of the cries are enough to create in him unbearable pity. How apt for our topic. The mass media are a larger and better echo chamber than all the valleys of the Alps. Through that medium cries from all the world figuratively reverberate and reach us. I do not think anyone would question that fact, even though the total symphony of sounds has other variations. How many cries of joy and anger are mixed in? What mood predominates? Is the tone altogether too mournful? These matters are problematic and worthy of study, but a bigger problem immediately comes to mind.

In Russell's case the echoes reverberated in his heart, the ancient seat of the passions, and thus aroused "unbearable pity," what I shall properly label a moral or social sentiment. He reminds us of that neglected general concept—my first major theme.

36

The echoes through the media surely reach our ears. They should enlarge our sympathies if only by expanding awareness of the suffering of others. Immediately, we are led to ask whether in fact they do reverberate in our hearts and arouse such sentiments as pity. If not, why not? I do not think we have the answer in past research, because we have rarely formulated the question in quite the way that the concept, sentiment, would shape it.

By way of illustration, consider a new study in Israel that is a genuine contribution and innovative approach to exploring social-psychological functions of mass media. Katz, Gurevitch, and Haas (1973) asked individuals to rate the importance of thirty-five different personal needs and how well each was served or gratified by various media. One of these thirty-five indeed implied an important sentiment—in their phrasing the need to "overcome loneliness"; in Russell's phrasing, the "longing for love . . . because it relieves . . . that terrible loneliness." So did a few others; but most of the thirty-five items were not sentiments.

Guided only by the concept "need" Katz, Gurevitch, and Haas would not be led to ask whether one felt, and no man in his right mind (except Russell and a few moralists and psychologists) would have said that it was important to feel, unbearable pity. It is not a need or desire that one has and seeks to satisfy, but it is a sentiment that the media may conceivably help arouse in adults or inculcate in children.

Katz and his colleagues tried to assemble, by reference to the literature, "as comprehensive a list as possible of social and psychological needs said to be satisfied by exposure to the mass media." But no competent psychologist's published catalogue of needs would include sympathy, indignation, revulsion, contempt, shame, remorse—which Adam Smith (1969), William McDougall (1960) and others have described as the most painful of sentiments—or kindness, trust, *ressentiment*. None of these entities are needs or drives. That they influence our conduct and the conduct of others and that they may be brought to us, like it or not, by the media and other sources of socialization is the case. Just how much comes via the media we do not know.

It is clear that sentiments have a great deal to do with the quality of life in society. Apropos the point, note the odd item that crept into Katz, Gurevitch, and Haas' list. The respondents were asked how important it was "to feel pride that we have a state." That social sentiment, to some an extension of what McDougall (1960) called the "self-regarding sentiment," would not have been found in any conventional catalogue of psychological needs or drives. It just does not belong there. The item must have been included only as a result of the researchers' "own insight into the specific functions of the media in Israel," which they examined in order to supplement the original list of "needs" culled from the literature.

The sentiment "pride in the state" is clearly of utmost importance in Israeli social life. It crowned the list of thirty-five needs. The percentage of the sample saying it was "very important" to them—90 per cent—was higher than the figure obtained for any of the other needs. The inquiry documents that the radio, television, and newspaper media are "very helpful" in arousing or strengthening that sentiment in substantial majorities of the sample. Only through the fortunate accident of the special site of the study, and through the very broad and loose usage of a concept, do we obtain such a striking demonstration of the importance of sentiments and the influence upon them of the media.

In contrast with Israelis, I doubt very much that recent experiences of adult Americans or the way the new generation has been socialized would have led anywhere near 90 per cent to have said that pride in the nation was very important to them. We have not recently formed a new nation under heroic conditions. But the distribution of that sentiment among adults and children, the ways in which national pride has been shaped gradually by events and by the media—at times becoming enlarged, perhaps even overblown, and at other times diminished, perhaps even washed away, by other sentiments such as shame—these are important problems here too.

Although many sentiments are pleasurable, such as pride that causes no pain until it is shattered, others are a source of pain, such as Russell's unbearable pity. Individuals, of course, desire to avoid pain. Thus it might seem that research on the gratification from, and uses of, the media—especially when it is guided by the model of escapism—would yield evidence on the avoidance of communications that aroused painful social sentiments, thus providing one possible answer to our earlier question.

The echoes through the media of cries of pain may not reverberate in our hearts, because somehow we tune out, or deafen ourselves, to escape from unbearable pity. Spencer, a classic writer on the sentiments, talked of moral callousness, the calluses we must build up to reduce excessive sensitivity, although he had in mind specialists—surgeons, soldiers, and fox hunters, specifically—whose professional activities would be impaired by too much sympathy. Following Byron's line in Don Juan: "And if I laugh at any mortal thing, 'tis that I may not weep," McDougall (1960), the great modern writer on the sentiments, stresses that laughter is our protection against sympathy carried too far. And so we watch entertainments, the answer might go, or treat tragedy as comedy.

In the long run, entertainment may lead some people not away from but back toward more painful content. It may serve the function of a buffer, insulating the audience from what would otherwise be an unending symphony of unbearable cries, from which they all would have to flee (Hyman, 1963). By this logic, tragedy can be treated for what it is because there is some comic relief elsewhere. We need not build up our own calluses; the partial insulation we need is provided for us. We can still hear the cries, perhaps just because they are diluted, and they do indeed reverberate in the hearts of some of us. To be sure, individuals differ in their thresholds for pain, and for some no mix other than pure entertainemnt whatsoever would be tolerable, but surely the buffer will increase the number who hear the cries.

Conceivably, research might find an alternative answer to our question. Buffering or deafening ourselves may not be necessary at all. The echoes, even though intermittent, reach our ears in such a stream and with such a shrieking intensity that we have lost the capacity to hear them. The model is that classic disorder known as "boilermaker's deafness," such workers having been exposed so long to the intense noises of that trade that they become selectively deaf to these frequencies because particular receptors in the ear have been literally destroyed.*

The irony is that research guided by the "escapist" model has generally been inattentive to our theme and thus has produced little pointed evidence on exposure to, or reception of stimuli to, painful sentiments. Researchers guided by this model often examine whether children or adults use the media to escape from the unpleasantness of their own daily lives, to forget their private problems, or to satisfy their unfulfilled needs by being caught up in the entertainments and fantasies presented by the media. But that kind of content might still, if only at the imaginative level, present all sorts of unpleasant plights and play upon the audience's sentiments. Katz and Foulkes (1962) put it well. "Even if it is true that alienation or deprivation tend to drive people to seek refuge in the mass media, it is not at all self-evident what they find when they get there."

Thus, it is possible that old-fashioned audience research is more suggestive for our problem since it describes the distributions and patterns of differential exposure to types of media content. But here, too, the conventional categories for classification are not pointed enough to discriminate the exposures to various kinds of sentiment-arousing material. Note, for example, the sympathy-arousing content of what we might classify as an "entertainment"—the daytime radio serial of thirty years ago. This is not merely of antiquarian interest; it bears upon the socialization of the cohort of young women who are the grandmothers of today.

> Human existence is pictured as being continuously threatened by catastrophe. There is not just one problem which has to be faced by a character or a group of characters, but an uninterrupted chain of more or less severe nuisances. . . . An unsophisticated serial listener who accepts these programs as convincing and true must carry away the impression that human life is a series of attacks to be warded off by the victims and their helpers [Arnheim, 1944].

The television soap opera, thirty years later in 1970, is no different judging by Katzman's (1972) content analysis. Here is the summary, followed by the detailed box score, which totals up to eighty-five problems in one week:

> On the whole, the world of the soap opera was full of troubles. Problems seem to keep the shows moving along. They are not major problems like war, forest fires, outlaw bands, or national security. Rather, they are "realistic" problems of shady business deals, illness, young people and drugs, marital infidelity, and so forth.

---

*The model of "boilermaker's deafness" is intended only as a metaphor. That we may actually become de-sensitized, however, to sensory and emotional stimuli by repeated stimulation is well known. In its application to media exposure, see, for example, the discussion of "blunting" and "emotional habituation" in the report of the National Commission on the Causes and Prevention of Violence (Lange, Baker and Ball, 1969, pp. 404-405).

1 blackmail
1 bigamy
3 threats or instances of violence
2 murders
2 other deaths
1 poison
1 illegal drug traffic
3 cases of business difficulties
3 professional men on probation or fired
2 cases of drunkenness
4 youth involved with drugs
4 offspring of parents not married to each other
1 adoption of a child
5 cases of family estrangement
2 mental illnesses
4 psychosomatic illnesses
5 cases of physical disability
4 pregnancies
3 successful medical treatments
2 instances of important medical research
3 romances in trouble
3 new romances
4 marriages in trouble
8 clear cases of marital infidelity
2 cases of potential marital infidelity
3 divorces or annulments
1 reconciliation of a married couple
7 impending marriages

Any audience escaping from its own problems was plunged into this bloodbath. It evidently was not too much to take, judging by the size of the audience, but it may have been so much that it verged on the ridiculous or grotesque. Yet this sort of fare could create, to adopt Cooley's (1956) fine phrase, "imaginative sociability"; it could arouse in those not overly sophisticated a sympathy for the human condition—perhaps even to the point of unbearable pity. Similarly, news programs contain not just cold fact but, as already implied, the cries and injustices of the world, which might shape the sentiments as well as the knowledge of the viewers. The problem is that the categories are cut so as to blur our point because they have not been constructed with reference to their "sentimental" content.

What is the relevance of all this to socialization? Go to the root meaning of the term: the process by which the individual learns to become social, a member of society. To socialize, as the Oxford English Dictionary defines it, is simply "to make [someone] fit for living in society," meaning that he is taught to be sensitive to the coexistence and demands of others. The sentiments or complexes of ideas and feelings about social relations, about the self vis-à-vis others (ignore for our purposes sentiments about nature, the supernatural world, and the animal world) are thus fundamental. They set the social tone.

Of course, a child is prepared for a particular kind of social life. Thus, the term always has an added meaning: learning through various agencies the distinctive patterns that fit an individual into the particular place and subgroup in which he lives. These include not only sentiments but all sorts of phenomena. But surely we should not exclude from our studies the sentiments we learn. Yet they have been neglected in our attention to, for example, the socialization of impulses and drives; attitudes; knowledge and beliefs; and political, social, and occupational roles, norms, and values. In studying the socializing influences of the media, I stress the socialization of sentiments, about which we know so little.

In examining this neglected area, the same research designs that have worked to demonstrate the formation, growth, persistence, and change of other patterns under the influences of various agencies—parents, peers, schools, churches, etc., and/or mass media—can be applied. After all, the basic methodological problems in tracing some developmental process and revealing some causal agent are the same whether we study sentiments or other patterns.

Designs that have already served us well can serve us once again: longitudinal studies following samples of particular children through time; quasi-longitudinal studies juxtaposing groups at various ages and stages of development; comparative, quasi-experimental studies of children from contrasted social settings and exposed to contrasted institutions; descriptive, observational studies of the ways parents and other parties guide children and interpose themselves between the child and the larger world and affect his responses to those experiences; content analyses of the guidance provided by such agents; or intensive, quasi-clinical studies of the ways individuals search for, select out, and learn from the flux of their experience the normative cues that guide them; or true experiments that simulate some real life-experience and measure change following exposure to such a treatment—all these designs have their proper place in a program of research on the socialization of the sentiments and the contribution of the mass media.

Investigators, to be sure, must use a little creativity in adapting these designs to the new purpose. Ironically, the general literature provides no detailed blueprint that can be followed mechanically to study the influence of mass communication on the socialization of any pattern, let alone the socialization of sentiments, since that ubiquitous force in contemporary society has been neglected because of attention to other traditional socializing agencies.

A reading of the chapter on socialization in the most recent edition of *The Handbook of Social Psychology* (Zigler and Child, 1969) will convey the irony. This encyclopedic review has more than 150 pages and over 600 references but makes no explicit reference whatsoever to mass media, although the summary of the studies on aggression (for those in the know) implicitly deals with the media.

Considerable guidance on the design of research, however, can be obtained by turning instead to the specialized literature on the ways in which mass communication has specifically influenced the socialization of particular patterns. The studies by Child, Potter, and Levine (1946); Himmelweit, Oppenheim, and Vince (1958); Maccoby and Wilson (1957); and Schramm, Lyle, and Parker (1961) will be reviewed later. These few alone present a diversity of designs. General discussions of the function of mass communication in sociali-zation, such as those by Roberts (1973) and Wright (1959) also provide guidance.

What will challenge investigators is the construction of the instruments for measuring the sentiments that are aroused and formed in the course of socialization through stimulation by the media and other social agencies. Clearly, new investigators cannot just copy instruments from the many others currently working in the field of mass communication or elsewhere, since the study of sentiments has fallen into terrible neglect. But they can find guidance in conceptualizing and measuring sentiments if they go back into the distant past or recall the occasional modern investigator who has not forgotten about sentiments. Some of the classic writers, reviewed later, show us fruitful lines of theorizing; some of the moderns suggest the kinds of verbal instruments and observations of behavior that have been used as indicators of sentiment and can be incorporated into new inquiries.

Three well-known studies, modern albeit not from this year or yesteryear, will convey how central sentiments can become in the experience of audiences for mass communication and how readily they can be measured among children and adults by large-scale surveys, focused interviews, or content analysis.

In the parallel surveys of the reactions of adults (Sheatsley and Feldman, 1965) and children (Siegel, 1965) to the news of President Kennedy's assassina-tion, responses to a list of statements "representing the ways some people felt when they first heard that the President was dead" revealed among adults that "the first reactions of nine out of ten Americans were *sympathy* for Mrs. Kennedy and the children"; that four out of five were bereaved, "felt deeply the *loss of someone very close* and dear"; that "five out of six admitted to deep feelings of '*shame* that such a thing could happen in our country' "; and that about three out of four felt *moral indignation*, "felt angry that anyone should do such a terrible deed" (Sheatsley and Feldman, 1965, pp. 155-156, emphasis supplied). The findings were almost identical for the children. In light of the four sentiments aroused in so many, chosen by the respondents from a list of 17 possible cognitive and affective responses, Sheatsley and Feldman are indeed right in their judgment that "the death of a chief of state can reveal a great deal about the sentiments that normally surround the incumbent of that office" and, one might add, that are stimulated and transmitted by mass communica-tion.

Merton's (1946) *Mass Persuasion*, as many may recall, was an analysis of the reasons why Kate Smith's radio marathons in 1943 were so effective in persuading the American people to buy war bonds. But what many may have forgotten is that Merton's central hypotheses were that the sentiments aroused, rather than rational self-interest or pecuniary gain, were the potent force, and that his content analysis of her words and deed and character, and his focused interviews about the audience's responses provided confirmation. Over and over again, his text underlines the importance of sentiments. The program involved "technicians in sentiment," the "management of pathos." The performance activated "remorse," "pathos-laden sentiments." Against the societal back-ground of "distrust," Smith in her person and her deed incarnated "bene-volence," "altruism," "humanitarianism." "She appealed only to 'higher' sentiments. . . . To tinge such contributions with commercialism would profane the sentiments centered about war bonds." Even among those who resented her, the key to their reactions was that her arguments were too "sentimental." These three studies and others still to be mentioned should suffice to create renewed interest in the sentiments among mass communication researchers, and to give them confidence about and cues for the development of appropriate measuring instruments.

Research on sentiments would shed light not only on a new sphere of socialization that is important of itself, but also—automatically—on many *old* topics for which our research findings remain shallow or enigmatic. By way of a simple illustration consider the finding of Katz, Gurevitch, and Haas (1973) that television served to assuage loneliness, a finding that I am sure is sound and not limited to Israel. It fills up the emptiness contained in the flux of feelings associated with loneliness, and it creates "imaginative sociability." But why, in the first place, is the sentiment of loneliness so common in people, even when they are not recently bereaved or in the midst of a terrible crisis, when they do need the help of others?

Being alone has not always been regarded as a distressing experience. Indeed, some wise men have sensed that it can be a most contemplative state, even a blessing. As Riesman, Glazer and Denney (1950) put it in their great phrase, in the midst of others we are still a "lonely crowd." Perhaps the media (television, for example) help create the sentiment of loneliness, the ideas and feelings we have about aloneness, and thus have a wonderful thing going for them, like advertisers who create a need that only their product can satisfy.

AGGRESSION AND SYMPATHY

The way in which old but enigmatic findings could be clarified by inquiry into the socialization of sentiments is best illustrated by a perennial problem: the effects of exposure to violence in the media on children's own tendencies to violence. It is hard to think of an area that has been studied more. On top of the sophisticated and subtle earlier literature, already overwhelming in magnitude, about fifty new studies were commissioned and presented in support of the Surgeon General's recent report (1972) on the problem. I would not even attempt to review this huge literature—it defies any attempt at a brief summary.

Fortunately, the earlier literature has been ably examined by Berkowitz (1962, chap. 9), Maccoby (1964), Weiss (1969, vol. 5, pp. 124-141), Roberts (1973), and others; and Bogart (1972-1973) has given us a thorough and thoughtful critique of the six volumes issued by the Surgeon General. Not all the subtle questions have yet been answered, but the biggest question has been. Entirely too much violence has been documented repeatedly for the American mass media. It does increase aggressive tendencies among at least some children, and since it seems to benefit hardly anyone, why have it the way it is.

Yet there is one big question, obvious to those concerned with sentiments, that remains unanswered. This despite the fact—if I may indulge in a bit of perverse humor—that the field of violence has been worked to death. There is one dimension of the problem that is lacking in most of the research.

Start with the simplified model: whenever there is a violent act that is not trivial, there is a victim who bleeds, cries in pain, suffers loss of property or some more subtle form of distress, or who is threatened by force with such consequences. We need not call Russell as an expert witness to know that the victim should arouse our sympathy.

Now we face what is enigmatic about the effects demonstrated in children after observing aggressors and their victims engaged in violent encounters in the media. If it is regarded as "natural" that observing such scenes should increase children's aggressive tendencies, it is equally natural to assume that it should also increase their sympathies. Both are primitive patterns. Cooley (1956), in describing the young, talked of "primitive kindliness." And Lois Murphy (1937), in her studies of nursery-school children forty years ago, enumerated endless acts of sympathy by two- to four-year-old children toward other children who were in distress, either because they were victims of an aggressor or because they had been accidentally hurt.

Perhaps our sympathies, or those of our children, are not those of a Bertrand Russell, but sympathy for those in distress has always been recognized as a fundamental sentiment. To be sure, not even a young Russell might feel unbearable pity for a bobo doll, or a flower choked by a weed, perhaps not for a cartoon character who is too far from human in representation—these being some of the victims that the children observe in the experimental simulations and real media presentations whose effects are being traced. That, after all, might be too sentimental a response. Logic, even what Pascal called the logic of the heart, tells us that such victims feel no pain. Set such studies aside—no great mystery surrounds them. Aggressions of that type meet only weak opposition from us because there is no real victim to arouse our sympathy.

But when the child observes a real victim he should be taking away from the experience at least a grain of sympathy as well as a quantum of aggression. His total repertoire of social behavior, pro- and anti-, should have grown. To someone who looks at studies of real victims through the twin lenses provided by a theory of aggression and a theory of sentiments, the findings indeed appear enigmatic, and the mystery surrounding them needs to be solved.

Follow one of the clues that Lois Murphy (1937) left us three decades ago. She and her staff watched forty children for 432 hours and recorded no less than 5,000 social episodes. I quote her observations at some length to stress the clue. She emphasized "the striking prevalence of both aggressive and protective patterns in all the groups" (p. 64). The quantitative analysis of total scale scores revealed that:

Sympathetic-behavior scores correlated positively with aggressive-behavior scores, under all conditions. . . . An item analysis . . . is even more interesting. . . . The most dramatic relationship which appears here is a correlation of .91 between item 4 (joins attack on one child by another) and item 10 (defends child attacked by another). Item 25 (attempts to comfort another child with pats, embraces, and the like) gives a correlation of .58 with item 19 (pushes or pulls another child without regard for his discomfort) . . . [pp. 167-169].

These paradoxical findings are clarified by the realization that there is "a tendency for outgoing behavior of all kinds, both aggressive and sympathetic" (p. 167), and that "children who are active in a situation calling for aggressive response are apt to be active in a situation calling for sympathetic response" (p. 169).

In contrast to Murphy's children, where has all the sympathy gone in our children who are now observing violent television or simulations of it? Could it just have vanished over the last forty years leaving only naked aggression? I doubt it. Murphy's children, of course, grew up before the age of television. Some might turn this fact into compelling proof, arguing that the sympathy has not just vanished, but that it was driven from the scene by the very institution of television. I doubt that, too. The key to the mystery may simply be that many modern researchers, unlike Lois Murphy, make their observations over too brief a time interval to catch a sequence in which both aggression and sympathy have been aroused or, in their aggressive concentration on aggression, fashion measuring instruments that simply provide no place for sympathy to be entered into the data.*

If our modes of measurement were more inclusive, more extended, perhaps typological, we could make a better case. We might find some children in whom both aggression and sympathy were heightened, a mixed blessing at best. Sympathy could be made to grow in other ways, not just by paying the price in increased aggression. Such a typological approach might reveal the starkest finding—a large number in whom aggression increased untempered by any growth of sympathy. Within the large number now scored simply as showing no increase in aggression, the concealed but admirable type whose sympathies had grown at no price in increased aggression might conceivably be revealed as considerable, or so few in number as to make the picture still starker.

The Surgeon General's group, titled the "Scientific Advisory Committee on Television and Social Behavior," was not unmindful of the broader mandate, implied by the title, to study both pro- and anti-social behavior. Indeed in the concluding chapters of the general report on "future research" and "the unfinished agenda," there are pointed references to the social sentiments and the matters I have raised, and relevant remarks are scattered through earlier chapters. The irony is that most of the empirical studies in the five supporting volumes provide no evidence on the problem. The few that do strengthen my argument.

Tannenbaum's research in progress provides some evidence, but most impressive is Stein and Friedrich's (1972), in which nursery-school children aged three to five were observed for a protracted period: an initial three weeks for baseline measures, followed by four weeks of exposure to several contrasted treatments of television content (aggressive, neutral, or pro-social), and a final two-week period for post-measurements of effects.

---

*Monica Blumenthal, one of the writers of the National Commission Report (Lange, Baker and Ball, 1969), made a good suggestion apropos the point, which seems never to have been followed up. "In addition to . . . studies of the short-run effects of the mass media on . . . violence, we need to begin consideration of [its] long-term effects . . . on the adult character. We need to develop measures of empathy, which are now missing from the set of tools available for making psychological measurements" (p. 491).

That is just the kind of design needed. One finding, to quote the Surgeon General (1972), was that "the high-status children showed an increase in *pro-social* behavior after viewing *aggressive* programming" (vol. 1, p. 112, emphasis supplied). Bogart (1972-1973), in his review, singled out the finding and remarked, "*Curiously*, the aggressive programs also seemed to increase social interaction, including cooperative interaction. . . ." (p. 502, italics supplied). The general effect would not be curious at all to the student of sentiments, although it is curious that the finding was limited to the upper stratum. (The pro-social behavior of the lower stratum was increased by the pro-social programs.)*

I am not suggesting that sympathy follows reflexively from every vicarious experience with "violence" in the media. There is not enough evidence to support that argument. Rather, there are good reasons to argue against it. There is much evidence that exposure for some instigates nothing but aggression. This does not mean that the study of the sentiment is irrelevant to our problem, but only that the *simple* model presented will not carry us much farther. However, even the simple model will carry us a little bit farther. In Gerbner's content analyses for the Surgeon General (1972), no pain was conveyed in over half of the violent episodes, and in the Barcus study, only 4 per cent of the human victims were injured or killed. One is reminded of the capsule content analysis by Himmelweit, Oppenheim, and Vince (1958): "In one fairly typical Western we found that 149 shots were fired, yet no one was killed and only one man seriously injured, a second one slightly" (p. 183). There simply weren't enough real victims to arouse our sympathies and perhaps the lesson learned here was that aggression is a relatively harmless game anyone can play.†

Experimental evidence in support of the point is provided by studies in which a person's helplessness or the degree of injury is manipulated and the effects on subsequent aggressive or altruistic acts by the spectator are measured. In general, helplessness and the knowledge of severe injury increased helping behavior and reduced subsequent acts of aggression by the spectator (Berkowitz, 1962).

---

*Although the findings are based on adults, Almond and Verba (1963, pp. 265-273) found class differences in five countries, the lower groups having a more distrustful and misanthropic view of people. This sub-cultural pattern could obviously influence the young who would be more likely, therefore, to see others as objects of fear or suspicion rather than as objects of sympathy.

†The National Commission on Violence (1969), in reviewing the research available at that time concludes that "aggressive impulses may be held in check if the viewer has been made especially aware of the suffering that may result from violence. Production codes for most of the media include prohibitions against the portrayal of physical agony and suffering and too much punishment. Question: When this kind of *de facto* self-censorship operates to 'sanitize' violence by 'prettying up' or entirely omitting the real consequences of aggression, is the result again an unwitting creation of the very conditions found most conducive to the instigation to aggression? Laboratory research suggests that it is" (p. 244).

The Commission also quotes the astute observation on Westerns by a critic, Robert Warshaw: "Our eyes are not focused on the sufferings of the defeated, but on the deportment of the hero." And the Commission adds: "It is just these painful sufferings of the defeated victim, however, that may allow the provoked viewer to 'think twice' about acting out his own aggressive impulses" (p. 407).

Berkowitz followed up his major research program on the instigation of aggression with a program of research into pro-social behavior (1972). Some of his analyses of social class differences among adolescents in England and the United States in norms about helping may help us understand the "curious" findings by Stein and Friedrich (1972) noted earlier.

The subtle question we must examine, however, is not how many victims and how much victimization, but who is a victim and who is an aggressor and toward whom do our sympathies and other sentiments flow. Here we must turn to a more complex model. In Murphy's (1937) most dramatic finding, there was a correlation of .91 between joining in the attack on one child and defending a child attacked by another. The aggressor in the first instance might have been a previous victim of the present victim, and so the child's sympathies and other moral sentiments may all flow in his direction, rather than in the direction of the new victim. What we decide is aggression in the first place and what we take to be justified aggression may affect our sympathies, and our sympathetic behavior may in turn be aggressive.

Adam Smith formulated much of this so well back in 1759 in his *Theory of Moral Sentiments*. According to his "principle of propriety," our sympathies, for example, will not go out to a previous victim "upon bringing the case home to our own breast" whose actions are "extravagant and out of proportion" to his cause (p. 18). By this principle, the new aggressor (but old victim) may lose our sympathies, and the new victim, though in the wrong and a former aggressor, may regain them.

One might pursue Smith's principle, exploring the degree to which no impropriety is attached to the extremes to which a wrong is righted by violent means on television. Not only that, the child generally observes such an aggressor being commended and rewarded. The child has an incipient principle of propriety that may have to be strengthened so that his sentiments that justice must be served are not carried to excess.

If no impropriety were sensed by the spectator, one might assume that all his sympathies would flow in the direction of the "aggressor" whose cause is just. He commands our sympathies, compels our admiration, draws our moral sentiments his way. He seems to have everything going for him, and might be just the kind of exemplar who would increase the spectator's own tendencies to aggression. Yet Smith does not see it that way. Although he recognizes that "the villain . . . is as much the object of our indignation as the hero is that of our sympathy and affection," and states that we do find hatred and resentment sympathetic, nevertheless, he presents a model of the process that may seem strange to us. "Our sympathy is *divided*." "Our fear for what the one may suffer, damps our resentment for what the other has suffered. Our sympathy, therefore, with the man who has received the provocation, necessarily falls short of the passion which naturally animates him" (Smith, 1969, p. 44, emphasis supplied).

The model may be extreme, and Smith may have been wrong about the contemporary division of our sympathies; yet he makes us wonder why the new victim does not have more going for him, and why the aggressions of the child spectators are as easily released as they seem to be in the studies of the problem. Surely there ought to be more sympathy for the victim, who sometimes is treated with impropriety, who at worst should still get a piece of the sympathy when it is divided, and who, when he is innocent, ought to command our *undivided* sympathy.

Adam Smith has given us a lead in his formulation of the basic process underlying sympathy, although he has been hotly criticized by the few who have written systematic treatises on the sentiments. We sympathize with a victim—old or new—because we see ourselves in his situation and "we then tremble and shudder at the thought of what he feels" (Smith, 1969, p. 4). The process of identification, though not explicit, creates the link between our vicarious experience from the media and our response.

But there is another implicit feature in Smith's argument that I think provides the more important clue for us. When we realize that we, ourselves, would suffer in a situation, we must carry the process one step further—and back to the victim. We must conclude that he suffers in the same way we would. Now it is perfectly possible that sympathy is aborted at that point because we conclude that he is less sensitive than we, or completely insensitive. He is a stoic Indian or some other category of insensitive creature. Smith suggests to us what might be called an "ethnocentric theory of sympathy," and we might well explore the way the media help to define others as lacking our capacities to suffer, and therefore not being victims for whom we feel unbearable pity.

Thinking in the vein suggested by the notion of ethnocentrism, it is that those least likely to deserve our sympathies are our "enemies." In addition to being defined as less human creatures with lesser sensitivities, they may have been defined as not deserving our moral sentiments. It is ironic that, despite all the attention paid to the way violent *fantasies* in the media instigate violence among our own children, little attention is paid to the way the violent *realities* of war, refracted in particular fashion through the media, may socialize our children into aggression or sympathy.

Long ago, in examining evidence on the role of family in political socialization, I noted that out of perhaps a hundred intra-family correlations between the attitudes of parents and their children, the only *negative* findings were in the area of attitude toward war (Hyman, 1959, pp. 70-72). The children did not resemble their parents but the evidence from unbiased sample surveys—not from the social composition of groups of demonstrators—indicated that the younger generations were if anything *more* bellicose, more pro-war (Erskine, 1970). What had socialized them and where had all their sympathies for the victims of war gone were unanswered questions.

In the Vietnam war, truly the media have pictured the suffering and echoed the cries of pain of the victims, and the evidence is just beginning to suggest that there has been a sharp change in the newest generation of youth (Erskine, 1972-1973). But this is only juxtaposition, not proof that the media have had much to do with it. An innovative, small-scale study of a cohort of high-school seniors, conducted by Hollander (1971), should inspire us to pursue inquiries in the area of the socialization of sentiments, which may underlie our attitudes toward this institution of organized violence. Hollander asked the youth in his study to assess the relative importance of various socializing agencies in determining their ideology about war in general and the

Vietnam war in particular. In contrast to church, family, friends, and the school, the media are reported to be far and away the most important influence, and television the most important among the several media. The several suggestive studies—far too few, given the importance of the problem—must be expanded.

Whatever the ethnocentric circle to which we are sympathetic, Adam Smith is most explicit about another variable that governs our responses. "It is by the imagination only" that we transport ourselves into their situation, and the outcome depends on "the vivacity or dullness of [our] conception" (Smith, 1969, pp. 3-4). Thus we are led to the study of individual differences, but parsimony requires that we at least consider whether the presentation itself is so dull as to reduce the vivacity of anyone's conception.

Writing in 1909, when only print was around, Cooley (1956) welcomed "the new communication [that] spread like morning light over the world, awakening, enlightening, enlarging" but he did recognize its limitations.

> We may *read* statistics of the miserable life of the Italians and Jews in New York and Chicago; of bad housing, sweatshops and tuberculosis; but we care little more about them than we do about the sufferers from the Black Death, unless their life is realized to us in some human way, either by personal contact, or by *pictures* and imaginative description [Cooley, 1956, pp. 88-89, emphasis supplied].

I think we can guess what Cooley would say now, at a time when pictures and imaginative descriptions from the newest medium bring the whole world into our homes. We can dismiss the hypothesis that the pictures are too pallid, and return to the hypothesis that the dullness of our own conceptions, along with other variables reviewed, accounts for the lack of sympathy in many of us, despite our exposure to the problems of others. That may leave only a few who are capable of making the most of their socialization into sympathy via the contemporary mass media, but we should not see this in the worst light.

Russell again provides a good illustration. Very few children or adults have his imagination and exquisite powers of sympathy and can respond to the echoes in the media as he did. We cannot even claim him as a victory for the *newer* mass media. Although he lived so long that he came to know the world of television toward the end of his days, he grew up long before it and radio and movies appeared on the scene. He was a child of the world of print of a hundred years ago. His case provides the ideal material to satirize a not uncommon point of view about the role of mass media in socialization.

Some who examine the effects of the mass media in instigating violence in children discount such effects on the grounds that there are individual differences in response; that those affected adversely are predisposed, perhaps because they are less than healthy; and that the size of that group relative to the general population is small. For sure, the policy implications of studies of differential effects cannot be drawn without background data on the prevalence of the various types in the population. Thus, experimental studies of communication and socialization must be joined with descriptive surveys of the child population to yield what Daniel Katz (1967) called a "social psychological taxonomy."

But even if the *numbers* who are potentially "at risk" are few, this does not dismiss the problem. Bogart (1972-1973) put it well in his review of the Surgeon General's report:

> Unfortunately, the Surgeon General's Committee had nothing to go on when it faced the inevitable question as to what proportion of young people are susceptible to the antisocial effects of TV violence. This represents a major flaw in the research program, since the question might have been anticipated. It is possible to draw inferences from independent, cross-sectional studies of the child population to determine what proportion appears vulnerable to the kinds of anxieties or frustrated rages that can be activated by violent fantasy. Even if this proportion is small (and the evidence suggests that for some critical subgroups of the population it may not be small at all), its size is no index of its potential for social disorder [p. 517].

The criterion, however, cuts both ways. Just as the size of the group affected in anti-social directions by the media is no index of its potential for social disorder, so, too, the small group that may have been benefited in their growth by the media is not an adequate index of its potential for social good. Russell, for example, was one in a million, but what a weight he had in the affairs of the world. If his growth was influenced only by print media let us not dismiss those "small" mass media from current consideration. If those at risk are less than healthy, we have perhaps all the more, not less, ground for concern. If those who benefit the most are uncommon children from rare circumstances, like Russell, let us not dismiss these either in weighing the scales.

These thoughts will soon lead us into our next major theme—small-scale and large-scale socialization. But there is more to be said on social sentiments, since a discussion of sympathy in no way exhausts that spacious problem of the role of the media in socializaing our sentiments.

ANTICIPATORY SOCIALIZATION, REFERENCE GROUPS, AND *RESSENTIMENT*

In my treatment of the way in which mass communication may socialize our sentiments, I have emphasized one benign sentiment, the growth of sympathy for those who are in misery or victims of violence, and touched upon another usually regarded in an attractive light, the arousal of *moral indignation* toward wrongdoers. It would be unfair to leave the impression that mass communication in socializing our sentiments is only a force for good. A brief discussion of *ressentiment* will balance the presentation and show once more the way in which the study of the socialization of sentiments, conducted jointly with study of other patterns of socialization, can deepen otherwise shallow findings.

To set the stage for the problem, we must first discuss the *anticipatory* socialization function of mass communication, which itself has not been adequately studied. When Cooley (1956) saw the new communication spreading "like morning light over the world," he noted not only that it was "awakening," and "enlarging" but "filling with *expectation*" (p. 88, emphasis supplied). Communication tells us of the existence of other groups whose lives are more attractive; and, along with other forces it helps create new reference groups to which we aspire.

But mass communication plays an even more important *anticipatory* socialization function by helping us prepare ourselves for a new status and role in life. We have not been members of the reference groups to which we aspire; thus, we have had no opportunity to learn their ways. Nor can our parents—out of their own experience—help us; they are our primary group, not our reference group. The media can show us how. To be sure, we cannot learn everything simply from pictures and words. Recalling William James' distinction between "knowledge about" and "acquaintance with," we must recognize that observation does not give us practice in performing a role; we may, despite exposure, lack the intimate acquaintanceship we really need. But we can learn some of what we lack. The children Schramm, Lyle and Parker (1961) studied mentioned that television "helps me know how other kinds of people live." Long before that, Herzog (1944) established that radio daytime serials were not merely consumed as entertainment and escape, but that the audience sometimes identified with the characters and regarded their behavior as worthy of imitation.

Thus, the media can be an important source of otherwise inaccessible knowledge, not only to the children but also to those parents who may be ignorant but wish to help their child into another and better world than they had. We tend to think of anticipatory socialization generally in terms of class and social mobility, but in the United States we certainly should think of it in the context of moving out of a racially segregated minority group and into contact with other groups or into an equalitarian society whose patterns, whatever they may be, are not those of the minority group.

Two studies will suggest the way in which the media can contribute guidance to children engaged in anticipatory socialization. Gerson (1966) studied hundreds of Negro and white teen-agers in the San Francisco area in the early 1960s. Presumably, the Negro families included many migrants from the South. Most of them lived in a residentially segregated area, so primary-school experiences of most of the children had been under segregated conditions. Upon entering high school, they were thrust into a relatively novel, integrated school situation.

While Gerson did not deal specifically with inter-racial behavior, he found that over half of the children reported using a variety of media to check whether their own ideas about proper behavior were correct, and also to obtain new ideas and advice about appropriate behavior. The Negro children, however, were more likely to use the media as an agency of socialization, suggesting that they aspired to learn the ways of the larger society, guidance on which is less available to them from conventional sources.*

In a more experimental study, Maccoby and Wilson (1957) showed a movie to grade-school children. All of these children were white, but were divided among lower-class and middle-class families. The two main characters in the movie were a middle-class and a lower-class boy, both depicted in attractive ways, but differing in their characteristics and behavior. The audience was classified not only in terms of their social origins, but also in terms of their occupational aspirations. The screen character with whom the lower-class boys identified was dependent on the class to which they aspired, rather than on the present class of their family. In a later memory test of what they had learned from the film, the boys were also more likely to remember the behavior of the character with whom they had identified. The general way in which the media may function to aid anticipatory socialization is clear from these two examples.

The cues to be learned are in the media, often presented to the spectator by the prestigious model or reference individual, and a process of observational learning or modeling ensues. The slender base of direct evidence on which I have had to lean, of course, can be buttressed by a mountain of indirect evidence. Conclusions on the child's learning of aggression from the media are predicted, in a great many instances, on experimental evidence that imitation of the *aggressive* model occurs. Why shouldn't the same process apply to a non-aggressive and prestigious model? It is ironic that the abundance of theory and evidence are rarely examined for their general applicability to realms other than aggression.

Pointing to the parallels between aggressive and non-aggressive behavior may sharpen our understanding of both processes. I have suggested that learning the social patterns in a non-membership group by exposure to the media may fall short of perfection. The individual needs practice in the milieu of the new group to develop skill and sophistication in the role and styles of behavior. I think it is axiomatic that intimate acquaintanceship is required to learn some complex patterns well. The *faux pas* of the social climber is a stock item in literature and life.

Why, then, is it assumed by the students of aggression and the media that it is easy to learn the complex skills of aggression from mere observation, without any practice? I know that I will never shoot as well as Marshall Dillon no matter how long I watch him on television and I think that would also be obvious to a child. Among all the inhibitory factors that researchers have studied, they never seem to remark on the inhibitions a child raises for himself as he ponders the skill he needs and lacks to win a fight.

Perhaps some of the positive research findings are again an artifact of the instruments employed, which measure rudimentary acts of aggression that are

---

*Two analyses of 1970 data from independent national samples document differences among Negroes and whites in attitude toward and viewing of television. They also report differential patterning by age and socio-economic status in the two groups. The array of findings supports the view that television may be a more potent force in the general socialization of Negro youth and also serve the function of anticipatory socialization (Bogart, 1972, especially pp. 19-20; and Bower, 1973, pp. 45-49).

very easy to learn and perform. One might even venture the guess that many a child who tries out the aggressive skills observed on television learns the hard way that he had been played for a sucker, and never tries it again. The effects thus may be extinguished, although serious damage may have already been done to the child or to the person toward whom he displayed aggressiveness.

Another parallel and contrast between the two spheres of learning is worth pondering. In a most thoughtful essay in the earlier report on *Violence and the Media*, by the National Commission on the Causes and Prevention of Violence (1969), Catton remarks:

> People ordinarily learn in the process of being socialized that they can check doubtful impressions of the world around them which they have obtained from one source by seeking information from other, independent sources. The ubiquity of television ... tends to undermine the independence of anyone's alternative sources ... they may "confirm" his impressions because they have been watching the same shows. But, having thus obtained the same image from several sources which seem independent to him, this viewer's impression hardens into a conviction [p. 304].

The argument applies with even greater force to the sphere of anticipatory socialization into the patterns of a normative reference group. The child's peers are his primary group, a *membership* group. They have no independent knowledge of the patterns in the non-membership reference group he has adopted. They too had to learn most or all of it from the media.

One of Gerson's (1966) analyses is especially relevant to this discussion and provides intriguing findings. A scale of items yielded scores on "integration into the peer" group, and Gerson makes the reasonable assumption that the peers were predominantly from the youths' own racial groups. In the instance of the whites, integration made hardly any difference in the tendency to use the media for sources of socialization, the integrated perhaps leaning a bit more on the media. But among the Negro youths, the non-integrated were far more likely to socialize themselves via the media than the integrated Negroes or the non-integrated whites. Non-integration for these youths is to some extent a hidden indicator of the fact that they have adopted different reference groups, but it also means those Negro youths had no other source of normative guidance and, perforce, had to rely on the media.

The stage is now set for the discussion of a nasty sentiment that may be cultivated through the media. In itself, studies of the role of the media in anticipatory socialization into the patterns of a normative reference group would provide findings on an important and neglected problem. But those findings would have added depth if the dimension of sentiment were incorporated into the inquiries.

In the examples cited, the media present attractive normative reference groups and reference individuals, with whom we may identify, plus the cues the aspirant needs to engage in anticipatory socialization. But we all know that there are twin reference group processes: comparative as well as normative. Is it not reasonable to suggest that the higher-status groups in the media are also taken as points of comparison, and that the lower-class and Negro children in the audience then experience a vivid sense of relative deprivation? Whether one selects one reference group or another, whether one identifies with or compares himself to a given reference group, how the deprivation is interpreted and experienced, and what reaction follows—these matters are complex and not yet fully understood (Hyman and Singer, 1968). But certainly one of the consequences of relative deprivation is the arousal of *ressentiment*.

Scheler, who presented almost the saintly side of the sentiments in his work on sympathy, also presented the seamy side in his treatment of *ressentiment*, whose "origin," as he noted back in 1912 with foresightedness about reference group theory is

> connected with a tendency to make comparisons between others and oneself. . . . Each of us—noble or common, good or evil, continually compares his own value with that of others. If I choose a model, a 'hero,' I am somehow tied to such a comparison. All jealousy, all ambition, and even an ideal like the 'imitation of Christ' is full of such comparisons. . . . [From them may follow a] progression of feeling which starts with revenge and runs via rancor, envy, and impulse to detract all the way to spite, coming close to *ressentiment*. . . . This fire of a gigantic ressentiment could be fed by the media presentation of attractive lofty reference groups, whose life is out of reach [Scheler, 1972, pp. 46-47, 53].

In the old days, as content analyses show, the media conveyed a vivid contrast between the lives of the poor and the rich, the black and the white. Now, to be sure, content analyses suggest that things have been changing. Negroes, for example, are depicted in less stereotyped and downtrodden ways. But, ironically, the media may be damned whichever way the matter is presented to the viewer. If he engages in what Runciman has called "egoistic" comparisons, he may still see himself as a deprived member of his own group; if he engages in "fraternalistic" comparisons he may have seen his group as deprived relative to other groups (Hyman and Singer, 1968). There are possibilities for either kind of deprivation and for *ressentiment* when one's group is presented as better or worse off. I leave us and the media with this dilemma and turn from the theme of the sentiments to other aspects of socialization.

SMALL-SCALE AND LARGE-SCALE SOCIALIZATION

The extreme example of Russell, a single individual but a weighty one, was intended to make us realize the improtance of small- as well as large-scale socialization. There are pockets of uncommon men contained within the mass, and also small numbers of common men who do not react in the common way to the media, being more benefited or harmed than most. These effects, as I also argued earlier, should not be ignored. There are enclaves within the larger mass, some small and some large, who use the general media in special ways and who have their own separate media. Problems such as the one illustrated by my one example of the pattern reported among Negro youths should not be submerged in our research. Some media are smaller than others, but they still deserve the name, *mass* media, and satisfy most strict definitions of mass communication.

One has the intuition that the biggest, newest, most glamorous, and perhaps most entrancing medium of all—television—has so attracted our attentions and concerns that we, me included, neglect the older, smaller media and the role they play, if only in small-scale socialization. Indeed the audiences for these other media in the United States and other western countries are not small at all in absolute numbers; and in other countries, where television exists hardly or not at all, it is the other media that are truly the most massive of mass media. Within the larger or smaller media, there are sub-species—all sorts of special categories and varieties of mass communication—some of which now create only peculiar small-scale patterns of socialization.

David Riesman's memorable typology of communication—the mass media, the class media, and the ass media—will surely widen our horizons. I do not think he ever put it into print (perhaps it is better reserved for interpersonal communication), but I have not forgotten it and it is too stimulating for our topic to lose. Perhaps there are many alternatives—not just these three gross types—to what are presently the prevalent forms of communication that we could make into future, larger-scale communication if they deserved it. We shall never know what might best be maximized unless we study empirically a wide variety of such small-scale entities. I shall try to explore some of these areas in the hope that we can expand and redirect some of our research into communication and socialization.

Varieties of Books

I start with the smallest mass medium of all, books. Surveys report that a substantial majority of adult Americans have not read a single book in the last year. One recalls the child in *Wee Willie Winkie* who had reached the age and stage where at last he said, "Now I can truly read," and then added, "now I will never read anything in the world." But then, Kipling tells us, as Punch pushed his schoolbook into the cupboard with the other dull books buried there, out tumbled "Sharpe's Magazine" containing pictures and verses, and Punch suddenly realized what he had fallen into. "This . . . means things, and now I will know all about everything in all the world." And "he read till the light failed." The poet speaks the truth.

Even if the majority of Americans do not read, there are still millions left who do. Even if Punch is a rare type, the number may be too big to ignore. And, indeed, the kind of awakening that Kipling describes can be documented from real life. In his autobiography, Mahmut Makal tells us that, as a boy from a Turkish village, he had been educated to be a village teacher. In the process, he was exposed to the print media. Almost like Russell and his passions, Makal reports:

> You may wonder where I get this passion for newspapers. When I left
> the primary school . . . I had no notion even that anything was

published other than school-books. . . . Then . . . I suddenly got a taste for papers and periodicals. . . . It was as though whole worlds of fairy tales were disclosed to me in the pages of every newspaper, magazine, and book; and that terribly narrow world of mine became wider and wider [Makal, 1954, p. 99].

We may underrate how early books influence a child's socialization process. Long before children can read by themselves, they are being read to by their parents. Books, like other media, work by a "two-step flow of influence" brought to bear upon the child at a most formative stage—perhaps earlier than television intrudes.

There are an endless number of books, many of them with tiny sales and no consequences for socialization. We must pick strategic problems within this sphere. From the many content analyses of books, we get occasional hot ideas from researchers who have restricted their universe to books that have a *high probability* of being socializing forces—because they have the label of authority, because specialized institutions compel large numbers of people to read them at a most formative stage of their lives, and because the lessons to be learned from them are presented insidiously and persuasively. These restrictions go far to reduce the ambiguity of inferences from content analysis. Child, Potter and Levine (1946) provide a good example in their classic content analysis of all the third-grade reading primers adopted in American schools in a certain period, which were found not only to serve the manifest function of teaching reading skills but to serve the latent function of teaching characteristic American values.*

An even better instance of the latent content of primers, pushed very early into the child by the authoritative institution of the school, is provided by Ellis Freeman's (1936) examination of the arithmetic book used in a bygone era. He found as many as 643 problems that

accept and stress the concepts of capitalism and of our familiar commercial practices. These 643 consist only of those which . . . place stress on commercial transactions in which monetary gain was ever the motive. There is selling, buying and reselling, rent, working for wages, employing others for wages, and interest on loans [pp. 264-265].

---

*In a similar study, fourth-grade primers used in the United States over a period of 150 years were sampled and content analysed for trends in moral teaching, and in material likely to encourage needs for achievement and affiliation. Moral teaching showed, as expected, a regular and sharp decline over the last hundred years studied, but changes in the other variables are not what one might have predicted (DeCharmes and Moeller, 1962).

McClelland has done this on a comparative scale, for primers used in the second to fourth grade in forty countries, scoring the emphasis on need achievement. In all these studies, the content may be, and generally is, taken as a reflection of prior cultural patterns, but the medium then perpetuates the culture by socializing the next generation (McClelland, 1961).

The Cubans evidently discovered Freeman's point independently, and really put it to work in the mass literacy campaign launched by Castro in 1961. The manifest function was teaching the three Rs, but the not so latent function was political socialization. I quote only one of the long series of exercises from an arithmetic primer to be employed in the educational campaign:

Of the 18 employees of a business, 9 are militiamen, 5 belong to Committees for the Defense of the Revolution, and 4 form part of a Battalion of Voluntary Workers. How many employees of this business are contributing their efforts to the progress of the Fatherland during this period of sacrifices? [Fagen, 1964, p. 63].

Those of us who see our present era in a secular light may be as startled as I was by the statistics on sales of bibles and religious books. Sixty million dollars a year buys a lot of English-language bibles, and they all cannot be located in hotel rooms. One new version alone, published in 1971, was reported to have sold more than 5 million copies by spring, 1973. The good book surely has the aura of authority, and a network of institutions helps the lessons along. I would think a survey of children's use of and response to the bible's lessons would be in order, if it has not already been done.

Bradburn and Berlew (1961) examined various forms of communication—street ballads, stories of sea voyages, and dramas—current in England from 1400 to 1800, and found that the emphasis on achievement in these literatures preceded later waves of economic growth. These literatures spurred subsequent generations by transmitting, from whatever its origins, the need to achieve. The role of the atlas in such a process of socialization should also not be neglected.

Atlases constitute another class of printed works that may have important consequences for socializing our view of the world. They have an air of authority and are presented to children, although not at the youngest ages, via powerful institutions so that their lessons may be latent and insidious. Atlases are the purest case of a medium projecting a picture of the world in which the very nature of art and technology is distortion. Slight acquaintance with the history of map making and the responsiveness of the audience of the past will suggest the importance of this particular medium for socialization (Bagrow, 1964; Brown, 1949; Tooley, 1949 and 1958).

The proliferation of atlases in the seventeenth century graphically displayed the achievements of the explorers and enlarged popular conceptions of the world. Some atlases constituted a class medium, being too expensive for the ordinary man; but a mass medium was also created to meet popular demand. Thirty pocket-size editions of Ortelius's *Theatrum* and seventeen similar editions of Mercator's *Atlas*, both world atlases, had been printed by 1651.

As picture books, atlases can be followed even by the young, the simple, and the uneducated. The complexity of the medium—the conventions, symbolization, simplification, and abstraction inherent in all maps—is usually apparent only to the highly trained mind, which is what makes the medium insidious. The pictures are ordinarily taken at face value, but brief reflection will suggest many areas of discretion for the producer of the pictures and subtle consequences for the socialization of the audience.

Consider, for example, one form of insidious slanting by all map makers since Ptolemy. The North is always on top; the South always on the bottom! One wonders why the South American and the Australians have not made more of an issue about that. I suppose the answer is that it has become so taken for granted that nobody takes note—but perhaps it is a source of the Southern mentality.

That convention relates only to the "orientation" of the maps. Now consider conventions relating to scale, and to what I might call "centering" and relative "weighting," as these might affect our picture of the world and our ethnocentrism. A comic map in the April 8, 1973, edition of the *Times* makes the serious point about scale and centering. With the caption, "Cartographers think a map is an objective thing, but when you live in Liechtenstein, you know better," that great principality of 61 square miles is pictured as occupying approximately the central seven-eights of Western Europe, with France, West Germany, and other countries as tiny appendages sprouting from the edges of Liechtenstein.

The scale of a map may be distorted along any dimension—geographical area, population, GNP, etc.—but, as far as the principle of centering goes, the resulting representation has no more distortion than any serious atlas. One can put himself or his country in the center and map everything else around it, and put himself on the first page and everyone else in the back pages. It is arbitrary whichever way one does it. But it may affect our ethnocentrism, just as earlier man was affected by the Ptolemaic map of the universe, which showed the earth at the center of things, rather than the sun.

In Soviet atlases, the Soviet Union is in the center of things, just as in our own atlases the United States is. One may say, of course, that we are all being faithful and objective in the way we depict our true magnitudes since we use a uniform scale for size; but a more subtle principle of weighting ourselves up and others down is involved. We give forty-eight pages to the maps of the United States (maybe fifty by now), and only one or a few pages to, for example, the whole of the Soviet Union. They may do it just the other way round. We are highly differentiated into parts, other countries are one glob. In effect, a form of stereotyping has crept into atlases.

The London *Times Atlas of the World* states, by way of introduction, that "nothing can protect the maker of an atlas against political and international pitfalls." It then goes ahead and does an admirable job, at least by my layman's standards. But what impresses me most are some of its special maps to represent social and economic, rather than geographical, facts about the world: the world distribution of food—not just production but also consumption level and type of diet, the distribution of energy, the density of population and population change, the distribution of language and religious groups, changes of sovereignty, and the like.

Thus, atlases not only present or distort geographical features of the world, but can convey pictorially and effectively a variety of complex facts about a society and about relationships among societies. It would be desirable to socialize and educate people of all ages in these important respects. One wonders not only about how much damage present atlases may have done but also how much or how little of the potential of the medium has been realized. One is reminded of the vision of Otto Neurath, who hoped by pictographic statistics—more correctly by what he called *isotypes*, "picture language," and "picture education"—to educate ordinary men in the complexities of social life.

Children's encyclopedias constitute another class of books that, like atlases, are important for socialization of the young; their contents and effects, as far as I know, have not been examined by communication researchers. Children's encyclopedias have an aura of authority, are attractively designed with pictures, etc., are brought into prominent use through the institutions of the library and the school, and have a high probability of being employed. They are the easy way out for the child who has a report or research to do, presenting all knowledge on all topics in capsule form.

To illustrate some of the implications for socialization into roles, I have done a very primitive content analysis of children's encyclopedias. I chose *The Book of Knowledge*, beginning with the 1956 edition. (This should not be construed merely as an historic baseline since encyclopedias have a long "shelf life": People do not trade them in after two years, as they might cars; the one that served the oldest child will be used years later by a youngest child; and, I would guess, libraries do not scratch their old encyclopedias all that quickly.) I then looked at some of the articles bearing upon the role of women.

Under the title "Homemaking" (1956, Vol. 8, p. 2881-2885), embellished by pictures that show only women happily engaged in domestic pursuits, the article begins: "Homemaking is the most important job in the world." Other sentences claim: "What a pleasure it is to hear a woman say proudly 'I'm a homemaker,' in answer to a question about her occupation." "Homemaking never need be tiresome. On the contrary, it can be the most satisfying of careers."

Acting as the only coder, so my judgments may well be subjective, I skipped to the 1963 edition of *The Book of Knowledge*, which carries two articles—"Homemaking" and "Home and Family Life." These seem to me to show a marked change in the treatment of the role of women. The latter article uses much more "equalitarian" pictures, showing both the father and mother implicated in the domestic duties; in the former article, although all illustrations are confined to mother and daughter they are pen and ink, cartoonlike drawings that have a much less authoritative tone than the earlier, realistic photographs. The new "Homemaking" article, written by the very same author as before, remarks that "children, *boys* as well as girls, ought to learn how to run a home successfully. . . However, the mother of the family cannot take all the praise or all the blame for the home. Every member of the family is a homemaker." The article on "Home and Family Life," by another writer, remedies the narrowness of the one on "Homemaking" by a comparative and somewhat anthropological analysis of the variation in family structure and household composition in different societies, pointing out the relativistic character of institutions and concluding that "families are emerging in which leadership is shared equally by father and mother," and "modern families are in a state of change." In the 1972 edition there are entries for "Women's Liberation" and "N.O.W.," and brief summaries of the goals of such movements and organizations. The articles on various occupational roles—"Nursing," "Lawyers," and "Doctors"—still show, in the newer editions, somewhat subtle traditional treatment of the role of women, if only by the pronouns and pictures used. However, an article on "Role of Women" in the 1972 edition describes historical changes and emphasizes a variety of social, religious, and political factors that have shaped the role. Capping the piece are three photographs of the women Prime Ministers of Ceylon, India, and Israel.

"Secondary" Socialization: Multiplying the Effects of Small-Scale Socialization

The child's encyclopedia, presented as one example of a particular medium contained within the smallest class of mass media, books, serves to emphasize what I have called "small scale," but not unimportant, socialization of the young. But the particular aspect of encyclopedia content examined—the role of the mother and homemaker—illustrates a class of potential effects that might be called "secondary socialization," following the stimulating suggestions of Davison and Yu:

> Perhaps we have ignored "secondary effects" in studying the role of the media in socialization. For instance, syndicated newspaper columns and popular magazine stories on how to bring up children, directed by parents, may have greater effects than all the TV programs directed to children. The same may be true of popular "baby-care books," which circulate in millions of copies. [From a memorandum sent to contributors to this volume.]

If a small-scale medium works specifically and strategically upon the way in which a socializer handles his or her role, it indeed multiplies its effects and, in the long run, becomes large scale. My example is indeed very long run from one point of view, since the children who learn about the proper role of the housewife and mother from the encyclopedia will not begin to perform that role until many years later. But Davison and Yu's remarks make me think of another type of secondary socialization: media effects that change the orientation of the child, while he is in the process of being socialized, towards his socializers—parents, teachers, clergy. This, in turn, may weaken or strengthen the other socializing agencies; it indirectly multiplies and elevates the immediate importance of the small medium. The encyclopedia example also illustrates this possibility, since the relationship to the mother may be changed by the way she is presented to the child in these authoritative articles. If the medium that is contributing to the definition of the role has an adult audience, the secondary effect is the one suggested by Davison and Yu. If the medium has a child audience, the secondary effects may be of both types, one occurring in the short run and the other much later in time.

Some evidence on my short-run point is provided by Ai-Li S. Chin's (1966) comparative study of the way in which family relations are presented in modern fiction in Mainland China and Taiwan. I draw on only one portion of the findings, those relating to a very small-scale medium, a literary quarterly in Taiwan, whose contributors are mainly young members of the new, educated elite, but whose short stories apparently have a wide following and impact. Even if we were skeptical about the direct effects of this medium in socializing youth, the way in which the powerful socializer, the parent, might be undermined is clearly conveyed. I quote a brief excerpt captioned "Fathers and Sons."

> The stories involving fathers and sons are uniformly on a highly charged emotional plane but in a consistently negative tone, surrounding the theme of the mutual rejection of role obligations. . . . The portrayal of physical aggression, mutual blame, shame, lack of understanding, and sheer heartlessness reveal an impoverishment of the traditional filial dimension . . . [pp. 15-16].

In this light, early studies of small media are restored to their proper importance. For example, Clark Vincent's (1951) trend analysis of changes in the advice on infant care of brochures, books, and periodicals is cited almost nowhere—not in the chapter on content analysis in the 1954 edition of the *Handbook of Social Psychology*, nor in the chapters on the effects of mass communication and on socialization in the 1968 edition of the *Handbook*—suggesting that we have not been mindful enough of secondary socialization and its multiplier effect.

In this same vein, Gerbner's (1972-1973) comparative studies of the image of the teacher, based on content analysis of films, radio, television, and magazines in ten countries, assume importance not only in terms of possible effects on recruitment into this occupational role and the way the occupant might ultimately perform that role, but also in terms of the secondary socialization effects—the way the teacher is portrayed may modify the pupil's response to the socializing influence of his present teachers.

As this last example will suggest, large-scale media—movies and television—can also affect secondary socialization and thus multiply their effects, becoming bigger yet. Interestingly enough, one of Gerbner's findings suggests that they do not often follow this route to enlarge their effects, teachers rarely being portrayed in comparison to other occupational roles and far less than is proportionate to their numbers in the occupational structure of our society.

With the heightened awareness that a small-scale medium may have larger-scale secondary socialization effects, let us turn to some very special subvarieties of communication within the class of small-scale mass media.

Interpersonal Style of Socialization Within Small-Scale Mass Communication

A tradition of research has developed that sees mass communication as becoming interpersonal only through a two-step flow of influence in which influential individuals in the media audiences transmit and ramify the influence of impersonal communication from the media by passing the messages along in interpersonal transactions. Thus, the effects are ultimately spread and multiplied. The human agents of socialization, the links in the process, can draw upon new information sources while remaining potent and flexible in suiting the lessons to the capacities and needs of the particular audience. The mass media are, by contrast, seen as too standardized and impersonal. Flexibility, however, should not always be seen as a force for good (in some societies, the ordinary socializers may be too conservative), and standardization as all bad; nor should we necessarily judge the mass media as being perceived in so impersonal a light. I speculated on these matters long ago (Hyman, 1963). But the more familiarity one has with the endless variety of mass communication around the world, the more one senses how malleable a tool it can be—how often, without benefit of a special interpersonal link that may be obstructionist, the subvarieties can be recast in a highly personalized form.

Consider, for example, one variety of program within the total radio broadcasting of Northern Rhodesia in 1953. According to an audience survey, after song programs and news "Request" was the most popular program, but almost all listeners heard it with enjoyment. "This personal program consisted of messages sent to and from individuals in various towns and villages," and "listeners said they liked this program because it was 'quicker than a letter' " (Powdermaker, 1962, p. 242). Radio had become a kind of free telephone call for these individuals on the copperbelt far from their native villages. They and their primary groups were linked in a traditional socializing process via this apparently impersonal, modern, mass medium. The rest of the audience was listening in on a kind of party-line. Even when not telephoning themselves, they might well be learning from others in the same human predicaments.

That this was not an isolated instance is evident from the form of interpersonal communication grafted onto the print medium in Northern Rhodesia. The "Tell Me, Josephine" column, begun in 1960 in the *Central African Mail*, a mass circulation weekly paper, provided an avenue mainly for men to be guided and socialized by Josephine, a wise woman, during a transitional phase of modernization. "Her identity is never revealed, so that she remains for readers a mysterious yet intimate counselor" (Hall, 1964, p. 142). I quote from the many exchanges in a printed collection some correspondence that relates to the self-regarding sentiment and a possible identity crisis.

"My eye was taken out because I had a blindness and now I plan to get the plastic kind. My girl says it must be brown like all our eyes, but I want a blue one. Shall I have my blue eye, or would my girl leave me?"

"I don't see why you should not have the colour you fancy. . . . But don't forget everyone will know it is a false eye, being blue. Why not tell her you will replace it with a brown one when you are tired of looking different from everyone else?" [p. 44]

That this was not an exotic feature peculiar to the African scene is clear from Ai-Li Soong Chin's (1948) content analysis of a similar feature in a Shanghai periodical. The writers were mostly youths caught in the tides of change sweeping China in that period and confronted with dilemmas of resocialization. Again, the relationship is seen as intimate and the counselor as wise. "The editor may be characterized as a teacher-friend. . . . He is often addressed by the letter-writers as the one with 'high education,' 'wisdom,' 'experience.' " Apropos the importance of sentiments he is also addressed as having "compassion" (Chin, p. 5).

A similar personalized form of mass communication, serving the same function for Jewish immigrants in the United States was the "bintelbrief"—exchanges of questions and answers in the letter columns of Jewish newspapers in New York (Metzker, 1972). Of course, the institution is known to all of us in such forms as the "Dear Abby" columns, in which the correspondents may not be marginal men caught in the process of resocialization, but surely are individuals caught in the dilemmas of existence and asking for guidance from the far from impersonal "mass media."

I do not think it is an unwarranted assumption that such personalized exchanges via the mass media have a socializing influence but, to be precise, I have presented no evidence of any effects on the audience. A last example will provide empirical support for my assumption and show another variant on the particular form. The teen-age radio program, *Mind Your Manners*, originated in Hartford, Connecticut, in 1947, was picked up and carried for a long period over the entire NBC radio network and for almost a year on television. The advisers were a teen-age panel "talking to teen-agers" . . . "through the instrumentality of the medium," and the advice seekers were youths who wrote letters that were then discussed on the air.

Forer (1955) attempted to study the "effectiveness of this mass medium program as a socializing agent." Two of his points are worthy of note, and make us ponder our usual model of the socialization process and the factors that govern its potency. The panel involved peers, rather than parents, but unlike usual socializers and agents of social control, they were not members of the teen-agers' primary group who came into contact with and could sanction them. Indeed Forer went so far as to describe the panel as an "anonymous agent." And he noted that many of the problems reviewed by the panel "are never actually answered." He noted that the "importance given the problem by its public presentation often serves as the 'solution' " (p. 187). Among a large sample of teen-agers in Connecticut, 69 per cent of those who knew of the program said "they would follow the advice given," and between 10 and 15 per cent said they would follow the advice over that given by members of their immediate family. About 50 per cent said they would take the advice of the panel over that given by their own teen-age friends.

These are clearly varieties of mass communication that are small in scale in proportion to the total number of forms; they can be potent and flexible socializing forces.

Deviant Varieties

Some forms that seem to fall far outside the domain of the mass media may provide unusual opportunities to study the socializing or resocializing influences of communication. Deviant and tiny for now, they may be on their way to becoming bigger and conventional forms in the future; and right now they may exert subtle pressures for change within the mass media. Indeed, the history of one of these forms, from the little I know and have read, suggests that very historical process.

Consider the underground press, particularly on the high-school level. It has been estimated that there are about 500 underground papers in the country, 100 of which are clustered in the Los Angeles area. Added together, they form a not so minuscule force. Written by peers and surely relevant to some of the major themes already reviewed, the tone of the underground press is one of "outrage" and "indignation," to quote one analyst (Heussenstamm, 1971). That it speaks to the sentiments is suggested by the very titles, which may be ironic but often are biting: The *Loudmouth*, The New York *Roach*, the *Wretched Mass News*, the *Rat*, the *Bullsheet*, the *Crocodile*, *Heresy II*, *Last Harass*, *Le Chronic*, *Katz, Katz, Brayns & Braun*.

In the best traditions of our field we may judge the effects of the underground press as negligible, arguing that the audience is highly selected and predisposed to the norms of the counter-culture, and see it as a reflection rather than a cause of social unrest. But surely, in terms of "secondary socialization," it must work to undermine the conventional socializers, if it does nothing else.

The fear of co-optation within these enterprises may be seen in a positive light as indicating the pressures toward change exerted on the mass media. They are not taking over the deviant media; they are taking on some of its style, sensing, if only for commercial reasons, that there is an audience that wants that kind of content. As a result, a much larger audience, not necessarily predisposed, gets exposed to this deviant content and, in the process, may be socialized into new ways.

In the instance of another deviant form of communication—rock music—which had initially been only small in scale, this seems to be the historic process (Hirsch, 1971). The songs of social protest—those describing a bohemian life style, first played only by unknown groups, produced by unknown companies, and broadcast only over small radio stations—were soon picked up by large producers and the mass media. Thus, large numbers of youth now receive these messages. The evidence of large-scale audience studies suggests, however, that the socializing effects of the messages are small. It is mainly the music, not the words, that are heard. In the terms of information theory, the sound is the noise in the channel that interferes with the message. But perhaps the songs will get less "noisy" and the messages correspondingly clearer.

Innovative Forms

Not through pressure or imitation, but through innovation, new forms of mass communication with powers of socialization may come into being. A final example brings us back to the grand theme upon which I began—the enlargement of sympathy through expanding awareness of the human condition. It also reminds us of that other great passion of Russell's—the search for knowledge. A news story about *Kodomo Niusi*, or Children's News, a nightly Japanese program, asks:

Have you ever flicked on your television and sat down to watch the news of the miseries of the world only to have your children grumble: "News? Aw, do we have to watch that stuff again?" [*New York Times*, Dec. 16, 1972]

The Japanese have evidently found a way to make the news appealing to elementary school children—partly by special coverage and also by using commentators who are young women and therefore give a "gentle familiar impression" to the material. The average Japanese audience is reported to be 5.4 million viewers, which includes many grandparents living in the extended household who themselves act as socializers of the children. *Niusi* avoids scenes of violence, but there is plenty of material left to arouse compassion. The producer, who majored in child psychology, remarks: "I like children very much." No doubt he is on his way to large-scale socialization of children into a passion for knowledge and a sympathetic understanding of others.

4

FUNCTIONS OF MASS COMMUNICATION
FOR THE COLLECTIVITY

W. Phillips Davison

The thesis of this chapter is that mass communication researchers should give as much attention to the functions of the media for organizations as to their functions for individuals. Organizations, like individuals, make use of communications, and are affected by them, in a variety of ways. The structure of large and complex organizations, in particular, and the degree to which they are able to fulfill their purposes, depend in part on the mass media channels available to them for receiving and imparting information.

While the principal focus here is on formal organizations—such as political parties, business enterprises, or labor unions—some of the following observations apply to social units that are not ordinarily thought of as organizations—family groups, neighborhoods, or nation states. The term "collectivity" has therefore been used as a reminder of the diverse nature of the groupings being considered. This term is admittedly too broad, just as "organization" is too narrow. We are not concerned with crowds or mere aggregates of individuals; there must be a significant degree of interaction among the people involved.

As noted by Lerner (in the following chapter), organizations have often been studied as communication systems. These investigations have usually dealt with the internal flow of messages. Sometimes a biological analogy is used, and information channels are compared to the nervous system of an organism (Miller, 1965). More commonly, an effort is made to relate patterns of internal communication to the effectiveness of the organization in carrying out its purpose (Price, 1968). Most such studies have been concerned primarily with interpersonal or inter-unit communication (Voos, 1967).

By contrast, relatively little effort has been devoted to exploring the role of the mass media in organizational life. Mass communication researchers have been more interested in the impact of the media on individuals than on organizations. Surveying the field at the end of the 1950s, John and Matilda Riley (1959, p. 538) noted that "the traditional approach to mass communication . . . has been largely concerned with the content of the communicated message and the responses of isolated individuals." The group, or collectivity, was brought into the picture principally as an intervening variable that mediated the individual's response. Thus, Shils and Janowitz (1948) found that the individual soldier was little influenced by enemy propaganda when his primary group ties were strong and when the larger organization to which he belonged was functioning efficiently. Kelley (1958) studied the role of group membership in the individual's resistance to persuasion. Klapper (1960), in summarizing the quantitative literature on the effects of mass communication, concluded that group affiliation was one of the principal factors that mediated these effects. One can find exhaustive analyses of the literature concerning the impact of communications on individuals (Weiss, 1969), but there are no comparable treatments of the functions of communications for organizations.

That is not to say that the functions of mass communication for collectivities have been completely ignored. They have often been treated in connection with the problems of particular organizations or institutions, but there have been few attempts to formulate generalizations that apply to a range of collectivities. We have a substantial body of literature that touches on the impact of communications on aggregates of individuals, as in voting studies (Lazarsfeld, Berelson and Gaudet, 1948; Berelson, Lazarsfeld and McPhee 1954), but the organizations to which these individuals belong are treated as independent variables. Works on collective behavior and mass phenomena contain insights on the role of the mass media, but their primary concern is localized interaction and the role of rumor (Lang and Lang, 1961; Smelser, 1962). At the present state of knowledge it would be difficult to write about the uses of mass communications for organizations as Katz, Blumler, and Gurevitch (in this volume) have done for individuals.

Perhaps it is impossible to build a body of propositions regarding mass communication and organization similar to the corpus of propositions regarding mass communication and the individual. It may be that collectivities are too diverse in character and that only limited generalizations are possible. The leap from the nuclear family to the nation state, or from the neighborhood society to a large corporation, is indeed a grand one. There is a danger that propositions applicable to such a wide range of phenomena would have to be so broad as to be valueless. Even if one limits oneself to organizations of a given size or level of complexity, differences in structure and function may make generalization difficult. But the degree of difficulty, or the prospects for success, cannot be assessed before a systematic attempt has been made—and such an attempt has thus far been lacking.

THE IMPORTANCE OF RESEARCH ON
COMMUNICATION AND ORGANIZATION

Whether or not development of a body of propositions regarding mass communication and organization is possible, it is highly desirable. In planning for utilization of new communication technologies, for example, one is forced to ask about their significance not only for the individual but also for all types of social organization—from political parties, police departments, and industries, to families, neighborhoods, and voluntary associations. Intelligent speculation about the impact of new communication technologies on society would be easier if more knowledge about the relationships between communication and organization were available. Is it possible that mass communication channels can substitute for face-to-face channels in medical, educational, or other organizations, thus decisively altering their structure (Mandelbaum, 1972)? Will children be taught by television, and then come to school to socialize with their friends? Or, as Meier (1962, p. 60) asks, "Why not transmit the symbols over a somewhat greater distance instead of moving people?"

Social planning in general would benefit from such a body of propositions. If a new type of organization or collectivity is to be established, what kind of communication system will it require? Or, will alterations in the structure or content of our present communication system enable certain types of existing organizations to function more efficiently? We know that most needs of individuals are taken care of by larger or smaller social groups or organizations—needs for food, clothing, shelter, security, affection, and so on. Some group needs, in turn, are satisfied by the mass media. Can one therefore reason that individual needs would be better met if the mass media were more efficient in satisfying group needs? Or are the contents of the mass media determined by the nature of social groupings? Henderson (1973) asserts that, except in totalitarian societies, groups lie at the base of the mass communication process. In studying the reversion of Okinawa to Japan, he found that sentiment on the issue first formed and then grew to massive proportions among individuals and social organizations; communications about the subject flowed through interpersonal and organizational channels. Only in the final stages of reversion were the mass media involved. Does media content, then, mainly echo group communication processes?

The study of communication and organization leads one into a consideration of house organs and their role not only for the particular collectivity they serve but for society as a whole. Where does a house organ leave off and a general medium begin? The *New York Times* has been referred to as a house organ for the political leadership of the United States, but it serves a more diverse public, too. Is it possible that a general medium can perform the functions of a house organ for a number of groups simultaneously?

What happens to communication within a group when a house organ is started? We read in Cole's (1962) history of Fabian socialism that during the early years of the movement the members assembled at evening meetings, and articles and other materials were read to them as they sat in circles. Then, in 1891, *Fabian News*, a four-page publication, "for members only" was established. This, in turn, led to the founding of the *New Statesman* which, however, was not an official publication of the organization. But what happened to person-to-person communication within the organization during this long period, and what changes in its structure were occasioned by the new communication channels? Furthermore, how did the *New Statesman* change the relationship of the Fabians to other organizations, and how did it affect the mass media serving British society in general?

Blumler and Ewbank (1970), in a study of British union members, found that only 31 per cent of them recalled reading a union journal, but 70 per cent could name their shop steward. When person-to-person channels are so much more inclusive, is a house organ worth the resources devoted to it?

Questions about the human, material, and financial resources devoted to house organs, as well as about their place in society, are not trivial. The number of such publications in the United States cannot be estimated with any accuracy, but one periodical directory (*Standard Periodical Directory*, 1973) lists upwards of ten thousand of them. The list is headed by approximately three thousand college and alumni magazines; then come some two thousand miscellaneous house organs. It is not known how many of the one thousand journals devoted to labor and union affairs, the two thousand dealing with religion and theology, or the one thousand ethnically-oriented publications can be classified as house organs, but the proportion that should be so classified must be significant. While most of these periodicals are small, some have circulations running into the hundreds of thousands. And this does not include the myriad of mimeographed and more casual serials that are issued by almost every membership organization. Numerous radio stations serve as voices for religious and other groups, and television stations increasingly are being encouraged to provide at least some services approximating those of a house organ to neighborhoods, ethnic and special interest groups.

What place do house organs occupy in the communication network of the larger society, and what place could or should they occupy? Might they be able to provide more efficiently some of the services now attempted by the general media? Perhaps, for instance, they could take advantage of the relative homogeneity of their audiences and include more economic or cultural information of particular relevance to certain social groups. Or, perhaps, house organs should be seen as part of the infrastructure of the general mass media. According to the latter view, one of the functions of the house organs would be to collect information about the special groups they serve. The general media would then monitor the house organs and select out the information that appeared to be of relevance to wider publics. Some monitoring along these lines is already done by the general media, but rarely systematically.

These questions, and others of equal difficulty, are unlikely to be answered in full by any body of propositions developed in the near future. Specific studies adapted to individual problems—e.g., the costs and benefits of establishing a weekly newspaper in a low-income housing project—would still have to be undertaken. But if one could start with hypotheses based on a higher level of knowledge about the general relationships involved, research on specific questions would proceed more rapidly and produce more fruitful results. Perhaps our initial goal should be to develop understanding about mass communication and organization to a level comparable to that currently available about mass communication and individual political behavior.

THE CURRENT STATE OF RESEARCH

There are several bodies of literature that include particularly relevant data and insights on communication and organization, although these disparate sources have never been brought together and studied with a view to determining how they supplement and complement each other. Rather, each has traditionally been regarded as a self-contained unit, not necessarily related to the others.

One of the most obvious bodies of literature concerns communication in business organizations and the communication needs of business. Another focuses on political communication in general, and on the way governments, parties, and pressure groups make use of the media. A third deals with the role of communication in the development process, and in particular with ways in which mass media can help to establish or strengthen political, economic, and cultural institutions.

Studies of public relations, advertising, and international propaganda occasionally contain information about the functions of mass communication for collectivities. Closely related to these are "image" or "attention" studies, which describe the way a particular organization is seen by specified audiences, or measure the amount of attention given the organization by the mass media. Those investigations are usually more concerned with external publics than with the organization that originates the communications or is being discussed. Nevertheless, they may also provide insights into organizational operations. Thus, a massive fifty-nation study of coverage of the United Nations in the world press, radio, and television notes that a scheme for monitoring international communications could improve the functioning of the world organization by helping it to identify "hot spots" throughout the globe (Szalai, et. al., 1972).

Then there is a diffuse and elusive array of historical and sociological studies dealing with organizations and social movements. These usually mention mass communication in passing, while discussing some other subject, but the unselfconscious manner in which these references are presented makes them all the more valuable as basic data. They are free from the suspicion that the importance of mass communication has been magnified by the author's preoccupation with the subject, or that the presentation has been biased by an interest in one or another hypothesis regarding communication.

Because the above literature has not been systematically analyzed, it is possible to present only a crude and impressionistic inventory of the functions of mass communication for collectivities. Three primary processes appear to be involved: an organization must be able to form, act in fulfillment of its purposes, and relate to its external social environment. Communication makes all these processes possible. Small organizations usually find face-to-face, or at most point-to-point, communication adequate for their needs. As organizations grow larger and more complex they tend to rely increasingly on mass communication. This tendency can be observed in countless cases: a group forms on the basis of person-to-person contacts; recruits more members from among the friends and neighbors of those who already belong; and ultimately starts its own journal, sends out press releases, and receives mention in the mass media. Conversely, material in the mass media may facilitate the formation of primary groups or may assist existing organizations in pursuing their purposes.

The same mass media channels may be used by different individuals or groups to satisfy different organizational requirements. Thus, a study of

Wisconsin state officials found that elected executives were likely to use the press to build program or personal support—for purposes of group formation; legislators relied on the media to inform themselves about the activities of other parts of the state apparatus—to enable them to function within the political structure; while administrators saw the press largely as a means of conveying information to the public—as a means of relating to the external social environment (Dunn, 1967).

COMMUNICATION AS AN ORGANIZING FORCE

Under some circumstances, mass communication facilitates the creation of organizations by focusing attention on an issue and alerting individuals who share common attitudes about the issue to the desirability of forming some kind of association. More commonly, the media serve as intentional or unintentional recruiters for small groups that wish to expand their membership.

The classical description of the way the press enables discrete individuals to join together in purposeful groups has been given by Tocqueville (1956, pp. 202-203):

> The effect of a newspaper is not only to suggest the same purpose to a great number of persons, but also to furnish means for the execution of the designs which they may singly have conceived.... A newspaper then takes up the notion or the feeling that had occurred simultaneously, but singly, to each of them. All are then immediately guided toward the beacon; and these wandering minds, which had so long sought each other in darkness, at length meet and unite.

Tocqueville docs not give us specific examples of this process, and it is difficult to know how often it actually occurs. The model suggested by Henderson (1973) seems more likely: namely, that the mass media eventually pick up themes developed among existing groups.

Nevertheless, approximations of Tocqueville's model can be found. Nationalistic political organizations in Egypt during the British ascendency there tended to develop around individual publications (Berger, 1962, p. 426). Congruent developments have been noted in other parts of the world, where journals of a particular ideological, religious, or philosophic tendency served to draw together people with similar interests. It has been argued that the black press in Chicago played an important part in building a collective cultural life for the black population in that city (Kreiling, 1973). Homosexual publications have been credited with turning a loosly-knit subculture into more highly organized groups: "Such publications give voice to, indeed they create, shared feelings and common orientation; they consolidate and stabilize for the reader his identity and reality of his group" (Carey, 1969, p. 26).

The mass media perform a somewhat similar function in nation-building when they help diverse peoples to recognize their common interests and the usefulness of working together toward shared goals (Schramm, 1963, p. 38).

Indeed, Deutsch (1953, p. 71) defines membership in a nationality as "the ability to communicate more effectively, and over a wider range of subjects, with members of one large group than with outsiders." However, the extent to which mass media are able to create complementarity of communication within a nation state is difficult to establish. They may much more give expression to ties already established by other means.

Better documented is the ability of mass communication to serve as a channel for small face-to-face groups that wish to become mass organizations. In such cases, rather than serving as a lodestone or catalyst, a medium provides facilities through which appeals to a wider public can be made.

The history of almost any political party or voluntary association is likely to show that the mass media played a major part in recruiting members. In his account of the Nazi Party in Germany, Hitler (1944, pp. 388ff.) described how shortly after World War I "six or seven men, all unknown, poor devils, came together with the idea that they would build a political movement." They tried repeatedly to hold mass meetings but nobody came. Notices of the meetings were composed on a typewriter or by hand and distributed to acquaintances, but the results were disappointing. Once Hitler wrote out eighty notices himself, but when it was time for the "mass meeting" to come to order only the same seven faces were there. Then the little group started to have their notices duplicated by machine and distributed more widely. Over the next months attendance at meetings rose to 11, then 17, and finally 34.

By this time the struggling political group had collected enough money to announce a meeting through an advertisement in the *Münchener Beobachter*. They rented what they considered a big hall, with capacity for 130 people. Success this time was "amazing." Over 100 came to the meeting, and collectively donated 300 marks. This solved the organization's immediate financial problems and enabled it soon to become a mass movement. The Nazi Party, as a significant political force, started with an advertisement in the *Münchener Beobachter*.

This example, while illustrating the power of the mass media to enable large groups to form, is also a cautionary tale. As long as Hitler and his fellows distributed their notices to friends and acquaintances, nobody came to the meetings. One may speculate that those who knew the early Nazis personally dismissed them as cranks, fanatics, or worse. The party that was to cause a cataclysm of worldwide proportions was held in check by gentle but effective primary group pressures, much as a rural community is often able to accommodate a number of mentally abnormal persons who in a more impersonal urban enviornment would be institutionalized. But when the Nazi Party made its appeal through the mass media—and here the mechanically duplicated notices must also be taken into consideration—the primary group constraints were no longer effective. The original seven members were able to reach into the total population of the Munich area to find kindred spirits. And even though for several more years they were able to attract only a small percentage of all Germans, this small percentage was large enough in absolute numbers to make the party a serious political force.

When it comes to group formation, the mass media serve equally the just and the unjust. They can help to mobilize large numbers of those with vicious prejudices, paranoid tendencies, or aggressive intentions. Or they can promote the formation of organizations devoted to the improvement of the human condition, the cause of peace, or the advancement of the arts and sciences. The capability is there for all to use.

New communidation technologies enable large organizations to form much more rapidly than was possible even a few years ago. Not only do television, radio, and the print media together saturate the populations of the industrialized nations as never before, but computerized data systems combined with print-out capabilities make it possible to send personalized messages to millions of individuals simultaneously. This enables an organizer both to appeal to the undifferentiated public and at the same time to reach into primary groups where potential members or supporters are especially likely to be found.

The manner in which the two capabilities can be employed is illustrated by the "citizen's lobby," Common Cause. This organization, founded at the end of the 1960s by former Secretary of Health, Education and Welfare, John Gardner, claimed 200,000 dues paying members before the end of 1972 (*Report From Washington*, December 1972). It made astute use of press releases, public appearances of its organizers, newspaper advertisements, posters, leaflets, and other established means of attracting support, but it also engaged in a large direct-mail campaign. Those who joined the organization early were requested to send in their Christmas card lists, the names of those in local citizens' groups who pursued goals similar to those of Common Cause, and the names of out-of-town friends. Membership forms and information about the organization were then mailed to the persons whose names had been submitted, as well as to other lists of likely prospects. This combination of public and individualized appeals seems to have been remarkably successful. Early in 1971, the organization's newsletter reported that "membership in Common Cause is growing at a rate that astonishes the old pros in the organizing field." (*Report From Washington*, February 1971) As the organization gained a mass following, its ability to attract news coverage also increased. Through news reports in the general media, even more potential members and supporters learned about it.

The organizing capability of the media is extensively used by groups ranging from neighborhood associations to national states and international movements, but it has received little attention from students of communication. We should not only learn more about the processes involved, but should also examine the social implications of this capability. Under what conditions are mass communications likely to be an effective force in mobilizing individuals to work together toward given goals? When are they likely to be unsuccessful? How might various categories of unorganized individuals be helped to form associations, and what are the implications of doing so? Increasingly precise answers to questions such as these are likely to influence the future shape of our society.

MASS MEDIA AND THE INTERNAL
FUNCTIONING OF ORGANIZATIONS

Communications facilitate the internal functioning of most organizations in at least four ways: they help to ensure coordination of the organization's various parts, provide technical information that assists members of the organization in doing a particular job or playing a specified role, furnish intelligence for decision making, and foster group morale and a sense of belonging. The extent to which mass communication—as opposed to other channels—satisfies these needs in any given organization depends on that organization's size and structure. The mass media involved may be directed to the public at large, may be designed for specialized audiences within the general public, or may be house organs.

Writers on business organization often stress the importance of communication channels that provide for flows of information in both directions between management and other levels. "It is only through the give and take of a two-way flow of communication that management can effectively manage" (L. Brown, 1970, p. 387). Stress is also often placed on the necessity of keeping each part of an organization informed of what other parts are doing, although this is not the case when coordination is insured mainly at the highest level.

All organizations require information channels linking leadership to the membership, and most of them also require lateral channels that keep the various elements of the organization, or even the individual members, in touch with each other. Small groups usually can satisfy their communication needs on a face-to-face basis, although telephone conversations, memoranda, and other written messages may also be involved. As organizations become larger and more complex, increasing emphasis is placed on written communications (often sent in many copies) and on more complicated electronic hook-ups, sometimes including public address systems. Very large organizations usually publish house organs to supplement other channels and may engage in periodic opinion surveys among their members.

The larger and more loosely organized a group, the more likely are the general mass media to perform some of these internal communication functions for it. A study of British trade unions found the press, radio, and television to be a valuable part of the system of communications within the labor movement; indeed, the mass media provided the principal channels through which the membership could be reached by the leaders (Blumler and Ewbank, 1970). Similar observations have been made with regard to government organizations, where the general media are an important factor not only in informing those in lower ranks of the policies set by the leadership but also in keeping each element in government aware of what others are doing (Cohen, 1963, pp. 135-138; Davison, 1974a).

The general mass media are less likely to convey information to the leadership about what is happening at lower levels, at least in formal organizations. A study of a number of complex organizations found that events at lower levels were rarely reported in the press, and even those that were reported had been known to the leadership for some time (Kaufman and

Couzens, 1973). In large and diffuse organizations, such as nation states or major religious denominations, the mass media play a more important role in conveying information from the membership to the leadership.

House organs are often devoted largely to strengthening internal lines of communication within an organization. A discussion of company publications, for instance, notes that they can fulfill the following functions, among others: they can tell workers about each other to promote a "one big family" feeling; they can interpret company policies to the workers; and they can serve as a sounding board for employee attitudes (Woods, 1962). Since most house organs are controlled directly by organization leaders, in practice they usually devote more attention to downward communication *to* the membership, rather than upward or lateral communication.

Mass media also serve the function of providing group members with information that they can use in doing a particular job or playing a prescribed role. In an industrialized society, this seems to be true even in the case of small organizations, such as the family. Thus, cook books, baby books sex manuals, and a large proportion of the content of popular magazines instruct individuals with regard to various roles and activities that are important in family life. One may speculate that at least some of the media consumption of children is for the purpose of gaining information that will enable them to play the role expected of them in the family or play group. The following finding, which is reinforced by others, is suggestive: the greater the parents' concern for education, and the higher the status of the chief wage earner's occupation, the more the children read newspapers (Liu, 1973). One possible explanation for this finding is that children whose families expected them to be able to discuss current events turned to newspaper reading as one way of satisfying these expectations. In regard to play groups, Riley and Riley (1951) describe television viewing as one way children acquire ideas that can be used in peer group games. The mass media provide these children with information that assists them in role performance.

Eisenstadt (1955) found certain types of communication content common to all the Israeli ethnic communities he studied. Some of the content he labeled "technical," which was defined as information needed by immigrants to orient themselves in a new society. Another category consisted of "normative" communications, which told the new arrivals how they were expected to behave, especially when various roles made conflicting demands on them. Most of this information was provided on a person-to-person basis, but some was derived from the mass media.

The importance of mass communication in providing information necessary for role and job performance in large and complex organizations is obvious. A company that employs many kinds of specialists cannot instruct them all in their specialties or keep them up to date on new developments. Much of this task is performed by the specialized mass media—e.g., by publications directed to engineers of all stripes, architects, or biochemists. Indeed, a major portion of the periodical press in the United States consists of publications that assist people in the performance of professional jobs. These include several thousand periodicals devoted to applied science and engineering, the social sciences, medical specialties, natural science, and so on (*Standard Periodical Directory*, 1973).

The general mass media provide large quantities of job-related information to those whose occupations require familiarity with current political affairs. In the words of a State Department official, "You can't work in the State Department without the *New York Times*. You can get along without the overnight telegrams sooner" (Cohen, 1963, p. 138). Indeed, officials in all foreign offices appear to spend a great deal of time keeping up with major newspapers, as well as with radio and television news (Davison, 1974a). The same is true of many teachers in such fields as the social sciences, law, and journalism.

A third way in which the mass media serve the internal requirements of organizations is by promoting morale and a sense of identity among the membership. This is one of the principal functions of house organs, which may be used to build loyalty, increase group prestige, promote morale-building social activities, and report on awards and distinctions received by organization members (Woods, 1962). Favorable mention of a group, or of persons who are identified as belonging to the group, in the general mass media may be even more effective in fostering morale and identity. Thus, one of the reasons the citizens of Berlin conducted themselves with such courage during the blockade of that city in the winter of 1948-1949 was that they were exposed almost daily to reports from the world press that praised their resolute behavior (Davison, 1956). And, on a microcosmic level, the writer has vivid memories of what happened when a local newspaper music critic praised the performance of a choir in which he was rendering indifferent service as a second bass: at the next rehearsal the choir director was ecstatic; and the volunteer singers performed well beyond the limits to which their natural endowments entitled them.

However, McQuail (1969) does a service in reminding us that some mass media content may be dysfunctional for group morale. The information coming to the attention of an organization's members from outside sources may lead to cross-pressures, less self-confidence, and a lowered consensus.

A fourth function often performed by the mass media for organizations is to provide the leadership with information necessary for making policy decisions. Green (1973) notes that management must have a flow of substantive information, or operational intelligence, in order to make good decisions at acceptable risk. Wilensky (1967) points out that some of this intelligence comes through mass media channels, and that such information, derived from public sources, may be superior to that received through private or secret channels.

Studies of decision-making in large organizations usually disclose that the mass media have played a role. McCamy (1964), in an examination of decision-making in foreign policy, characterized the mass media as one of the "influential agents" that influence the minds of those who assume responsibility for a course of action. In another study (Blumler and Ewbank, 1970), the strategies of British trade union leaders were found to be based in part on currents of public opinion that "may have been stimulated and channeled by the available means of communication." Significantly, 45 per cent of the full-time union officers read the *Guardian*, the *Telegraph*, or the *Times* on weekdays, while only 7 per cent of the union rank and file did. On Sundays, more than half of the officials read the *Times*, as opposed to 14 per cent of the rank and file. The mass media, observe Blumler and Ewbank, "give voice to assumed national needs, which the unions are expected to take into account when framing their own policies."

American business leaders are avid consumers of mass communications, which they require if they are to take account in their own decisions of what is happening in the world. In the group of executives studied by Bauer, Pool, and Dexter (1963), the principal relevant sources of information were the prestige newspaper press (especially the *New York Times* and the *Wall Street Journal*) and the news magazines. These general media were supplemented by a wide variety of specialized publications—often directed to specific branches of business—that sometimes served to underline the importance of information that had been included in the daily news flow (e.g., the report of a government study commission) and sometimes presented additional information. Although these business men also relied heavily on person-to-person channels for information required in decision-making, the persons to whom they turned for advice tended to have an even wider range of the mass media at their disposal.

If one examines the files of any organization that is of such a nature that it keeps files—whether a small civic group, a singing society, a business firm, or a government agency—one is likely to find newspaper clippings, magazine articles, perhaps leaflets or pamphlets. Sometimes the reason for the retention of these items is clear, but sometimes it is not. Are the clippings and other materials relevant to the operation of the group, to its internal morale, to the roles of its members, or to the decisions of its leaders? Perhaps the secretary-treasurer or other official who filed these items was not clear *why* they were important to the group, but somehow knew that they *were* important. The task of the social scientist is to specify the "why" more clearly.

COMMUNICATIONS DIRECTED OUTWARD

It is not uncommon, within a small but formally organized association, to find a "corresponding secretary" among the group's officials. As the title implies, the corresponding secretary takes care of communication with outside individuals and groups. The duties of this officer may include answering letters, distributing information about the organization's objectives, and dealing with government agencies.

Other titles having to do with outgoing communications may be found in most large organizations, the number and nature of such designations depending largely on the group's purposes. There may be information officers, public relations officers, an advertising manager, a sales manager, a chief of the department of propaganda, or a director of public education.

Volumes have been written about these outgoing communications, but attention has been devoted mainly to how they are composed and disseminated, and to the effects that they have or are presumed to have on external publics. There has been surprisingly little thought given to the functions that they serve for the organization itself. Why are they necessary? Or why, even if they are not necessary, do they survive?

One reason for the inattention may be that the needs served by outgoing communications are assumed to be obvious. Incoming letters must be answered; governments must inform the population about laws and regulations and distribute other information having to do with the public interest; advertising is necessary to promote sales; the public relations function is intended to preserve good working relations with relevant individuals and organizations; propaganda is indispensable if the group is to gain support for its objectives, influence the behavior of other collectivities, and recruit new employees or members.

The "obvious" functions served by messages directed by organizations to outside individuals and groups fall into four partly-overlapping categories:

1. To persuade. Communications in this category include those designed to sell products, solicit votes, influence health-related behavior ("see your dentist twice a year"), advance ideologies, build a favorable public image, and recruit personnel.

2. To inform. These messages provide people in the external social environment with information they need in order to deal with the organization in question. Just as an individual must introduce himself to a new acquaintance an organization must provide certain basic information about itself: its purposes, business address, names of principal officers, and so on. If it produces a product, it must also give the public instructions about how to use the product: how to operate an automobile, cook a processed food, or take a medicine. Government decisions may be regarded as products of government, and these require explanation and interpretation. In some cases, the product is information: for example, the findings of a research laboratory, or the reports of a government economic bureau.

3. To negotiate. Messages in this rubric are designed to arrive at accommodations or agreements with outside individuals and groups. The agreements may have to do with buying or selling, the use of scarce facilities, the coordination of activities, or any other aspects of an organization's operations. Negotiating may also involve informing and persuading.

4. To gain information. This category includes not only questions but also other communications that are intended to tap sources of information—e.g., communications that are designed to continue a dialogue with a potentially valuable information source.

These organizational needs may be acknowledged, but perhaps outgoing communications satisfy other needs that are not so obvious. Students of religion have sometimes said that a church cannot be healthy unless it conducts vigorous missionary activities. An advertiser has maintained that the purpose of much advertising is not to sell goods but to massage management egos (Samstag, 1966). A small religious cult, whose prophet foretold the end of the world, increased its proselytizing efforts when the world did not self-destruct on the date specified (Festinger et al., 1956). Governments spend millions on foreign information programs and exhibitions to impress their own citizens as well as foreigners.

It may be that an organization, like an individual, requires reassurance and a sense of identity if it is to function satisfactorily and that outgoing communications are necessary to assure these qualities. Perhaps organizations, like individuals, need attention; and an inexpensive way of gaining attention is to speak. People sometimes seek to increase their self-confidence by dominating the conversation. Why should it be otherwise with organizations? Some political propaganda is designed not to persuade voters but to motivate campaign workers. Some advertising is intended to build the morale of salesmen or to influence distributors, not to sell products. Perhaps all organizations make use of outward-directed communications in order to build their own self-image.

Information disseminated by organizations that appears to represent an effort to persuade or inform may in addition have an information-seeking function. The group may actually be seeking to elicit a response that will provide reassurance or be useful in policy-making. An obvious example is provided by the "trial balloons" released by government agencies. Here the principal purpose is to learn what others think about a proposed policy or action. One may legitimately ask whether other types of communications directed outward by organizations, regardless of their ostensible purposes, are not actually attempts to gain information—especially information that will bolster the self-image.

An organization's outgoing communications, just as its incoming ones, may be largely person-to-person or point-to-point in nature. Even a government or large corporation may rely heavily on conversations among individuals when it comes to negotiating or information-seeking. The mass media are more likely to be used when it comes to informing and persuading, and little is known about the extent to which outgoing communications are designed to secure mass media attention in order to provide reassurance and promote internal morale.

SOME PATHS FOR EXPLORATION

In view of the relative lack of emphasis so far placed on functions of mass communication for organizations, an obvious first step would be to describe these functions in more detail and to relate them to organizational characteristics and requirements. For instance, Eisenstadt (1955) notes that the greater the differentiation of roles within a community, the more there tends to be reliance on impersonal mass media. Does this observation hold with respect to groups other than the ones he studied? And what other relationships between mass communication and organizational structure can be established?

This area of inquiry includes a number of questions of high political temperature. What degree of access to the mass media do organizations of given types require in order to operate efficiently? And if they achieve this degree of access, does it impose penalties on other collectivities and individuals? A study of environmental information in the San Francisco Bay Area mass media found that approximately 40 per cent of it originated with public relations practitioners (i.e., organizational spokesmen) and about 20 per cent consisted of rewritten press releases (Sachsman, 1973). Before we cluck disapprovingly, we should know more about the functions that these communications serve for the organizations that released them, for the organizations that consumed them, and—of course—for the attentive public.

Another investigation found that many editors favor extension of freedom of information laws to cover public utilities, feeling that press-business relationships should be defined in the same way as press-government relationships (Rubin, 1972). Can such a demand be supported in view of what is known, or could be known, about the functions and dysfunctions of mass communications for business organizations? What costs would increased surveillance entail—for the utilities and for the public? Would these be balanced by corresponding benefits?

This leads us to ask about the degree of access to the mass media, and the degree of privacy, required by various levels of government. If government is denied adequate means to reach the public, or lacks the degree of privacy necessary for internal consultation, society as a whole suffers. But society also suffers if government dominates the channels of communication and excludes the public from policy-making. What is the proper balance?

The extent to which organizations have access to the mass media is relevant to the needs of individuals as well. Complaints are frequent that in the days of huge mass communication media the individual has little opportunity to gain a public hearing. Nostalgically, a contrast is drawn with days when small newspapers served small communities and almost everyone who cared to do so could avail himself of the freedom of the press. One possible solution to the problem of individual access is vicarious access through organizations. The individual who has something to say does not necessarily turn to the mass media directly, but may express himself to one or more organizations to which he belongs. If the ideas expressed find resonance within the group, they are then more likely to come to the attention of the mass media—through a house organ, a press release, or some other way.

If individuals are to gain access to the mass media through organizations, then the internal communication patterns within collectivities become even more significant. Julian (1966) has suggested that coercive organizations tend to distort internal communications. Lipset, Trow, and Coleman (1956) point out that the leadership of a formally organized group does not necessarily have to dominate the group's internal communication channels. Within the union they studied, the International Typographer's Union, it was possible for a variety of views to be brought to the attention of the membership. Both of these studies suggest that further attention to the structure of mass communication channels *within* organizations would be desirable.

It has been recognized for some time that new communication technologies have an impact on organizational structures and activities. Cott (1971) and others have pointed out that the conduct of American election campaigns has been greatly altered by the advent of television. Instead of trying to shake as many hands as possible, candidates serve as actors in events that are likely to be included on the evening television news broadcast. An insurance company executive mentioned to the author that entirely new group structures had been created when the principal offices of his company were linked together electronically; officials who had common interests (e.g., in obtaining a greater share of the budget for certain purposes) were then able to make common cause, while groupings based on geographical propinquity diminished in importance. A political scientist (Marvick, 1970) has speculated that two-way computerized communication facilities could serve the intramural communication needs of loosely-knit organizational structures composed of people with a common sense of purpose working in a coordinated effort. Nevertheless, much more thought has been given to the implications of new communication technology for the media themselves, and for individuals, than to their relevance to the needs of organizations.

How well are organizational needs of various kinds served by existing mass media, and how could they be served better? Which types of organizations, and which types of needs, receive disproportionate attention? Which are ignored or slighted? Are additional types of content desirable in order to serve organizational needs more completely, and should this content be carried in general mass media, specialized media, or house organs?

Finally, can an organization's communication requirements be satisfied at a lower cost? Many possibilities for reducing costs suggest themselves. Perhaps, in some instances, mass communication could substitute for face-to-face communications, saving the time (and often travel) that the latter entails. It may be that mass communications primarily serving to provide reassurance for a group, or to bolstering its sense of identity, could be replaced by less expensive mechanisms. Can the benefits of advertising be secured with lower expenditures? Much thought has been given to reducing abuses in advertising, but little attention has been devoted to reducing its cost. In view of the huge resources devoted to advertising, even a small percentage reduction in costs would represent a substantial saving.

Research that would shed light on these and other questions regarding the functions of mass communication for collectivities should not be difficult to undertake. Most obviously, the enormous but diffuse literature should be reviewed more systematically. It would be particularly valuable to examine histories of organizations and movements, case studies of business firms, and accounts of institution-building in developing countries. Careful analysis should make it possible to form more precise hypotheses about the role of the media in the formation, internal functioning, and external relations of various types of organizations. This avenue of research would entail a substantial fringe benefit: it should help to relate the bodies of writing on public relations, advertising, and propaganda more closely to the main currents of social science thinking than has been possible thus far. Indeed, one reason the literature on advertising and public relations has been of little interest to most social scientists is that the relationships of these activities to the structure and functioning of the organizations that sponsor them have ordinarily not been studied.

More case studies, designed in the light of hypotheses about the functions of mass communication for organizations, are desirable. Doctoral dissertations and master's essays could make substantial contributions here. The case studies should deal not only with existing and successful organizations but also with organizations that failed or that never grew to a significant size. It might be possible, for instance, to explain the demise of the International Workers of the World in terms of its policies governing the use of mass communications (Brooks, 1969). Did it fail in part because its ideological appeals, while impressive to intellectuals, were of little interest to its membership? In contrast, one might examine the use of mass communications by more successful labor movements in the United States, and by Marxist unions in Europe. More attention to Lenin's use of mass communications in the early stages of organizing the Communist Party would probably yield new insights. Very detailed analyses of day-to-day organizational communications, analogous to the detailed studies of communication among individuals in small groups (Bales, 1950) might also shed new light on organizational needs.

Community studies, illuminating the relationships among organizations, individuals, and the media, would be especially valuable. It should be possible to specify organizational needs that were well or poorly satisfied by mass communication in order to determine the extent to which existing groups created a "market" for media content and to find out whether organizations do in fact provide indirect access to the mass media for their members. Community studies would also enable researchers to examine communication patterns that were functional for one group but dysfunctional for others.

Some community or neighborhood studies might be designed on an experimental basis. A weekly newspaper with one type of content could be introduced into a neighborhood, while a newspaper with another type of content was started in a similar neighborhood. Organizational life in the two neighborhoods could then be compared, and both communities could be contrasted with a third area that had no locally oriented mass media. Similar experiments could be undertaken with cable television or computerized information systems. Such experimentation would be quite expensive, although it is possible that situations approximating an experimental design might be found: e.g., two communities, one of which was served by certain mass media and another that lacked such services.

Finally, content analyses could be undertaken in order to identify types of information in the mass media that might satisfy specified organizational needs and to determine how much of this information was available. Content analysis would be most valuable if undertaken in conjunction with some other mode of inquiry that would enable the researcher to ascertain which organizational needs were actually being served by mass media content and which were being slighted. It might turn out that organizations, like individuals, do not take advantage of the full range of information available to them

One reason that research on the functions of mass communication for collectivities has been slighted may be that the survey instrument, widely used by social scientists, is more difficult to adapt to organizations than to individuals. Adaptations of this and other instruments will be required, and new research techniques should be devised for use in this area. However, it would seem possible to make good progress even with the research tools presently available.

5

MASS COMMUNICATION AND THE NATION STATE
Daniel Lerner

Communication, in our lexicon, is the neural system of organization. Wherever people must act together (an informal definition of organization), there they must exchange information (an informal definition of communication). Communication, in the sense of shared information, is the organizing mechanism of social action. It is analogous to the organizing functions for body action performed by the neural system, which transmits the "information" that informs the skeletal and muscular activities of the human body. This is why the neural system often is referred to as our physiological "message center." Like all analogies, this one is treacherous if pushed too far; like many analogies, it is illuminating as a starter for inquiry and reflection.

The proposition—that communication shapes organization—is applicable to all varieties of collective behavior in social institutions: large and small, formal and informal, hierarchical and egalitarian. It is true that large, formal heirarchical organizations tend to have more one-way (and less multiple-way) communication than small, informal, egalitarian organizations. But the kind and amount of communication is an empirical question, like all questions of quality and quantity to be determined by controlled observation of particular cases. The essential theoretical point is that every organization must have a communication system of some shape, size, and sort.

We do not impose this proposition by theoretical fiat. Rather, we derive it from the common concern with communication found in every study of organization known to us. The studies range, in the wise words of Edward Sapir (1930), "from the glance of a pair of lovers to debates in the League of Nations." They include the family (Flavell, 1968; McLeod and O'Keefe, 1972), the neighborhood and city, the hospital, the corporation, the nation, as well as bilateral and multilateral and global negotiation. Even the United Nations is studied as a "world forum," i.e., a multinational message center for the exchange of information.

Our main concern here is with the particular form of social organization known as the nation-state. For, in the era of modern history that experienced the rise of "masscomm," the "media" have been mainly owned and operated—

or at least regulated—by official agencies of the nation-state. So it remains, especially with the more recent electronic rather than the print media, in the world today.

We shall examine four main areas of concern to current and future research on mass communication as organized by nation-states. First, we shall identify a set of contextual variables of social organization that may help to revise the original guidelines. Second, we shall reformulate the key variables of the classic communication paradigm. Third, we shall specify some characteristics of poor countries that further differentiate the key variables identified previously. Fourth, we shall conclude with some observations on the policy process as a guide to communication research.

CONTEXTUAL VARIABLES

We propose four "contextual variables" of social organization for future conceptualization and research on communication. They are contextual because they set the conditions under which national communications systems operate. In this sense, each contextual variable provides parameters for the operation of the classic set of variables in the communication paradigm. The contextual variables are: (1) size and shape, (2) mobility and participation, (3) disposable income, and (4) options and decisions.

1. *Size and Shape.* These societal contexts are critical for mass communication insofar as they determine density and dispersion of population. Where the land-to-man ratio is high—i.e., where a population is lightly dispersed over a vast terrain—mass communication tends to be low; on a cost-benefit calculus, it becomes expensive and is perceived as less urgent than other societal needs, such as road or rail. Thus, Greenland "needs" mass media less than Canada, Canada less than the Soviet Union, and the Soviet Union less than China.

Clearly, size and shape are "multivariate" terms: the United States and Indonesia are about the same "size," just over 3,000 miles from one end to another, but because of their differing "shape"—the United States being a unitary land mass (before the inclusion of Alaska and Hawaii), Indonesia being a conglomeration of islands, peninsulas, archipelagoes—Indonesia has been harder to "cover" than the United States. (In another relevant "context," it obviously matters that the United States is rich and Indonesia is poor.)

Historically, a cluster of other relevant factors has been related to size and shape—ranging from such simple factors as population density to such complex ones as language. Until recently, the United States had a relatively evenly deployed population (in regional and urban-rural terms) and a single national language (at least in school, media, and public affairs). Indonesia will take a long while yet to achieve any such state of equilibrium in distribution of population and unification of language.

What may well accelerate the process are the new technologies of mass communication. "Available" only in the last few years, they will probably not (for cost reasons) become "usable" for several more years for many countries of the world. I refer, of course, primarily to the high-cost technology of communication satellites as exemplified for commercial use by the Comsat-Intelsat system and projected for educational use by the NASA series of ATS satellites.

In the future application of satellite technology, size and shape are likely to be key variables. It is obvious that large countries with highly dispersed populations will be more intensely interested in using satellites than small countries with concentrated populations. This will be true whether we refer to relatively more developed countries (e.g., the United States, Canada, Japan, the Soviet Union) or less developed countries (e.g., India, Brazil, China, Indonesia). Indeed, the pattern of concerns is already discernible in the international negotiations over satellites of the past five years.

2. *Mobility and Participation.* Since I have already discussed these "key variables" at considerable length in earlier publications (e.g., Lerner, 1958), I shall confine my comments here to their impact upon media development.

One principal point is that mobility increases, I would guess exponentially, with the number and variety of mediated communications produced in a society. Consider the single social process of childbearing and nurture. In traditional societies, this process was handled according to certain established routines passed orally from generation to generation—usually from grandmother to new mother by demonstration, perhaps with a few cautionary observations by midwives.

What happens when the young mother lives in a highly mobile society, far away from the grandmother? First, there is a rise in telecommunications (on broadband spectra, telephone and telegraph count as mass communication). Second, millions of paperbacks by Dr. Spock are sold. Third, a "maternity clinic" industry, equipped with all available media, is created. The prospective mother (and usually father) is trained, audiovisually, to identify the sounds of infantile crying and the sights of infantile excreta. The media are pervaded by debates over breast vs. bottle, demand vs. schedule feeding. Fertile polemics fill the air as "diaperology" of infants is equated to the great historic issues of freedom vs. control. Why all this? Because the grandmother lives far away from the new mother—i.e., because of mobility.

The second principal point follows hard upon the first: mobility, which increases mass communication, raises participation, which increases the flow of messages even further. It is staggering to think now many millions of people, billions of sounds and sights, are concerned with feeding and toileting the new baby just because the grandmother lives far away. Jackie Gleason has made the point succinctly: "As I walk down the aisles of a supermarket and pass the thousands of cans of dog food, I'm glad to see how good dogs have it these days. When I was a kid, they just ate with us!"

If the effect of mobility upon the increase in number and variety of communications is exponential, then the effect of participation may be asymptotic. For, mobility multiplies participation. Young mothers who live far away from the grandmothers come to rely upon ("participate in") the media for many decisions beyond feeding and toileting the new baby. I shall pursue this line only briefly under the rubrics "disposable income" and "options and decisions."

3. *Disposable Income.* This concept may well be the most important contribution ever made to the history of human freedom. I refer in minor key to Adam Smith's dictum that "man is never more innocently engaged than in making money," in major key to the hypothesis of Riesman, Glazer and Denney (1950) that the "cash customer" is the great participant in modern societies—i.e., the person who reads newspapers, tunes in radio-television, votes in elections, and, I would add, expresses opinions.

The historical meaning of disposable income may be explained in terms of the "cultural lag" (*pace*, Karl Marx) that followed Gutenberg's invention of movable type in the early fifteenth century—a full half-century before Columbus bumbled upon the New World. Since navigation was then a better "paying proposition" than communication, Columbus *et seq.* received large shares of the Royal Treasury—then the principal source of "disposable income." The issue was not settled by British defeat of the Spanish Armada in 1588. Nor even, except among the Atlantic nations, by the War of 1812 and the Monroe Doctrine. It extended into the Pacific through the United States "Open Door Policy" of the 1890s and continues, in a new vein, with the Kissinger-Nixon reopening of corridors to China.

What, meanwhile, of Gutenberg's invention—more important in the long run, I believe, than Columbus' voyage? It took about three centuries for Europe to incorporate the technology of print into its social organization, with the "penny press" developed initially in eighteenth-century Britain. Why so long? What were the Europeans doing during these three hundred years? In a sentence, they were creating a new social class that could use a "penny press" in their own lives—a class of people who could read, who had an extra penny to spend, and who were willing to spend that penny on a newspaper rather than on cakes and ale. It illustrates, as does virtually all of subsequent mass communication history, the close connection between disposable income and media development.

4. *Options and Opinions.* While the penny press flourished in Britain, Dr. Samuel Johnson noted that "every Englishman, nowadays, expects to be promptly and accurately informed upon the condition of public affairs." This was a major new development in social organization. It completely transformed the relations between government and the governed and terminated the long historical era when a queen could say, when told of crowds crying outside the palace gates that they had no bread, "Let them eat cake!"

Indeed, the palace gates were pried open and most of the traditional societal walls came tumbling down. A new conception of proper relations between center and periphery swept the western world. The process has been vividly described by Carl Friedrich (1950) and Merritt and Rokkan (1966).

Among the principal consequences of this process was the multiplication of opinions and options among common men. Not only did the cash customer now read the papers and vote for his governors (retitled "representatives" and "public servants"). He also expressed opinions and selected options on a great number and variety of matters which, only yesterday, had been none of his business. It was this key variable that decisively separated the modern West from the rest of the world.

COMMUNICATION VARIABLES

Once we have ordered the contextual variables that set the conditions under which the mass media operate, we are obliged to establish ordering principles for the communication process itself. For, within any and every societal context the communication process, *qua* process, operates with an identical set of components: every communication transaction requires a sender who transmits a message through a channel to a receiver. This is concisely and cogently expressed in the classic paradigm invented by Harold D. Lasswell (1948): Who says what to whom, through what channel, and with what effect? This paradigm served communication research well—perhaps it is the source of systematic communication research—over the past quarter century.

The world policy has changed significantly, however, since the "great powers" of Europe fought each other for supremacy in World War I. To put the principal changes in summary fashion: (1) the imperial dominion of Europe over most of the world has ended; (2) two non-European "superpowers," the United States and the Soviet Union, have shaped much of world history since World War II; and (3) a "third world" has entered the global arena to interact with the great powers, in principle, on equal rather than colonial terms. These changes in the world political arena have occasioned parallel changes in the world communication network.

Of great moment as well, in the changing process of communication around the world, are three additional factors that have surfaced since World War II: (1) the great leap forward of communication technology, (2) the global diffusion of mass media, and (3) the new demand for "open societies" everywhere. While the third factor is hardest to determine empirically (as compared with the substantial bulk of quantitative data available on the first two factors), it may turn out to be the most important in shaping the future of communication with which researchers will have to deal. Let us look briefly at each of the three factors in turn.

The technology explosion of the past quarter-century has produced highly visible and audible transformations in the world communication network. The picture tube, the transistor, and the satellite have brought new sights and sounds into every variety of social organization on earth. These products of advanced technology, in turn, have produced relatively low-cost "spinoffs" (e.g., kinescopes, tapes, cassettes), which have greatly amplified and multiplied the volume of communication in the world today. It is fair to say that a true "world communication network" is the creation of satellites. Only in the past decade has this phrase become an operational reality.

As the new technology passed from the research and development phase into production, it turned out "mass media" (receivers) by the millions— and at prices that people were willing to pay. Many Americans who traveled in the South during the early 1950s reported the rapid rise of television antennas over even the poorest huts and hovels. These national reports were confirmed by the sales figures of media producers, as are the more recent reports of global travelers in the 1960s from the poorest countries of the world.

Thus, the new technology, diffused as mass media, has transformed social organization (as a more general rubric than political structure) by "mobilizing the periphery" of previously inert populations for relatively vigorous participation in the policy process. A whole new array of "audiences" has been created everywhere to interact with the new technologies.

Out of this has grown the demand, everywhere, for "open societies." The historical western pattern whereby cash customers became media consumers and then political participants (voters) is being reenacted on a world scale. The evidence strongly indicates that the future trends of social organization and communication with which research will have to deal are likely to be worldwide in form and content.

In concluding this discussion of communication variables, let us note the impact of recent and current societal transformations upon our classic communication paradigm. Researchers working in areas where the demand for "open society" has spread widely and rooted deeply find the old paradigm inadequate to deal with the new tensions building up between government and the governed. This applies to all traditional superordinate-subordinate relations (white over black, male over female, old over young, strong over weak), but it applies with special urgency to political relations.

The goal of most political regimes is "stability" (at a minimum to maintain themselves in power), whereas the demand of most political participants is "mobility" (openness to popular participation). This tension puts a premium upon studies that include the variables of "policy" (government purposes) and "feedback" (citizen demands). Accordingly we suggest the following reformulation of the classic paradigm: Who (source) says what (content) to whom (audience), why (policy), how (technique), with what effects (outcome), and who talks back (feedback)?

This adds to Lasswell's original paradigm two more "variables": policy and feedback. While the addition of variables usually is not advisable by the scientific law of parsimony, the policy and feedback variables are indispensable for communication researchers today, as we seek to pass from static to dynamic analysis of communication in varied societal and intersocietal contexts. Their functioning in the interaction between communication and social organization may well be the most important theoretical problem we face.

MASS COMMUNICATION AND DEVELOPMENT

The transformation of world society and communication sketched in the preceding sections is nowhere more marked than in the less developed countries (LDC's), those poorer countries seeking development, which comprise most of the earth's surface and population. Here, the contemporary tension between government and the governed expresses itself in the acute conflict between the constraints of poverty and the demands for development: economic, social, and political improvements. The conflict operates on both internal and international levels in virtually all developing countries.

On the internal level, the conflict between rich and poor expresses itself in a variety of "national socialisms" which have in common a diffuse ideology of populism. On the international level, the conflict tends to divide rich and poor countries into "haves" and "have-nots"—an ominous resonance of Hitler's international policy under the Nazi variety of national socialism. Some stigmata of Nazism are indeed visible in the LDC's, notably the spread of ethnocentrism and xenophobia. Few phenomena of the post-imperial epoch are more disheartening than the ethnic clashes among the ethnic poor, e.g., communal riots in India (Hindu vs. Muslim), Malays legislating against Chinese, Africans expropriating and expelling long-resident Indians (Lerner and Schramm, 1967, ch. 7 and 8).

The internal and external facets of the rich-poor conflict converge only rarely in LDC policy decisions, as when a Mossadegh nationalizes a giant oil company, or a Nasser "Egyptianizes" the Suez Canal. Such "propaganda of the deed" evokes popular support, even enthusiasm, among the native poor. But development does not grow by enthusiasm alone. Indeed, such spectacular acts are often counterproductive in both economic and psychological terms.

The initial psychological impact usually contributes to the "revolution of rising expectations" that has inspired and bedeviled populist sentiment in the LDC's over the past quarter-century. Great expectations are raised when a popular LDC leader "expropriates the expropriators." Now that the imperialists are routed, so goes the refrain, we shall prosper from the fruits of our own land and labor! But this rarely happens. Few LDC's have been able to break out of the vicious circle of poverty without the substantial aid of richer countries.

Why this is so has been made amply clear by development economists. A poor country is poor because it has no industry, one witty economist said in summary, and it has no industry because it is poor. To break this vicious circle requires quantum increases of money, technology, and human skills. In general (except for oil strikes and similar gifts of God or nature), such quantum jumps in LDC resources come from other countries rich enough to spare the needed resources. These richer countries turn shy with LDC regimes that expropriate their assets. Thus, the psychological enthusiasm engendered by the heroic act of expropriation tends to boomerang. The poor country and, especially, its poor people do not get richer. Great expectations turn into great frustrations.

This sequence underlies the "revolution of rising frustrations" upon which LDC regimes have foundered in recent years. Unfulfilled expectations lead to widespread frustrations among those people demanding betterment via development. Frustration leads, as the psychologists have long assured us it must, either to regression (withdrawal and retreat from the newly-raised expectations) or to aggression (e.g., the politics of the street, organized violence.) Aggression destabilizes social organization, the political regime crumbles, and the military takes over.

This sequence, culminating in military takeover, has been reenacted dozens of times in the LDC's over the past decade and continues today. Much of Asia and most of Africa, and Latin America is now under military regime or martial law. How has this come about? Why do the great expectations that arise with independence culminate in the dismal repression now epidemic among the LDC's?

The fundamental answer, I believe, is the "acceleration of history," propagated by the ideology of development and diffused by the mass media. Poor people everywhere have been led to believe that something like the levels of modernity achieved by the western world over 500 years could be reached by the LDC's in their own lifetime. This has turned out to be illusory. Hopes have been dashed and expectations turned to frustrations. The LDC's have discovered, like Wonderland's Red Queen, that relative to the rich countries they had to run twice as fast just to stay in the same place. Most of them, as Myrdal and Ward and others have demonstrated, have been getting poorer.

It would be pleasant to report that the managers of world communication have drawn the right lesson from the sad experience of the past quarter-century. Unhappily, that is not so. Indeed, the contrary seems to be the case—witness the overwhelming rejection last year, by the member states of the United Nations and UNESCO, of the untenable American thesis on "direct satellite broadcasting." Here is an instance in which commercial control of the new communication technology has operated along lines antithetical to productive interaction between developed and developing countries. I have already expressed myself at length elsewhere on this subject. I will here stress only that the great "acceleration of history" has been exacerbated in the LDC's during the past few years by the mass media.

Intelsat is the most spectacular of the new technological accelerators, for most of its members already are LDC's. I was told in Kuala Lumpur that the telecast of the Ali-Frazier fight created an unofficial national holiday. Every available television receiver was rented for the day by business concerns, which gave their employees time off to watch two black Americans punch each other according to rules and ruses alien to virtually all Malaysians. Elsewhere in the LDC's, people massed to watch strangely costumed persons walk on the moon; for these viewers the concept of "space" could have only an uncertain, or indeed a superstitious, sense.

Less spectacular than Intelsat, but probably more pervasive in recent years, is the impact of transistors. In 1968, I was assured by a mass communication specialist in Hong Kong that Chinese family structure remained strong and would "contain" the new media. Yet, in 1973, the streets of Hong Kong were filled with young Chinese blaring their pocket receivers—sometimes with two receivers glued to their ears to get a "stereo effect." What do they listen to? According to my learned friend, mainly the music and news of "underground stations"—certainly not the filiopietistic analects of Confucius. My learned friend has fundamentally revised his hypothesis of a few short years ago.

In underscoring this new "acceleration of history," I wish to stress the "people problems" it raises in the LDC's (and not only there). Some of these problems can be made to seem merely technical, e.g., what are the special effects of audiovisual media upon people who cannot read? But the core problems are psychological, socioeconomic, and ultimately political—with communication providing the neural ties that bind all these sectors together (or fail to do so). It is to the better understanding of these communication successes and failures that I direct my concluding suggestions for future research.

RESEARCH SUGGESTIONS

I have sought to indicate the key role of communication in mediating between public policy and social organization. Public policy embodies the values of a society as expressed by its governors; communication articulates and diffuses these values among the governed for their acceptance or rejection (partial or total); and social organization is the set of institutions (collective behavioral routines) that emerge from their interaction. Since the policy process continuously and endlessly shapes and reshapes the behavior of individuals and institutions, it provides a high-priority array of problems for communication research with a theoretical intent.

While communication research must take careful account of "contextual variables," its focus will be on "communication variables," modified from the classic Lasswellian paradigm to include "policy" and "feedback." The question "Why?" (policy) calls for fresh modes of analyzing communication content with respect to the sender's purpose. Clearly, all the extant modes of content analysis are applicable, from the historian's traditional *explication de texte* to Lasswell's computerized quantitative semantics.

These research techniques have served us reasonably well for the official utterances of political spokesmen (Sapir's [1930] "League of Nations"). But we have yet to devise and apply procedures that systematically clarify the unuttered messages contained in all communication, from Sapir's "pair of lovers" through all the mass media. These implicit meanings are the key to policy analysis, for they exhibit the common assumptions of any social organization. Where such common assumptions play a major role in communication content there is "political consensus"; where their role is minor we may expect "political conflict."

There is, in short, need for contextual studies of the policy process that will lead from description of past trends via systematic analysis of the conditions under which they occurred to the disciplined projection of policy alternatives. This is a terse statement of what Lasswell and I (1951) have called "the policy sciences."

A good example of such studies in internal communication is the Goldhamer-Marshall (1953) trend analysis of admissions to mental hospitals in Massachusetts over the past century; variations in the diagnostic labeling of mental illnesses are shown to be the "key symbols" in an historical communication process with important lessons for future policy. A good example in the study of international communication is Hans Speier's (1957) analysis of "atomic blackmail"; the dissection of Soviet communication content provided important guidance for subsequent American policy decisions (e.g., in the Cuban missile crisis).

For future communication research on the contemporary international arena, no set of problems appears more urgent than the putative "revolution of rising frustrations" in the less developed countries. While this revolution is generated mainly by the international media, it is sustained by internal communication. Over the past quarter-century, mass communication, exploited by the charismatic leaders of the less developed countries, has raised expectations everywhere in the world. In most places, these heightened expectations were doomed to frustration, leading, as the psychologists for decades have assured us they must, to either regression or aggression. Both reactions have tended to be counterproductive for development purposes. The aggressive reaction particularly has displaced demands upon the economic sector, generated largely via mass communication, onto the political sector. The political sector, in those countries and continents of the world that I have observed, is ill-equipped to handle such demands. Frustrations increase, regimes destabilize, the military takes over.

The revolution of rising frustrations raises many questions of critical importance for those who produce and consume mass communications. To illustrate but a few: Can we determine an optimum "dosage" of expectations for a sick society (as a physician does for an individual patient)? By what indices can any such dosages be objectified and generalized (as by the medical indices of age, weight, pulse, blood pressure)? How shall such an index as illiteracy be factored into the system of equations needed to deal contextually with the "organized complexity" presented to the researcher by any social organization?

The last question indicates the magnitude of the ignorance imposed upon current communication research by the diffusion of new technology into the first genuine "world communication network." Never before the last decade have millions of illiterates everywhere on earth been exposed continuously to news of the world. What, in detail, are the special effects of these new sights and sounds upon people who cannot read—as compared with people who have acquired the discipline of literacy? When we are able to answer this question, we shall be able to answer many more that shape our future.

MASS COMMUNICATION AND
THE POLITICAL SYSTEM
Davis B. Bobrow

One of the great continuing debates in the United States concerns the "proper" relationships between mass communication and the political system. The participants in this debate almost always seem assured of their virtue, of their monopoly on defense of the public interest. Much of the debate rests on assumed but dubious contentions of necessity (Pool, 1972; Will, 1972; Rivers, 1970). Democracy allegedly requires continuous efforts by the media to check the politicians. For example, columnist Rowland Evans quotes a famous newspaperman, Frank Kent, with approval: "there is only one way to look at a politician and that is down" (Will, 1972). On the other hand, national security and effective government allegedly require that political officials can readily communicate or not communicate with the people without harassment. And the United States media are supposedly harassing (Will, 1972; Ames, 1972).

Different stances on the "need to know" rest on the supposed incompatibility of alternative positions. Freedom from constraint of the media, or of the officials, is treated as a payoff in a constant-sum game: a gain received by one requires that the other incur a comparable loss.

Our concern here is neither to continue nor to attempt to resolve the debate; instead, the focus is on questions of normative priorities and empirical relationships. Too little is known about empirical relationships, although it is clear that the interests of each group of advocates are not restricted to what is asserted. My hope is to clarify the relationships between mass communication and characteristics of both the political process and its consequences. These relationships are two-way in nature. Two benefits should follow. First, we should gain a clear idea of what different normative preferences for the process and substance of politics imply for the gross structure of mass communication relationships with the political system. Second, we should be better able to devise specific steps to defend or attain our preferences.

It seems useful to begin with a definition of mass communication, but one that does more than differentiate it from interpersonal communication—one that links it to the political system. Let us refer by mass communication to systems of messages and means of generation and transmission (human and

93

technological) that have three properties: first, the messages and the media are intended for a large and spatially dispersed audience; second, the messages and the media are sufficiently standard to be readily comprehensible to and usable by a large fraction of the intended audience; third, the messages are available, because of media availability, to a large fraction of the relevant population. The political process relates to mass communication as it affects any of these properties: message content, media personnel and technology, cultural level of messages, or availability of the media output. If we accept this formulation we will still want to look at political attempts to control program content but we will also look at, for example, the pricing of electronic media receivers and hookups and decisions about the proportionate use of different languages in the media in a multi-lingual nation.

This definition deliberately does not try to pin down the term "large." A precise number, percentage, or probability of exposure would be arbitrary and meaningless without understanding the context of the communication system. Indeed, it may be wise to think of the "massness" of communication as a continuum along which media and program content vary in degree. For example, at an appropriate level of analysis we may wish to treat each of the following Chinese publications as mass communication: *People's Daily*, the regular bulletins sent to all political cadres in the People's Liberation Army with a circulation approaching five figures, and a review of the Western Press circulated to less than one thousand senior foreign affairs and defense officials. Also we may wish to distinguish between the "massness" of different stories or programs carried in a particular channel. For example, we may wish to distinguish between news stories in the United States press, which seem to require a high-school education or more for comprehension, and editorials, which seem to have a less stringent requirement (Moznette and Rarick, 1968). Similarly, we may want to distinguish between editorial cartoons in United States papers, which apparently are intelligible as intended to only a small fraction of the audience (Carl, 1968), and Chinese mass circulation politically oriented comics (*The People's Comic Book*, 1973). Under this relativistic perspective, we may want to score communications for "massness" as a function of the proportion of the population of the relevant social system that they reach. In any event, the relativistic approach would help our political concerns by including "closed" but large edition media.

Any attempt to pin down what we mean by the political system is even more troublesome. One strategy is to refer to the behaviors and relationships of formal government organizations, of persons holding or aspiring to office in those organizations, and of those who take part in the selection process. We could then determine for each relevant situation the identity and function of the actors. Used alone, this approach has two problems: first, some organizations and persons are difficult to categorize—public corporations, members of kitchen cabinets; second, efforts to generalize will probably founder on differences within and between nations. We need a more analytic and less concrete approach.

With acknowledgments to Lasswell (1936) and Lerner (in this volume), we can start by treating the political system as a matter of exchange and allocation: Who gets what from whom, when, and how? This forces us to look for both sources and recipients, the transfer between them, its timing, and its mechanism. Yet it does not reflect our concerns fully. First, we want to know the scientific and social reasons for the answers and changes in the answers to the questions above. Let us add "Why?" Second, we do not simply want to know what is going on in politics and the reasons for that state of affairs. We also want to know what difference those actions make; we want to address and influence consequences. Let us add "With what effect?" Finally, since our concerns lie primarily with behavior through time, dynamics, we want to close the loop in a way that sets the stage for the next run of the political process. The consequences of political activity and communication, if any, trigger responses that affect who can and will get what from whom subsequently. Let us add "With what response?" If we accept this framework, we can use it to explore the nature of relationships between mass communication and the political system. Perhaps more importantly, we can use it to help determine the collective consequences of different patterns of relationships.

At least one major problem remains. As stated, the framework can be applied to all levels of social organization, from the family to a world organization. It seems useful to narrow this range to the following class of situations. A key actor for at least one element in our framework is an institution charged formally, by either law or custom, with collective responsibility for the distribution of public and private goods and bads (Olson, 1965). This would require the involvement of at least some institution we customarily think of as political. It is helpfully inclusive in that it applies equally well to different political systems and levels of political analysis, e.g., local, state, national, international. Also, it covers situations where the exchanging actors are in the private sector, but the mechanism, content, and consequences of the exchange are affected by a public sector actor.

Our political economy approach obviously applies to much media content other than news, editorials, and so-called public affairs programming. It treats as potentially germane all media content bearing on the allocations of public and private goods and bads and, more fundamentally, on their definition. For example, it would include "eco-pornography"—advertising by major corporate polluters that stresses their concern with a clean environment and is clearly intended to affect allocations of the burden for environmental quality. It would also include comics that attempt to establish the status of various public offices and issues, such as Steve Canyon versus Doonesbury. As a final example, it would include all media content that attributes politically relevant characteristics to segments of a population, e.g., majority-minority, hostile-reasonable (Johnson, Sears, and McConahay, 1971; Guillaumin, 1971), or to a particular nation (Kracauer, 1949).

We can set up a framework that helps us to examine mass communication—political system relationships without assuming that the characteristics of one always affect the other. Indeed, the important first-order empirical question is when and to what extent the nature of the mass communication system affects the political system and vice-versa. Sensitivity should be established rather than assumed. When we turn to assess sensitivity it is important to distinguish clearly the following dimensions:

	Political Process	Political Program
Mass Communication Process	?	?
Mass Communication Program	?	?

Each system may be sensitive in one and not another dimension. From an evaluative point of view, we may like a particular process by which the political system identifies issues, makes choices, and implements policies without approving of the resulting program. We may approve of the way in which decisions about what the media will carry to whom are made without approving of the substantive outcome or media program, namely, what the content is and to whom it is sent. Indeed one of the confusions in much of the debate is treating the two dimensions as highly and positively correlated in normal implication.

Once sensitivity is assessed, we need to establish preferences for the processes and programs of each system. We then turn to the much more specific and situational task of inventing ways to achieve the particular systems we prefer relative to what now prevails. We may again treat the questions as ones of sensitivity, but in a much more "micro" sense. What specifics of autonomy and control, personnel selection, carrying capacity and concentration, and funding are necessary and sufficient to generate the precise effect we want? And, more difficult still, what specifics will simultaneously achieve both our process and program preferences? Or do we have to choose?

SOME GENERAL RELATIONSHIPS

To the extent that we can map a "latent structure" of basic relationships involving mass communications, political institutions, and publics, we will be better able to compare cases, organize a wealth of case detail, and structure our thinking in terms of trade-offs and bargaining outcomes. In principle, one could arrive at a set of underlying relationships through a formal inductive or deductive procedure. The attempt here is a much more modest, impressionistic one.

The most common view of relationships among mass communication, political institutions, and publics stresses the securing, organizing, and forwarding of messages by the media from sender to receiver. The media constitute an information transmission belt and the relationships between mass communication (MC) and the political system vary primarily in terms of how messages are secured and forwarded, who decides which ones are secured and forwarded, and the thematic distribution of the messages used. The message mediator view looks like this:

$$\text{Pol. Inst.}_1 \Longleftrightarrow \text{MC}_1 \Longleftrightarrow \text{Public}_1$$

$$\text{Pol. Inst.}_2 \Longleftrightarrow \text{MC}_2 \Longleftrightarrow \text{Public}_2$$

$$\text{Pol. Inst.}_3 \Longleftrightarrow \text{MC}_3 \Longleftrightarrow \text{Public}_3$$

The popularity of the message mediator view of relationships with mass communicators is not surprising given how important it makes them. Yet it has two more-generally valid considerations to recommend it. First, it corresponds with our intuitive understanding of the need for mass communication in large, complicated, and mobile societies. Otherwise, political officials could do little else but relay messages to the polity; publics would have little time for their private affairs and could not afford access without the reductionist and diffusing activity of mass communications.* Second, the view is sufficiently general to accommodate most preferred models of mass communication-political system relationships. Both Lenin and Mill would be happy since all alternatives about control and mission are left open: within this framework the media can be a Leninist "collective propagandist, ... collective agitator, ... and ... collective organizer"; or, in a more populist mode, they can "tell the citizens what they need to know to make decisions, the citizens decide, and the [media] ... play at least some part in communicating these decisions back to the policy maker for implementation." (Will, 1972, p. 24). Both "objective" and "advocacy" journalists can readily be accommodated (Wicker, 1971).

To avoid misunderstanding, several points should be emphasized. First, any attempt to apply the message mediator view to particular cases will have to carefully identify and discriminate among the actors in each of the three categories. Second, the three actor categories are analytic units, like buyer and seller or producer and consumer. For different situations, the same concrete unit can change roles. For example, officials in Congress can be under the political institutions category in some instances and under publics in others. Third, the framework as stated is in no sense domestic as opposed to international. It can be used for national and for transnational analyses. Finally, although the framework has great flexibility, the basic dimension of relationship is fixed: message transmission.

The message mediator view is inadequate in several ways. First, it limits the relationships to messages, even though there are several other important dimensions of relationship. Second, it does not contain any apparatus to explain how particular message relationships are set and altered. What is the decision calculus used by the participants in the different elements? How can we state it in general form? Third, it does not place the mediator relationship in a context provided by the parameters of non-mass communication.

An alternative way of thinking about mass communication, political institution, and public relationships is in terms of the positive and negative kinds of utilities involved for the different actors. If we can characterize those utilities we may then be able to work out deductively and inductively the decisions responsible for one rather than another message mediator mode of operation. One test of the extent to which we have located the most informative dimensions of utility is the ease with which we can relate them to the behaviors and contentions of representative individuals and institutions.

---

*See, for example, Lippmann's discussion of "contact and opportunity" and "speed, words, and clearness" (1922, pp. 46-57, 64-76).

In our discussion we assume that the actors regard resources as having positive utility, i.e., more is better, and effective demand incurred as having negative value, i.e., more is worse. We also assume that each actor tries very hard to satisfy on the resource dimensions of value (Simon, 1965) and to establish a "safe margin" of resources over demands. The "safe margin" notion is basically a perception, based on the experiences of the actor and his reference group, of the resource-demand balance necessary to ride out possible fluctuations in either without major losses. To the extent that an actor sees mass communication-political system relationships in a paranoid way or feels unable to reverse any negative step, there is no "safe margin." Attempts to maximize are pursued as much as possible. Note that we emphasize the perception of danger, not its reality. Thus we allow for the possibility that Washington-based Republicans and Conservatives primarily exposed to the *Washington Post* and the *New York Times* might perceive risk and bias even though nationally the press is more Republican than voter registrations, and carries news and editorials favoring GOP positions (Bagdikian, 1972).

Let us see if we can arrive at basic utility sets for each of our major actor categories: mass communication, political institutions, and publics. To simplify the discussion, within each we will not try to differentiate between individuals and organizations or clusters of organizations. To avoid misunderstanding, it must be clearly understood that the elements in the schedules for each type of actor are relatively universal across situations. Also, we neither assume nor hope that the priority given to the items in the schedules for each type of actor will be the same across situations. Variation in priority, the range of possible permutations, is what gives the framework implications which vary as the phenomena in question do in the "real" world.

Mass Communication

For the mass communication actors, major resources are access to message sources, contact with audiences, and funds and supplies. The effective demand to be restrained is that which prescribes what to carry and what not to carry accompanied by sanctions that bear on the resource dimensions. In all the mediation structures, regardless of political system, there is dependence on access to sources and contact with recipients. As access or the distribution capability on which contact depends are confined, the mass communication system faces a decline in its role in politics. What does vary is the importance of different population groups in different political systems and of different distribution capabilities for various media technologies. Accordingly, access and contact abundance or scarcity are matters of continuing concern to mass communication actors.* Recent manifestations of concern about access to message sources in the United States include discussions of presidential press

---

*See Lippmann's discussion of press dependence on official records and reader satisfaction (1922, pp. 321-329, 338-361), and Wise's discussion of war reporting (1967).

conferences, freedom of information and classification, and "shield" laws to protect the identity of sources.

Mass communication actors rarely have the simple alternative, dominant solution of simultaneously optimizing on access to all sources and recipients. Access to audiences, assuming that they have some volition in the matter, requires that the mass communicators maintain a minimum degree of fit between their programming and audience interest and a base level of credibility (Sherkovin, 1969; Doob, 1950). Awareness of this requirement can be seen in the media's extreme sensitivity to attempts by political institutions to raise the price of access to audiences as a result of media attempts to maintain access to message sources. Obviously, with certain forms of constraint on the media—censorship, prior restraint—mass communicators have no incentive to push access to dissenting sources since it will not affect what can be conveyed to audiences.

Funds and supplies are directly related to effective access especially to publics though also to political institutions. Funds affect staff size and coverage. Lack of funds and supplies tends to weaken the media's ability to bargain for access even if access has priority. Of course, it may not. Political institutions and mass communicators have long recognized the economic dimension in their relationships and its interactions with access and contact (Sinclair, 1919). Examples include: mailing rates, paid political and government advertising (Ames, 1972; Balk, 1971), anti-trust regulations and exemptions (Editorial, *Columbia Journalism Review*, 1970), and attempts to provide financial incentives for particular types of public affairs content (Powers and Oppenheim, 1972; Pietila, 1971). The supply relationship is equally important when it is not determined simply by a market mechanism. Examples include: the allocation of a scarce good, such as television channels, or licenses for shares of newsprint import quotas. The value of funds and supplies matters even in a situation of state ownership.

A crucial problem for mass communicators now becomes how to maintain or achieve a level of audience interest and involvement and of message source trust that secures access, contact, funds, and supplies at a minimum cost in incurred demand. The preferred solution for the mass communicator is to separate the locus of influence over funds and supplies from political institutions and publics that may affect access and contact (Cater, 1972). The extent to which this can be done is probably highly sensitive to: the extent of competition that the mass communication media face for the mediating role; the importance of the mediating role to political institutions and publics; and the extent to which funds and supplies are available, regardless of the preferences of political institutions and/or citizens.

If no funds or supplies are available except through the state, survival can be secured only by the compliance required to maintain access. If very great importance is attached to the mediating role and there are no alternative sources of funds and supplies, effective constraining demand will be very great. On the other hand, if importance is high and alternative sources are robust, the restrictive effects of incurred demand will be relatively low. Familiar discussions about considerations conducive to restricting incurred demand include reliance on: private sector revenue sources, such as advertising and consumer purchases; license taxes mandated to the media (Duscha, 1971); and structural changes that reduce alternatives to mass communication and status reasons for using them. Of course, it is not necessarily the case, given the set of utilities involved, that secure funding and the drive for access produce any particular pattern of media program content relevant to political matters. High levels of all resources do not produce increased political coverage or information unless these are a condition for the resource abundance. The United States commercial broadcasting experience supports this observation: what are in effect subsidies have had only limited impact on internal decisions in the mass communication institutions to engage in "public affairs" programming (Crandall, 1972).* The case of Japan's public television network (NHK) also supports that observation (Krisher, 1972).

It seems useful to point out, in passing, that our set of mass communication utilities is compatible with some familiar actions by United States mass communicators. The utilities suggest that mass communicators pursue access to and contact with others on their own terms but resist giving others access to the media. For instance, the president of NBC treats a rise in public access actions against broadcasting during the period 1965 to 1970 as a threat to press freedom (Goodman, 1972). Or, NBC, ABC, CBS, and the Washington Post-Newsweek broadcasting stations join forces and secure a Supreme Court verdict that time need not be sold to out-of-power political groups, among them the Democratic National Committee (*Washington Post*, May 30, 1973, p. 1ff). Their action is in the long-standing tradition of claiming that the doctrine of "fairness," i.e., equality of access by political opponents, limits freedom. Of course, even before the verdict access was not really available to third parties. This pattern of behavior probably reflects the desire to avoid: precedents in program regulation, reduction of revenues from profit-maximizing sales, and programming that might lessen access to incumbent officials. As we would expect, most innovations in access come from media outlets that must establish their *de facto* status as a public utility in order to survive financially or provide such access as a condition for profit-making opportunities.

Political Institutions

For the political institution actors, major resources are access to, information about, and support of relevant publics and other political institutions. These formulations are sufficiently general to apply, for example, to an administrative agency of a United States state government, a political party, or the President's advisor on national security affairs. They apply to both more and less economically developed countries and they are not limited to any particular type of political system.

---

*By limiting television competition, the probability of large audiences rises. In turn, it becomes feasible to sell advertising time at high rates.

With regard to incurred demand, political institutions seek to minimize responses that restrict their freedom to send and receive messages and create and direct support and skills. In all political systems, these utilities create a dependence on access to mass communication and, through it, to publics—in terms of both transmission and reception. The reason that political institutions care is that mediation affects what they can do in the allocation of goods and bads. From the point of view of the political institution, the utility of mass communication is not simply to transfer messages but to change the proba- bilities of support and skill behaviors on the part of publics and of other institutions. These changes in turn modify the feasibility and desirability of different behaviors by the political institution. It is not surprising, then, to find that "every official is in some degree a censor . . . every leader is in some degree a propagandist" (Lippman, 1922, p. 247). Once again the priority attached to different utilities varies. However, there are some recurrent problems in pur- suing the whole set of utilities simultaneously, whatever the priority ranking.

First, access in a transmission sense is obviously a requirement for creating and directing support and skill. However, increases in access do not necessarily increase management capability. They do so only if the increases do not disporportionately increase the access of sources that attempt to create incom- patible attitudes and skills or manage them for different purposes. An attempt by a political institution to calculate the value of increasing access to support and skills tends, then, to include an estimate of the ability to keep it restricted.

For example, this type of calculation confronts officials concerned about cultural autonomy in a nation that cannot yet generate sufficient programming to fill its media receiving capacity. A somewhat more complicated variant of the same problem occurs when the government of one nation wishes to accept the presence of foreign media in order to improve its international communi- cation posture—e.g., an Intelsat earth station or a *New York Times* bureau in Peking (*New York Times*, May 17, 1973, p. 2). Bargaining usually occurs to make the trade-off as advantageous as possible from the host government's point of view. The interaction between access and control has long been understood by regimes seriously concerned with control and media expansion, e.g., the South African government and television. Obviously, in the United States public broadcasting raises the same dilemmas for political leaders.

Second, this apparently simple decision rule may be insufficient for institutions in which change-oriented programs require the creation of major additional loyalties and talents. The control risk may be outweighed by the need. The political institution may have a sufficient share of current access capacity, or even a relative monopoly, but still have inadequate transmission volume and coverage. The importance of the need is a function of the variety of behaviors whose probabilities political institutions wish to change and the magnitude of the change desired. This principle works nicely in predicting some of the differences in stance toward mass communication of authoritarian and totalitarian systems. Also, it fits with the observed tendency of social reformers to give a higher priority to mass communication development that improves access, from political institutions to publics and vice-versa, than do social conservers.

Third, there may be a conflict between mass communication behavior, which services political institutions with information (feedback) about the publics and other institutions, and the support and skill management capability of the recipient. The dilemma is a familiar one: without feedback, adaptive behavior becomes unlikely; however, general awareness of the feedback information may decrease feelings of isolation on the part of dissatisfied parties, increase the cohesion of opposing coalitions, and in general increase constraining demand.

From the discussion to this point, political institutions would appear to have strong incentives for confidential feedback through channels to which access is limited. They do (Smith, A. L., 1972). However, two factors may operate to increase incentives for open feedback. Its absence may itself become an issue and increase demand or disillusionment. Obviously, precedent is important here. (Note that this factor is operable in nondemocratic as well as democratic systems although the issues are different.) The other factor for open feedback derives from the problems of filtering in multi-level bureaucracies. Top-level leaders are often dubious about the extent to which subordinate individuals and bureaus will forward information that reflects adversely on their performance. Accordingly, higher-ups often prefer parallel channels with clear incentives to forward warning information. Also, filtering may distort flows down as well as up. Top-level leaders may see open feedback through mass communication as the best way to alert hierarchically and geographically distant subordinates to the leaders' preferences rather than those of more immediate supervisors.

How can political institutions handle such complex, and at some points contradictory, incentives? Two common strategies merit noting. Both are intended to allow for some transmission of negative information but to limit its salience and magnitude. One is content control of a centralized mass communication system in order to limit the extent to which news that is bad from the point of view of managing political institutions is aggregated and displayed. This is illustrated by some policies governing French television. Another strategy is to fragment the media system. For example, by creating autonomous stations rather than national networks, bad news may be reported but it is unlikely to be aggregated. This strategy assumes no common information source and is relatively feasible when autonomous outlets have none. As Walter Cronkite has observed, there is no television news AP or UPI.

The problems discussed so far are relatively universal across political systems. There are other implications of the utility set that vary sharply according to the institutional nature of and limits applied to competition among political institutions. One important setting condition is the extent to which political institutions distinguish between regime and system legitimacy.*

---

*Lippmann (1956, p. 122) points out that there is a great difference between being one who strives for power in order to outdistance his rivals, and one who sees himself as the guardian of the order that regulates the rivalries. That is, will the one who wins the contest and becomes the ruler seek to maximize his own power, or will he be interested mainly in the well-being of the nation or the community?

When no distinction is made, the need for secure support and skill management by the prevailing regime becomes overriding and warrants monopoly of access. In effect, any demand constraints on the regime are regarded as extremely costly. If the distinction is made, monopoly of access seems less warranted and a given increase in demand seems less grave.

The distinction between regime and system legitimacy often seems particularly weak with regard to foreign affairs. The system is, after all, represented to foreign counterparts by the regime. Accordingly, it is not surprising that regimes that prefer monopoly access and are particularly anxious to constrain demand rely heavily on foreign policy ("national security") justifications. Vital, survival functions seem to increase the priority of the support and skill management value. The compelling nature of the argument is illustrated by the behavior of mass communicators in times of war (hot and cold): they increasingly equate regime with system legitimacy. Of course, the extent to which a particular response limiting the ability of political institutions to use national resources as they see fit really imposes a collective bad is a matter for case by case, factual analysis. Once we recognize that the basic utility structure of political institutions tempts leaders to make that claim, we should reserve acceptance of it.

Even if the distinction between regime and system legitimacy is firm, political systems differ in terms of the alternative regimes they consider legitimate and the selection process that certifies legitimacy. The narrower the definition of the legitimate regimes relative to the set of competitors in the system, the more likely the formation of coalitions that conflict on the issue of access to publics. If the rules in force favor the governing groups but the society has other norms, mass communicators are placed in a cross-pressure situation, which may threaten some of their utilities. That is what has been happening recently in the United States. If the definition of legitimate selection process is well-established and rather narrow, sharp changes in mass communication treatment of the process will generate concern among political institution actors for system legitimacy. The more competitive the political system, the more likely are the actors to behave ambivalently. At the same time that they bemoan the new mass communications role, they seek to take advantage of it to increase their own resources in the political competition. The behavior of the major United States parties with regard to financing for campaign media activity reinforces the point: Both take advantage of publicity buying and ignore its unavailability to "third" parties, but simultaneously seek ways to limit expenditures for this purpose (Dawson and Zinser, 1971; Dunn, 1972).

To conclude the discussion of political institutions, it seems useful to relate their utilities and those of mass communication to the often discussed notion of an "adversary relationship." To the extent that one exists, it derives from the political institution value for creating and managing support and skill resources. The adversary relationship seems necessary only if: political institutions seek to maximize, not satisfice, support and skill management; non-mass communication alternatives that can limit their latitude to mobilize loyalty and talent are absent; non-mass communication alternatives that satisfice political institution transmission and information requirements are present; and mass communication can procure funds, supplies, and contact with audiences in spite of political institutions.

Why are these four conditions necessary? If political institutions seek only moderate resource management objectives, they do not necessarily find constraining demand generated by the media hostile. If publics and other political institutions are stimulated to generate such demand by sources other than mass communication, the latter is not the sufficient cause of the problem. If political institutions are independent of the media for communication, they need not be in a relationship as intense as that of adversaries. Finally, if the media require political institution cooperation to survive they can be levered out of an adversary stance. If we accept this reasoning, it follows that the inevitability of an adversary relationship can be determined empirically and will vary from instance to instance.

More positively, the utility sets discussed to this point suggest some important interdependencies and a substantial probability that a pure adversary relationship will not be desirable for either political institutions or mass communication. The media require the ability to sustain audience interest and involvement, first, by providing items whose content deals with matters of value—and political institutions are the source of many of those items—and, second, by maintaining some trust in the veracity of that content. Political institutions require some credibility with publics and information gathered from them. At least to some extent, regardless of political system, these requirements can be met only if the media have some minimal credibility with publics. In specific areas, political institutions are often in a constant-sum relationship with mass communication. This is true even in totalitarian systems where propagandists and other types of officals disagree (Robinson, 1968; Hoffman, 1967) and political institutions often ignore complaints carried in the media (Klimek and Kubasik, 1970). However, at the most fundamental level, the utility sets suggest that mass communication and political institutions are in a non-constant-sum relationship with one another. The ability of each to bargain in specific areas depends on the extent to which they cooperate, at least partially, to maintain a minimal image of expertise and trustworthiness with publics. We know, at least anecdotally, that the two elites, like social psychologists (Hovland, Janis, and Kelley, 1953), recognize source credibility as an important asset in persuasive communication.

Publics

Publics constitute the third major category of actors. What resources do publics seek and what types of demand do they try to avoid? Within the framework of what are believed to be appropriate rights and obligations (Keesing and Keesing, 1956), publics seek the following four kinds of resources: information pertinent to the pursuit of their private interests; information that suggests the larger social order is in good condition or, if it is not, will be brought into good condition by the leaders of the group; the capability of expressing preferences on matters of private concern to their peers and to members of at least some higher status groups; and the capability of securing responses that either reflect their preferences or provide acceptable reasons to modify them. Publics seek to minimize demands that: deprive them of information pertinent to the first two resources, force them to consume other messages, and reduce established rights of expression and responsiveness. This set of positive and negative utilities appears generally applicable because it operates within culturally established boundaries which themselves differ substantially. The utilities enter into three decisions on the part of publics: exposure to communication; acceptance of communication; and origination of communication. The first and third decisions have implications for one another: time spent in exposure may detract from originating political communication through a variety of participatory activities (Nimmo, 1964).

Exposure decisions are governed by some limits on capacity—limits of time, economic expenditure, and absorption skills. All of these are somewhat, but not infinitely, elastic. In order to apply our calculus we need to recognize their flexibility and constraints. The release of time from work, the presence of media technologies that can be used during work and travel, surplus income, free or almost free exposure to media, literacy, and empathy—all these increase capacity. For example, if we view formal education as one indicator of capacity, it is not surprising that the political communication exposure decisions of publics are similar by educational level even for those within a political system who hold drastically different ideologies (e.g., members of the John Birch Society vs. Americans for Democratic Action). The same holds true across political systems (Grupp, 1969; Rogers, 1970).

Capacity goes unused if publics already feel that they have sufficient information to pursue private concerns. With regard to mass communication, information appetites, and thus the probability of positive exposure decisions, increase to the extent that other communication sources are lacking or seem uninformed. With regard to messages from political institutions, whether or not transmitted by mass communication, the probability of positive exposure decisions increases as these institutions are seen as continuing sources of information necessary to the effective pursuit of private concerns.

This formulation has an important implication for inferences about interest in political matters by publics. Low exposure indicates that publics believe information about political institutions is irrelevant to their private concerns only if the mass communication content is representative of the universe of political institutions that may be relevant. If it is not, and the relative ignoring in the United States mass media of statehouses and federal regulatory agencies so implies (Witcover, 1972a; Littlewood, 1972), we cannot distinguish between exposure decisions based on discriminating rather than blanket judgments of relevance. Relevance and sufficiency are the keys, and negative exposure decisions may be based on judgments of either or both.

Positive exposure decisions on messages from or about political institutions are particularly likely when at least one of the following conditions is met: publics see substantial increases in the subset of private concerns affected by political institutions; publics expect rapid change in the behavior of political institutions pertinent to established intersections with private concerns. The second positive utility, the status of the general social order (i.e., the health of the communities—national, town, ethnic, or global—in which membership is acknowledged) induces some positive exposure decisions even if information requirements for the pursuit of private interests are met or communication is irrelevant to them. Obviously, the probability of such positive decisions depends on: the size and diversity of the general order recognized by members of the polity, the expectation that mass communication and political institution messages will be informative about its status; and the need felt for reassurance about its status.

As stated, the pertinent utility does not provide incentives for exposure to information that reflects adversely on the status of the social order. Indeed, expectations of such negative messages may produce avoidance of communication. Information can reflect adversely on the social order not only by revealing its troubled state but also by suggesting that various forms of coercion and inequity are based on false premises. Of course, this does not imply that exposure to particular items of mass communication that either political officials or mass communicators view as political is equivalent to attention by publics to their political content. For example, viewing conventions or candidates on television may simply result from a desire for entertainment (Blumler and McQuail, 1968).

Acceptance decisions are not necessarily made more likely by exposure. At one extreme, publics may decide to expose themselves to messages from mass communication and political institution actors only to learn about attempts at manipulation. Acceptance decisions are made more likely by credibility and tolerability. Both are estimated through the use of information in addition to what is conveyed by the specific message and its contemporary source. Credibility and tolerability are assessed through both cross-sectional and longitudinal comparison. Convergent validity is a principle of mass psychology.

Cross-sectionally, messages from mass communication and political institutions are compared with messages from other channels, including personal observation. Longitudinally, current messages are compared with the known accuracy of previous mass communication and political institution messages, and with expectations based on experience. If scores are highly positive for both comparisons, credibility is high. If they are not, it suffers. For example, we would not expect messages about "Fun in the sun" in the All-Volunteer Army to be credible if members of the public are simultaneously being told by relatives and friends that Army life is awful, and know from prior personal experience that it is unattractive.

The tolerability assessment is made with regard to the ranking attached to items in the first two utilities: private interests and health of the social order. If accepting the message implies foregoing highly valued private interests or that the social order is in danger, rejection increases. If it implies both (e.g., for working-class whites, that a race revolution is imminent and can only be avoided by sharp reductions in their standards of living), the probability of rejection is extremely high. If at the same time the conception of the social order by publics requires trust in political institutions, one common way to avoid accepting the intolerable message involves denigrating the credibility of the media transmitting it.

Origination decisions tend to be positive only if at least one of two conditions is met. The act of communication serves to advance private interests, such as self-concept or status in the peer group. An illustration is the use of media by minority groups in the United States for "consciousness-raising." It produces behavior by mass communicators of political institutions that advances private interests or the state of the social order. The weighting of the second pair of potentially positive utilities—the capacity to express preferences and secure satisfactory responses—depends on their relationship with the first pair—which deals with exposure to messages. It follows that if political institutions wish publics to originate messages they must establish that one or both of these conditions are met. If mass communicators wish messages from publics to be channeled through them, they must convince publics that one or both of the conditions are met at no net marginal cost in private interests (e.g., exposure of radicals' plans to security agencies) or social well-being. To the extent that one or both of the two other categories of actors fails to establish the conditions stated, the flow from publics to political institutions through mass communication dries up or remains nonexistent. To the extent that political institutions and mass communicators attach positive value to that flow, they have an interest in meeting the requirements for publics to perceive appropriate incentives.

In sum, we have suggested that we retain the basic mediation model of the relationships between mass communication, political institutions, and publics. We have also stressed the need to associate with it sets of positive and negative utilities for each actor. While utility schedules in terms of priority within each set will vary situationally, the identity of the utilities may well be common. If this general stance seems sound, one can look forward to examining rather formally the implications for conflict and cooperation and for stability and instability of different permutations of utility schedules. This general benefit should be available eventually even if one disagrees with the utilities we have identified, the conditions under which we hold them to operate, and the trade-offs singled out for discussion. To the extent that one agrees with the utilities we posit, one can proceed to apply them to specific cases after specifying the values of the constraining parameters mentioned in our discussion, such as cultural notions of appropriateness.

CURRENT KNOWLEDGE AND MAJOR ISSUES

If the discussion so far suggests what we would like to know, this section may be seen as an overview of the current state of knowledge. After a general critique, particular attention is given to a few issues concerning the relationships between the structure of mass communication and the political system, and between decisions by one of our three types of actors and the politically relevant behavior of others.

Perhaps the most familiar approach to questions about relationships between mass communication and the political system is normative. What is the desirable degree of press freedom? Of government regulations? The answers

usually follow from a set of preferences about the nature of the political
process and some analysis of ways to insure realization of those preferences
(Siebert, Peterson, and Schramm, 1956; Rivers and Schramm, 1969). The
analysis usually consists of assertions rather than precise statements of relationships that allow for informative discussion of the question "How much is
enough?"

One problem with such general assertions is their lack of prescriptive
power. From one situation to another, the same principle can produce contradictory consequences with regard to how we would like the political process to
work. For example, one may favor uninhibited communication of government
business to "the people" through the media. Yet in the United States many
political liberals would praise Daniel Ellsberg's actions with regard to the
Pentagon Papers and deplore those of Joseph Alsop in revealing what was
allegedly Adlai Stevenson's "dovish" role in the Cuban missile crisis or that of
State Department security official, Otepka, in leaking information on possible
security risks (Peters and Branch, 1972).

Another problem is that no established ideology for the political process
contains only one value. Instead, these preference structures contain numerous
values and the extreme pursuit of any one can deny realization of many others.
Accordingly, prescriptions for mass communication-political system relationships need to deal with the trade-off decisions within particular ideological
frames of reference. For example, even the most extreme totalitarian system
must limit its quest for media content supportive of the regime by the need to
maintain the belief that the regime is aware of and trying to correct temporary
imperfections.

A third problem is that normative preferences deal overwhelmingly with
the political process rather than with policy outcomes. For example, they deal
with information that citizens should have rather than with the income or
health care that citizens should have. Yet we know that policy outcomes of one
kind or another matter to all participants in politics. And we know that the
content of and satisfaction with policy outcomes have substantial effects on
continuity and change in the political process. The relative omission of policy
outcomes may, in large measure, account for the static quality of much of the
more general literature on mass communication and for its unhelpfulness in
predicting the conditions under which the preferences for and relationships
between mass communication and the political system change.

The other very familiar approach to questions about the relationships
between mass communication and the political process is the historical, descriptive case study. Whether such studies are statistical or purely qualitative, their
usefulness is usually limited for at least two reasons. First, we have no notion
of the sort of sample of the universe of relevant instances that they provide.
Are they drawn according to random, stratified, and/or purposive criteria? Or
are they primarily selected on opportunistic grounds? To the extent that we do
not know what sort of sample the case material represents, it provides only the
most hazardous basis for generalization. In point of fact, a review of the
literature strongly suggests that it is heavily skewed toward economically
developed, western societies, and the United States in particular. Second, the
case studies rarely provide a credible causal analysis. Commonly, they provide

only temporal links between the events and attributes of the individuals and groups discussed. Obviously, this limitation confronts us with the possibility of numerous alternative explanations for particular behaviors by either media or political system actors. One characteristic of many of the studies that leads to ignorance about causality is their cross-sectional character. Even a strong correlation at a particular point in time between, for example, press freedom and competitive political parties, carries no information that helps us to choose between three alternative explanations. Did a free press help bring about competitive political parties? Did competitive political parties help create and maintain a free press? Is some third factor responsible for both? Without longitudinal analysis we cannot sort out these possibilities.

These general difficulties apply to studies that "blackbox" the decision process of political institutions, mass communicators, and publics, and to those that zero in on one or several of these in some detail. In both cases, generalizations are usually normative assertions, or at best inferences, about necessary but not sufficient conditions. And in neither case do we find very much work that formulates and tests mass communication policy for achieving particular political states of affairs in particular situations.

Obviously, this is a harsh verdict about the state of work on mass communication and the political system. To say that we know little is, of course, not to say that we know nothing. To make more discriminating judgments, it seems useful to turn first to the frameworks outlined earlier and then to some of the issues that they imply. To summarize the discussion so far, we suggested a number of aspects of mass communication that decisions by political actors can affect: message content, media personnel and technology, cultural level of messages, and availability of the media output. We also suggested a number of aspects of the political system that mass communication can affect: Who gets what from whom, when, how, why, with what effect, and with what response? We then argued that mass communicators, political officials, and individual and group publics engage in purposeful decision-making that leads them to seek or avoid some effects and not others; different preference priorities determine which of a variety of possible effects will be sought and achieved. While we recognize the importance of general social characteristics in constraining the latitude of choice, we argue that there usually is some latitude available.

These formulations present us with a large number of very complex issues to be pursued in specific situations. This is true even if we wish to omit the decision-making elements stressed earlier. We still have to consider the *set* of mass communication and political system linkages, and these linkages surely need not be mutually independent. With the possible exception of single landmark studies of Soviet and Chinese Communist mass communication (Inkeles, 1950; Yu, 1964), little has been done that systematically examines the relationships between the general characteristics of mass communication and the political system. Yet, if we are to take at face value assertions by experts that both mass communication and the political process are complex even in isolation, let alone in interaction, then the need to study them as complex systems seems obvious. And we have sufficient reason to believe with Forrester (1969, pp. 9-10) that complex systems pose special difficulties for causal analysis. In trying to explain a symptom, we can usually find a plausible cause near in time and space. But it may be merely a coincident symptom. The real cause may lie far back in a remote part of the system, and it may not be one or more prior events but may reside in the structure and policies of the system itself.

The extent to which an analyst can adequately predict and prescribe either mass communication or political system characteristics simply from information about their aggregate properties is an empirical question. However, should the predictions turn out to be weak, we clearly need to look into the relevant decision processes. Even if they are not weak, changes require different decisions by some actors, and we will eventually confront the need to deal with decision-making rather than to circle around it. A systemic approach must deal with the utilities of all three categories of actors; to contend otherwise is to attribute a degree of control to any particular one or pair that we have more than enough knowledge to reject.

The literature lacks studies dealing with the interdependent decision-making of political officials, mass communicators, and publics. Available instead are studies of fragments of both aggregate and decision-making approaches to problems. Many of these fragments are important and several will be singled out for discussion. However, it is important to maintain a reserved attitude toward the implications of the findings. The grounds for reservation are not the customary ones of divergent results. In fact, divergent results can be informative if we know why the results differ for either substantive or methodological reasons. Nor are convergent results necessarily informative, unless we have reason to believe that the situations examined are in some manner representative of the range of values on key variables. Rather, we do not usually have the contextual information that allows us to draw strong inferences from either convergent or divergent results of studies on mass communication and the political system. For convenience, the fragments discussed will be separated into those dealing with aggregate structural relationships between mass communication and the political system and those dealing with decision-making by one or several types of relevant actors.

Structural Relationships

Two sets of international issues have generated work on the aggregate relationships between mass communication and political systems. The first stemmed from the rise in the 1930s and 1940s of conflict between the United States and totalitarian regimes. The structural concern was the extent to which centralized government control of mass communication, including access to foreign mass communication, determined whether political institutions were competitive or monolithic, effective in implementing policies burdensome to citizens or hamstrung by dissent and controversy (including that fomented by foreign propaganda that reached citizens directly or through captive indigenous media), and capable of maintaining the secrecy allegedly conducive to delicate and complex national security policies or unable to operate with a judicious· amount of privacy (Inkeles, 1950; Lerner, 1951; Lasswell, 1927; Kecskemeti, 1950; Kris and Speier, 1944; Lasswell and Blumenstock, 1939; George, 1959; Daugherty and Janowitz, 1958). Studies based on this set of concerns have not been sufficiently either comparative or longitudinal to establish implications for government effectiveness (a matter of political consequences rather than process) of different degrees of centralized political control of mass communication. By emphasizing the contrast with a supposedly noncontrolled democratic media situation, the studies have often obscured the extent of political and administrator-propagandist conflict within totalitarian systems.

Implications for Political Development

A more technically impressive body of work came later and focused on the problem of political development. Operationally, political characteristics have usually been treated as dependent variables (Deutsch, 1953; Lerner, 1957). The characteristics of principal interests have been: the stability of regimes, citizen participation as indicated by voting turnout, and democracy as indicated by competitive political parties and autonomous legislatures. The most influential work was probably Lerner's, which posited the following flow of development in the evolution of a participant society:

> Urbanization comes first. . . . Within this urban matrix develop both of the attributes which distinguish the next two phases—literacy and media growth. . . . Out of this interaction [among the three factors] develop those institutions of participation (i.e., voting) which we find in all advanced modern societies [Lerner, 1958, p. 60].

Lerner's concern was with the infrastructure of mass communication, not with its content; with political participation—a political process characteristic—rather than with political programs or their consequences. A number of other analysts have attempted to pursue his concerns by analyzing simultaneously a large number of nations. The linkages they have found between the size of the mass communication infrastructure and voting turnout vary from study to study (McCrone and Cnudde, 1967; Tanter, 1967; Alker, 1966; Kline, Kent, and Davis, 1971; Adelman and Morris, 1971).

Three problems of interpretation should be noted. First, in some cases the statistical method used does not capture the interactions in Lerner's formulation. Second, the aggregate multi-national nature of the analysis does not identify the deviant cases or the supporting cases. Third, as Brunner and Brewer (1971) have emphasized, lumping nations together inhibits explanation of the processual connections that operate between mass communication and the political system in any particular nation. Thus, we are hindered from arriving at a powerful understanding of why some cases do and others do not fit the general set of contentions. Even if these problems could be handled successfully, which in principle is possible, the formulation is not intended to, and does not, provide guidance in the critical policy decisions that leaders of and donors to developing countries must make with regard to mass communication. As stated by Pool (1963), these policy decisions involve: the fraction of resources to invest in mass communication, the role of private and public sectors, the degree of centralized control and freedom of the modern media, and the cultural level of media output. The problems engendered by the almost complete reliance on voting turnout as the indicator of political participation are rather obvious.

Lerner (1963), Nesvold (1971), and others have gone beyond the increase in voting turnout to treat other implications for political development—in particular, stability. Their formulations emphasize an aspirations-expectations gap where aspirations are in large measure driven by mass communication. As frustration varies, so too does either the absolute volume and/or rate of change of political violence. It is important to note that the operationalization of political violence often excludes violence initiated by the regime in power. The problem of interpreting relevant results stems from the collinearity often reported between the measures of mass communication growth and measures of improved fulfillment of expectations. Nesvold (1971), for example, reports a negative relationship between newspaper circulation and political violence but also notes that circulation tracks with two other attributes negatively related to political violence (life expectancy and voting turnout).

The third structural issue relevant to political development differs from the others. Here, the independent variable is media autonomy, often operationalized as press freedom from the central government, rather than mass communication volume. Once again, the analysis is usually of large sets of nations (Gregg and Banks, 1971; Snow, 1971; Adelman and Morris, 1971), and it has the interpretive problems already noted for such analyses. It is also primarily cross-sectional. The most we can conclude from such analyses is that press freedom is strongly associated with, but neither necessary nor sufficient for, competitive political institutions along the lines of western democracy.

Mass Communication Ownership and the Political System

A rather different structural area concerns the interactions between political system properties and the general character of mass media ownership. We

Per Cent
MC Owned by
Public Sector

Per Cent Ownership
Concentration of MC

will deal here only with aggregate structural relationships. Two dimensions of ownership seem particularly important: sector (public versus private) and concentration (monopolistic or dispersed). The question is: What difference does the location of mass communication (MC) institutions in the plot below make for the aggregate nature of the political system? If location matters, and if we have preferred political system properties, then we will be interested in affecting ownership through such policy levers as taxation, anti-trust laws, license allocation, and centralization and decentralization.

There are strong views on these relationships. The Special Senate Committee (1971), for example, has deplored the growth of private sector concentration as inimical to a democracy and has called for special measures to increase dispersion. Announcements on United States radio stations stress that the private ownership of broadcasting in the United States is especially conducive to democracy. However, the evidence of the consequences of different ownership patterns is inconsistent and highly fragmentary (Anderson, 1971-72; Levin, 1960; Litwin and Wroth, 1969; Grotta, 1971; Rarick and Hartman, 1966; Brown, D. E., 1970; Grotta, 1970; Wolf, 1971; Toogood, 1969; Wedell, 1969). Part of the reason for the lack of clarity may be an unwarranted tendency to assume that public ownership implies concentration. That is not necessarily the case either geographically or across media. Nor does public ownership automatically imply centralization. Also, ownership attributes are not associated with any single pattern of restrictions on or incentives for access to the media. Privately owned systems, such as CATV, may be required to have a public access channel (Posner, 1972; Cable Television Advisory Committee, 1972). Publicly owned systems may insist in generating all their programming and media content internally. We probably need more complete specifications of the circumstances that, if present, determine the political system consequences of a particular pattern of mass media ownership.

What might more complete specification of structural relationships in this area look like? Here are some examples. If the public sector is highly centralized, and if it has concentrated in it ownership of most mass communication channels (within and across media), then political competition suffers. If the private sector is economically autonomous of the regime and its supporters, and if ownership is highly dispersed within and across media in the private sector, then political competition flourishes. Even such overly simply hypotheses would require somewhat more multi-dimensional analysis than usually reported.

In sum, our knowledge of structural relationships between mass communication and the political system yields little in the way of strong generalizations about the consequences of the size of the mass communication infrastructure, media content, or media ownership. An obvious exception is the necessary relationship between media and span of control geographicably and numerically (Innis, 1950). This still leaves us uncertain of the conditions sufficient for media expansion to increase the span of control. We do know enough to be sure that simply expanding mass communication will not insure the expansion of areas of administrative control.

Decision-Making Relationships

We shall focus now on classes of decisions by each category of actors that relate to political decisions by one or both of the other categories of actors. Three issues that have this property are discussed below: election treatment decisions by mass communicators and their effect on the behavior of voters (publics) and political institutions; regulation decisions by political institutions and their effect on the behavior of mass communicators; and news treatment decisions by mass communicators and their effect on political officials.

Election Treatment Decisions. The most studied area of mass communication-political system relationships is that of elections, in particular voter behavior (Lazarsfeld, Berelson, and Gaudet, 1944; Berelson, Lazarsfeld, and McPhee, 1954). General limitations on the impact of what the media carry are clear with regard to the behavior of mass publics during the course of campaigns. Those who change opinions most during a campaign and are most likely to be undecided at its outset are least exposed to mass communication (Katz, 1971; Dreyer, 1971-1972). They comprise a modest minority of the electorate. Others may expose themselves to mass communication coverage, but not for guidance in voting (Blumler and McQuail, 1968). Media endorsements are not particularly vital for electoral success in major contests (Blume and Lyons, 1968; Hooper, 1969; Roshwalb and Resnicoff, 1971), nor does last minute news on who is winning appear to influence the outcome of close elections (Tuchman and Coffin, 1971). Coverage does appear to stimulate turnout sometimes, which may matter in close elections (Blume and Lyons, 1968; Glaser, 1965; Torsvik, 1967; Simon, 1955).

Should we conclude, then, that media decisions to bias coverage in favor of one or another contestant, a frequently documented occurrence (Becker and Fuchs, 1967; Bishop and Brown, 1968; Graber, 1971; Witcover, 1972b) are unimportant? I think not for several reasons. First, patterns of bias and endorsement affect elections in which there is little basis for selective attention, e.g., candidates with no clear images or referenda and bond issues without clear connections to political parties (McCombs, 1967; Pierce, 1969; Atkin, 1971). Many of these choices have great importance for allocation decisions that are at the heart of politics. Second, skewed media content may seriously affect the nature of the choices that mass publics encounter when they come to vote. For example, the extent to which the media portray a candidate in a presidential primary as successful or faltering clearly affects his ability to raise funds, which in turn affects the subsequent pre-nomination competition. It also affects candidate issue position and the nature and extent of the commitments made before coming into office. A fuller understanding of these dynamics will only be gained from studies, such as the one now being conducted by Hofstetter,*

---

*Information based on personal communication with Richard Hofstetter, professor at Ohio State University.

that measure and compare over time media content, voter intentions, campaign manager assessments, and mass communicator decisions. The results of such integrated work are not yet available.

The relationships between mass communication and electoral decisions go considerably deeper than decisions during campaigns. Two aspects merit special attention. The first involves the consequences of decisions about the extent to which mass communication is national or local in coverage, visual and oral rather than print, and autonomous in selling and pricing access. Decisions to have national media programming emphasize the role of national offices, national government policies, political activities in the capital city, and national parties (Locher, 1970; Gilbert, 1967). Visual and oral media affect the priorities used in selecting candidates, the extent to which the candidate allocates resources to program rather than presence, and the extent to which campaigns center on personalities (Nie, 1970; Locher, 1970; Friel, 1968; Jennings, 1968; Rose and Fuchs, 1968; McGinnis, 1968). Finally, economic decisions affect political competition in terms of the emergence of new parties, the feasibility of bold issue positions, and the imporrtance of private and interest group wealth (Dunn, 1972; Atkin, 1971).

The second, more pervasive set of considerations pertains to the way in which mass communication shapes the significance that publics attach to the electoral process itself. While we do not understand the causes, considerable evidence suggests that mass communication exposure can, over time, generate in mass publics a "political malaise" about elements of low political self-esteem and perceived efficacy and a pervasive distrust of political officials (Robinson, M. J., 1972). The basis of evidence—television in the United States—is too narrow to assess the generality of the phenomenon, but it seems important to determine it.

Regulation Decisions. To what extent and in what ways do regulation decisions affect the decisions of mass communication actors? What are the consequences for the political system? By regulation we include the constraints—existing and threatened—that political institutions impose on mass communication operations. These constraints are, of course, not limited to programming content. They clearly include limitations on official information available to journalists and economic assessments and incentives. By requiring that regulation decisions alter mass communication decisions, we exclude what one might call ritual regulation: "rulings" that simply confirm the preferences of mass communicators. Obviously, such ritual regulation occurs most frequently in mass communication, as in other areas, when the individuals on each side move back and forth during their careers.

As we have stated the regulation issue, we have to know: (1) the regulatory actions; (2) mass communicator preferences in the absence of a regulatory action; (3) mass communicator preferences given the existence or expectation of a particular regulatory action; and (4) the difference that a gap between items 2 and 3 makes for the political system. With the partial exception of several recent studies of cable television (Comanor and Mitchell, 1971; Posner, 1972; Cable Television Advisory Committee, 1972), the writing on media regulation does not address more than any two of our four considerations. The others are treated by assumption.

Some examples will illustrate the shortcoming. Government classification allegedly inhibited the United States mass media from giving the "real story" on the Vietnam War and thus created unwarranted public acceptance of it. In fact, most information of value was leaked and reported. Lack of criticism resulted more from agreement with the official United States position than anything else (Fairlie, 1973; Witcover, 1970-1971; Friendly, 1970-1971; Stillman, 1970-1971; McCartney, 1970-1971). Those who charge that lack of regulation was responsible for unfortunate domestic dissent about the Vietnam War ignore other sources of information to the public, such as returned veterans, and historical trends of short-lived support for limited wars. As another example, some contend that information about social problems and government shortcomings will dry up if journalists are forced to disclose their sources and reveal their files (Isaacs, 1970). Yet, in the United States about 46 per cent of journalists do not even know if their state has a shield law, and less than half of those who have been subpoenaed feel it has hurt coverage (Blasi, n.d.; Baker, 1972). And examples of that are available, such as the Republic Steel Memorial Day Massacre, where disclosure under the pressure of subpoena contributed to civil liberties (Friendly, 1972). Even when the consequences of extremes of regulation are relatively clear—e.g., complete censorship versus none—the implications of intermediate positions are unclear and certainly not linear. For example, does greater restraint in Britain (Official Secrets Act) produce a less open political system than in the United States?

These examples provide several suggestions for an approach to issues of regulation. First, we must distinguish between formal and informal practices. The "leak," for example, is a common practice in areas of almost universal classification (Frankel, 1971; McCartney, 1971; Dahlan, 1967). Second, we must recognize that regulation affects the political system only as it changes the decision information available to participants in the political system. We may be tempted to underestimate the importance of interpersonal communication and direct observation. Third, no particular regulatory practice in and of itself necessarily favors a particular policy or political faction. For example, government-imposed requirements for program content may create a far more representative and open or a far more closed media. The result depends largely on what the media would do otherwise (McWilliams, 1970; Hvistendahl, 1970; Flanery, 1971; Donohew, 1967). Fourth, there may be a strong correlation between the threat of government regulation and self-regulation by mass communicators. In totalitarian societies, the prospect of censorship and prior restraint clearly has such an effect. In democratic societies, one finds numerous instances of the media only monitoring themselves in terms of accuracy and bias when faced with the prospect of increased external regulation. Indeed, in the United States there is little evidence that the media are prepared to engage in self-regulation except in the face of such a threat (Rivers et al., 1972; Isaacs, 1970; Commission on Freedom of the Press, 1947; "The Hutchins Report," 1967).

News Treatment Decisions. For half a century, we have recognized the extent to which political officials and publics depend on the "pseudo-environment" depicted in the media (Lippmann, 1922). In a complex media system, one might add, members of the media depend on other media of a particularly prestigious sort (Buckalew, 1969; Cohen, 1963; Cater, 1959; Rosten, 1937; Rivers, 1965; Nimmo, 1964). Regardless of the source of news treatment decisions—e.g., sales considerations, publisher's ideology, instructions from a propaganda ministry, content of other media—the consequences are in general similar: media content conveys the state of mind of important others (e.g., coverage of a mass demonstration informs politicians and distant publics of mass opinion [Lang and Lang, 1953]); it informs political officials and publics of the issues (Cohen, 1963; McCombs and Shaw, 1972; Shafer and Larson, 1972; Clark, 1968); and it shapes perceptions of who are particularly important and/or successful political officials and publics (Wilhoit and Sherrill, 1968; Lemert and Nestvold, 1970). It is not surprising, then, that attention has been paid to the gatekeeping decisions of mass communicators (Bailey, 1972; White, 1964; Friendly, 1967).

Obviously, the rules governing news treatment decisions vary widely. Several rules and their alleged consequences have received particularly heavy attention. Some contend that when media news treatment decisions reflect the views of political officials, the consequences include unwarranted public support for those officials and their policies (Witcover, 1970-1971; Friendly, 1970-1971; Paletz and Dunn, 1969; Wicker, 1971). On another dimension, some contend that criteria used to define news determine the ingredients and sophistication of official and public thinking about political matters (Lippmann, 1922; Fedler, 1971; Thoeny, 1968; Wilhoit, 1969). Examples of alternative news treatment rules are events versus trends, political crises versus incremental administrative acts, immediacy versus past. Those who make the argument go on to infer that emphasis on the first term in each of the pairs degrades thinking about politics.

Whether news treatment decisions do in fact have the powerful effects attributed to them in the arguments above is debatable. No one relies solely on the media. Even if public officials, for example, pay attention to mass communication to learn what people think important, they may well believe from other sources that those concerns are marginal. A similar statement applies to publics (Bauer, 1964). Indeed, if there is disconfirming evidence from other sources, then the degree of support for official positions that controlled media can generate seems to level-off and then declines. Nevertheless, audiences may maintain awareness of these media for surveillance purposes. As for the cheapening effects of some news selection criteria, once again an often unwarranted assumption about media impact must be accepted: "shallow" news produces "shallow" thinking and "in-depth" analysis produces "deep" thinking. That is only the case if other requirements for and propensities toward such thinking are at work. There is little evidence that differences in media coverage on this dimension are sufficiently potent to be responsible for fundamental differences in the quality of political dialogue. It is true, however, that given finite news space, selection according to one set of critiera drives out material that would be reported using different criteria. Whether the other material would be consumed and what the consequences would be are other matters. Rather than blanket conclusions about the political system consequences of news treatment decisions, it seems wiser to relate "gatekeeping" rules to the sets of utilities presented earlier. As the permutations of the utilities of different actors vary, so too do the political consequences of different gatekeeping rules.

NEEDED ANALYSIS

The discussion to this point has argued for certain research directions. We can limit ourselves here to restating them briefly and providing some examples of possible projects. The choice of specific projects depends on a host of situational considerations beyond the scope of this discussion. Research priorities, like priorities of any other kind, are relative statements. Accordingly, we will sometimes contrast what we are recommending with research that seems less badly needed.

Systems Treatments. If we are really concerned about mass communication relationships with the political system, then we must deal with the complexities of both media and politics. Isolated hypothesis testing of a specific aspect of the relationship will not suffice, except in context. Accordingly, we need studies that deal with all the key links between media and political system elements. The extent to which this is possible depends on our ability to identify problems that satisfy one or both of the following conditions: both the media system and the political system involved are small or homogeneous and accessible; even if the systems are large and heterogeneous, many of their elements are stable. Failure to work contextually may not deprive our results of the status of findings; it does deprive them of practical implications since context operates in the real world.

Interacting Decision Units. Consequences for the political system and mass communication are the joint product of decisions of at least two of the three categories of actors. The implication is that studies should include the utilities of at least two categories and how they affect each other. Accordingly, we favor studies that deal with the preference structures of, for example, the political leader of a nation and the chiefs of the mass media as they affect each other over time. We do not attach priority to a study concerned with only one of these.

Since stimuli take time to exert whatever influence they may have on complex systems, and since interaction between decision units also takes time, both the recommendations made so far require longitudinal studies.

Politics and Political Economy. On the basis of coverage in the literature, the major linkages between mass communication and political system behavior appear to be elections and central government control of the masses. In fact, these are but a modest part of political system activities and goals. They may exclude the most pervasive involvement of most citizens and most officials with allocations by political institutions. We particularly need to examine the relationships between mass communication and the major activities of governments present and future.

Mass Communication in a Competitive Market. While we have recognized the importance of non-mass media communication for general publics, we seem to do so less for political officials. In their total information environment, under what conditions are decisions more influenced by mass communication than by other sources? And what kinds of decisions do the mass media most affect (e.g., public statements versus budgets)? We know very little about the relative impact, credibility, and timeliness of different information sources available to officials. Without that knowledge, we must necessarily speculate on the consequences of mass communication content for their decisions. How do the mass media make themselves competitively attractive to a buyer (official) suffering under advanced information overload? Are the requirements for competitive attractiveness incompatible with providing information that alters otherwise probable decisions? Except in regard to voting decisions in a few countries, we know very little about the extent to which mass publics rely on available mass communications rather than other sources (e.g., friends employed by the government) to make decisions about political system issues.

Information Advantage. An important aspect of political behavior is estimating the behavior of others. Many of the issues about government regulation, in particular classification and intelligence activities, rest on assumptions about the information advantage provided by mass communication coverage. Yet, few studies have tried to assess the extent of the alleged advantage. When uncensored, who gains an information advantage from mass communication (e.g., the Hanoi government, United States Congressmen, or white-collar voters)? For foreign policy purposes, do controlled media provide a foreign analyst with more or less helpful information on some matters than uncontrolled media?

Advance Signals and Workable Policies. Different mass communication infrastructures provide those with access different capabilities for signalling distant and numerous others. As a policy strategy problem, political officials often have to calculate the trade-off between use of the signalling capacity to create readiness (support and skills) for a policy and the risk that those signals will commit them too early to a policy, so that they lose the advantages of surprise and arouse opposition. To what extent can old or new alternatives to mass communication provide the necessary advance signalling? Must it be confirmed in mass communication? Under what political conditions does it suffice simply to present a *fait accompli* via mass communication in order for a policy to work?

A Finite Mass Communication Budget. It is tempting to think of increases in mass communication as equivalent to some sort of addition to the total communication reception of individuals and groups. Beyond some point, that seems unlikely. People may have, under any particular set of economic conditions, a maximum communication time budget. If that is so, increases in mass communication beyond some point drive down other forms of communication. If the two forms have different relationships with and consequences for the political system, these must be explicitly recognized in communication policy.

With the exeption of the views that mass communication expands the size of political communities and creates instability within them (perhaps making them smaller), the possible relationships have not been subjected to rigorous scrutiny. Some aspects for attention are accountability of political officials and citizen beliefs in their own political efficacy.

More Attention to Publics. We have increasingly recognized that publics have their own reasons for deciding to "tune in" or "tune out" mass communications. However, we need to extend our interest in publics in at least two ways. First, we must assess the potential demand for mass communication content relevant to different aspects of the political system. After-the-fact assessment does not help us to determine interest in what the media do not carry; nor does it induce the media to experiment with different political content. One obvious step in anticipatory assessment is to discard the overly general categories of "news" and "public affairs programming" in favor of categories that reflect life concerns. Such assessment needs to be dynamic and concerned with the conditions that alter demand and the duration of any change in demand.

The second extension concerns the role of publics as message originators. With the exception of some recognition of the tactics used by minority activists to secure media coverage, we know very little about origination decisions. When do nongovernment actors turn to the media as a transmitter of their ideas? Do they see the mass media as a substitute for other channels perhaps not open to them or do they pursue a multi-step communication strategy in which the mass media are used at some particular point? If the latter, when does that point begin and conclude? What are the diffusion rates of mass communication strategies among nonofficial actors (e.g., from Blacks to Chicanos to Women), and are different diffusion rates conducive to different political outcomes? How does a nonofficial political group calculate the extent to which a high diffusion rate limits the period during which its possible innovative mass communication strategy will be effective?

Study of Preference Structures. The approach suggested here leads to several priority areas for research. The first is that of stability. What combinations of preferences on the part of the three categories of actors (mass communication, political institutions, and publics) yield stable solutions; and which are inherently unstable? Second, how are particular preference structures established and when do they change? If they change—for example, in response to new media technology, urbanization, more educated reporters, or more frustrated publics—how long does it take for the change in the determinant to alter the preference structure? Third, when we establish what we believe to be the operating preference structures for appropriately specified actors and situations and predict the actions that should follow, in what circumstances are our predictions right or wrong? Can we determine why? For example, perhaps we need to add other utilities, such as ideology about the rights and obligations of a journalist or a good Communist. Perhaps we have the right ingredients but because of poor information and measurement we have attached erroneous priorities to each utility.

As our ability to deal with these questions improves, we increasingly can prescribe the preference structures we wish to have and the means to achieve them. For example, the United States mass media now concentrate heavily on leading political personalities and pay little attention to the creation and execution of major national programs. We may wish that the situation were otherwise. The argument above is that through a better understanding of the origin and destruction of preference structures we can better determine what must happen for United States media to reverse the balance and to focus on major programs as they evolve. Obviously, work with preference structures requires that we can determine what they are and when they change. Given their sensitive nature, we cannot do so satisfactorily if we rely only on verbal self-reports elicited through interviews. We need unobtrusive activity measures. And these measures need to be sufficiently specific to link them clearly to priorities for different activities.

Since the point of research is to expand knowledge, and in this case particularly policy relevant knowledge, it seems advisable to consider directions that have had such results in other areas of public policy. That spirit has led to the suggestions above. These directions—systems analysis, formal theories of decision making, cost-benefit analysis, and theories of collective action—when pursued elsewhere have produced results that are relatively rigorous and of practical import. And the general approaches are workable for the analysis of both "grand" and mundane problems.

CHAPTER

7

PROFESSIONAL PERSONNEL AND ORGANIZATIONAL STRUCTURE IN THE MASS MEDIA
Ben H. Bagdikian

It is still possible to irritate most journalists by asking for a definition of "news." Though they spend their lives producing it, journalists with few exceptions do not understand what causes certain events to be acceptable as news and others not. "News" is not a uniform or stable commodity: its production is governed by so many conscious and subconscious influences and such inflexible demands that, like "poetry," merely to ask for its definition seems to threaten the practitioner.

What are the forces within professional journalism and its corporate structures? How do they shape what is called news? To answer these questions, primary consideration will be given to the 1,750 daily newspapers and 700 commercial television stations; to a lesser degree, the 8,000 weeklies and 6,000 radio stations will also be included. News—non-advertising matter and items not selected for entertainment—will get the most attention, but some will be given to entertainment on television where social impact is significant. The dynamics of news production will also be described because, by itself, it suggests what may be worth exploring in careful research.

Whatever news is, the chief influence on its production is the received conventions absorbed by the new journalist. It is still assumed in most newsrooms that this "definition" by tradition is an unquestioned doctrine handed down by apostolic succession from some unknown First Source who made an infallible determination that remains valid for all time. That this is the largest single factor determining what information the public will see and hear from its new media may be ironic, but it also suggests that good research may be therapeutic.

The fact that almost no practitioners have heard a superior or even a professor of journalism define this doctrine of definition by tradition does not diminish the general assumption that whatever happens in the production of news is based on a clear and certain determination. That is, of course, a self-fulfilling faith. Men and women come to work in news organizations and, usually without anyone ever instructing them on what to look for in the social environment and how to arrange its elements, they "know." The process is not entirely mystical. Professional journalists, like their consumers, are educated by what they observe in their own medium. A new reporter seeing what kind of stories get on page 1 with bylines or are aired during prime-time news does not have to be told what "news" is for that particular organization.

The standards for selecting information to produce news vary from organization to organization. The history of journalism confirms this—from the repetitious accounts of parliamentary acts printed in imported English newspapers, the partisan press of the early nineteenth century, the sensationalist inventions of Hearst and Pulitzer, and the impact of Adolph Ochs's insistence on "objectivity," to the growth of corporate journalism and monopoly with their economic constraints on controversy and partisanship.

Despite individual differences among news organizations, a number of forces combine in varying patterns to shape the news. These include a growing body of professional standards, received conventions, individual tastes of editors, budgetary constraints, editors' and writers' perceptions of their audience, internal and external rivalries, technology, business office pressures on content, government, relations between journalists and their sources, and the shifting conception of what is "legitimate" for entry into the news net. Each of these will be considered.

Warren Breed's "Social Control in the Newsroom" (1955) described the unstated values that shape reporters, editors, and their product—usually without explicit directions from the top. Daniel Garvey, in "Social Control in the Television Newsroom" (1971), found that the same unstated values apply to the electronic media. He also showed that the longer a journalist remains in an organization the more he conforms to and "believes" the values held by his superiors; hiring different types of people does not materially affect their ultimate conformity to the unstated desires of those higher up.

The values of leaders operating news media are created by a complex of elements, except in organs devoted entirely to ideological or other propaganda. Research data show that publisher intrusion into decisions on news is greatest for items that affect the economic interest of the organization or the publisher (Bowers, 1967). This intrusion is moderated substantially by professional standards and peer pressure, but it still exists, imbedded in the unstated conventions of the organization.

The smaller the quantity of alternative items from the outside world, the simpler and faster the selection of the day's news for a particular community. Since most newspapers of any size use only 15 per cent of the total material received in their newsrooms daily, practical standards for selecting so narrow a portion of the available universe are obviously needed.

ESTABLISHMENTARIAN BIAS

A major influence on non-local news is the product of the wire services—mainly the Associated Press and United Press International, but increasingly more interpretive and analytical reports such as the New York Times News Service and the Los Angeles Times-Washington Post Service. This accounts for the remarkable uniformity of regional, national, and international news in papers hundreds of miles apart and with vastly differing local standards.

Where syndicated and pre-packaged news constitutes the major output of a local news organization, an important portion of the remaining news inevitably reflects the self-serving bias of news sources. The lack of careful and comprehensive news gathering, selection, and writing by an organization's own staff usually means that the editors are dependent on the output of news sources themselves, either in the form of press releases used without substantial independent checking or indiscriminately repeated private and public declarations. This, in turn, creates a strong bias in the news in favor of groups who enjoy power and affluence, who not only have a stake in creating and sustaining a sympathetic public attitude toward themselves but who also have the affluence to support an elaborate public relations apparatus for skillfully pre-packaging information for entry into the news net.

Major governmental units, corporations, powerful institutions, and established special-interest groups with generous financing—almost all affluent and skilled—are all regular sources of major portions of "news," and over the years have become accepted as "legitimate." By contrast, many social groups of importance in public policy-making and attitudes—such as the poor, minorities, and unorganized consumers—lacking affluence and skill, usually have no comparable systematic entrée to the news. When such disestablished groups become compelling subjects of news, the news about them tends to be beyond their control; it comes through second parties that are established and accepted as "legitimate" news sources, such as government officials, police departments, or school administrations. For example, when blacks first took direct social action to protest continuation of the racial caste system in the United States, the news media did not have—and to a large extent still do not have—direct and systematic channels of information into the black community. As a result, media attention tended to be limited either to melodramatic, physical acts contrived to attract the media in the absence of "established" methods, or else to physical acts recorded as police actions and reported from that point of view.

The bias in favor of skilled and established news sources is a reflection of the obvious fact that the news media everywhere reflect the dominant values of society. While departures from such values are inherently newsworthy by conventional standards, they tend to be presented as interesting because of their eccentricity or bizarre nature, obscuring any serious social meaning.

Whatever the quality and quantity of information available to them, the executives who choose what the community will hear and see as "news" are conditioned by their own perceptions of the world and of their readers. In the United States, these executives are almost all middle-aged, middle-class, white males. They have usually achieved positions of status in their communities, and their personal social lives tend to reflect the values and goals of their social peers. This does not necessarily mean that they are unaware of or insensitive to other values—though it often does—but it tends to insulate them from other segments of society and from social change that does not immediately affect upper-middle-class life.

Such executives are also in danger of perceiving "the public" in terms of their social peers, with an apparent paradox that in some cases this seems to produce a view of "the public" as synonymous with the executive's social peers and in others a perception of "the public" as the opposite—uneducated, undiscriminating and unaware.

The social perceptions of the editor are important and have received insufficient attention. The same is true of his superior, the proprietor. In printed and broadcast journalism in the United States, the great majority of news proprietors are conservative Republicans (Mott, 1962; *Editor and Publisher* election issues, 1960 *et seq.*). This does not necessarily mean that their editors share these values but that tends to be the case. The monolithic suffusion of the organization with the proprietor's view is usually altered significantly by the necessity of maintaining the circulation of the newspaper (or the audience of the radio or television station), the desire to keep the staff stable and trouble-free, and the generalized assumption among professionals that ideological direction of news is unethical. But because the relationship between proprietor and editor is complex and varied, the performance of the staff is also complex and an uncertain reflection of the values of the leaders.

The editor usually hires the journalistic staff, keeping in mind the predilections of his proprietor and the professional needs of the organization—not always the same. He decides what the staff will do, which is the most important single step in the process of journalism. The perceptions and decisions of editors (as opposed to mechanical "gatekeepers" who do not create news policy but merely implement it) determine what is "news" in any given time and place.

The term "editor," like most hierarchical terms in journalism, has different meanings in different places, sometimes referring to the top executive with over-all power over both news and editorial functions, and sometimes referring to a relatively minor domain. Whatever his title, the chief editorial executive selects his subordinates and transmits his values through them. New visitors to newsrooms are usually surprised by the lack of constant communication among staff workers and the apparent casualness of decision-making on the news. In reality, the organization is suffused with the values of the executive, producing a unanimity, or near-unanimity, enforced not only by the punishment-and-reward system but also by the iron demands of smoothly processing information in a limited period of time.

There are instances in journalism, as in all hierarchies, of power struggles in which values become confused and subordinates are forced to join factions, and this often influences the news. This has happened among news executives in the dynasties of the Hearsts, the Pulitzers, the Reids of the defunct *Herald-Tribune*, the Grahams, the Cowleses and others. It sometimes happens that power struggles at the top produce opposing camps in news policy.

The same polarization can occur not with a power struggle at top levels of command but over dramatic social issues. This occurred on many newspapers and radio and television stations in the South during the school integration and civil rights struggles of the late 1950s and early 1960s. It was also discernible during the student rebellions and anti-war activities of the late 1960s.

Polarization of news policy can also occur when a single management issues a separate morning and evening paper with separate staffs. At times, competition between the two staffs is more fierce than between completely different managements, with conflicting stories or, more often, different emphases that deliberately do not develop provocative information originated by the other staff.

The impact of such differences is not often noticeable to the average reader since it usually does not influence the major outside news, except possibly in tone of headlines and use of illustrations. But it is quickly apparent to sophisticated news sources, which usually exploit the differences.

In the usual situation, the real conflict devolves on the chief news executive. He must satisfy his proprietor on one hand and avoid circulation losses from doctrinaire news on the other, learn to extract power and budget from his proprietor while maintaining the confidence of his professional staff. This seems to produce, more than anything else, a withdrawal from controversy in order to solve the problem of conflicting forces.

It is significant in a non-quantitative way that a common topic of conversation among editors at late-night informal sessions during their conventions is the problem of placating their proprietors while attempting to maintain professional standards of journalism. This conflict seldom is overt. Where it breaks into the open the editor is almost invariably dismissed, as in recent years in Savannah, Wilmington, and Houston (Bagdikian, 1964 and 1966).

In weekly papers, the editor-publisher polarization varies widely, but there is little doubt that most weeklies avoid controversy and act as volunteer bulletin boards for surface events. For one thing, staffs are small—publisher and editor often being the same person—which means that there is an insufficient critical mass of working professionals to represent a force for separate standards of performance. Also, most weeklies are filled with commercial promotion presented as "news" and avoid any stories that will disturb the status quo or require prolonged journalistic attention to one subject.

Where weeklies depart from this pattern, as some do, the results are often spectacular. There tends to be a reversion to old-fashioned muckraking and personal journalism with dramatic consequences in the community—and often bankruptcy for the publisher. Despite national attention to large publications that are attacked by the federal government, most legal harassment and suppression of newspapers has been among the minority of smalltown weeklies and dailies that disturb the status quo or report official malfeasance.

Broadcasting has its own pattern of news policy. There are so many different units in broadcasting that it is difficult to generalize. There are few data on the whole universe or even a random sample of broadcasting station performance. In addition, there is wide disparity between the nature of news produced by the three networks and a few big city television stations on one side, and that of the majority of individual stations on the other.

The average radio station does not employ a full-time professional journalist but someone who has a number of duties such as announcing, reading commercials, and reading items from a news ticker. Most local radio and television news remains unprofessional, and receives little emphasis. It is in such stations that there appears to be the greatest intrusion of commercial self-interest in the news. Typically, there are reports of sponsors' commercial activities, a few items read from a news ticker or a local paper, plus the most dramatic reports provided by the local police (Bagdikian, 1971).

By contrast, television and radio stations that maintain substantial news staffs have a significant impact because of the size of their audience and the vividness of their presentation. Standards in some of these operations are high and attract considerable journalistic talent.

TECHNOLOGY

Even under the most earnest news policies, there are frustrating technical inhibitions. Television crews are expensive; processing and editing film is done under severe time limitations. Because there are few crews even for the networks (compared with the number of reporters for metropolitan newspapers), assignments are usually undertaken with high expectation of action footage on the most obvious major stories. Since production is limited, film editors do not have the choices available to print editors and are under compulsion to use almost anything that is shot and processed in time for the major broadcasts. This comes from a natural desire for dramatic on-the-scene action and a prejudice in television against "head talk"—an individual talking about an event instead of live scenes from the event itself. The high value placed on action footage intensifies the traditional tendency to put a high priority on conflict even more for television than for radio or print.

The principal product of network news is the evening news program. Since the main events of the day, especially political events, have occurred in the late morning and afternoon, there is extreme pressure to process material for 6 P.M., material that almost universally is handled by newspapers on an overnight basis for the morning paper.

Constraints on television news can be based on non-news factors, too: on-the-scene reporting may be cut short because of headwinds that would reduce the speed of the chartered plane taking film to the nearest town, traffic between the airport and local studio, the obsolescence of local studio equipment, or the hostility of local affiliates over intrusion of a national network reporter.

The intrusion of commercial and managerial self-interest into news content on the networks does not seem to follow the pattern evident in printed and local broadcast news. There is less compliance with particular ideologies or advertiser interests in the news.

But another technical factor influences the nature of broadcast news. It is a one-thing-at-a-time medium. Since it survives by collecting large audiences for sale to advertising sponsors, great emphasis is placed on any program that can collect and maintain a maximum audience not only for its own economic value but for carry-over to the next program. This is especially true for the main televised news, at 6 P.M., since this is the start of prime time when television makes most of its money. So news programs are under pressure not only to be exciting enough to attract specific sponsors for the news itself but also to maintain interest throughout for delivery to the next sponsor's program on the same station. Competent but unexciting news can fail this mission. So whatever the professional journalistic standards that operate on a national and regional level for evening newscasts, the station is penalized if the news does not have both mass appeal and excitement to the very end.

Printed news, which operates in a medium no less interested in advertising revenues than broadcasting, has the same problem only on an insignificant scale. Newspapers present the reader with a wide variety of contents that he can accept or reject in seconds at his own convenience. An unexciting story on page 1 does not cost the paper a reader if there is something interesting elsewhere in the same paper. Most readers, usually over 85 per cent, have their newspapers home delivered so sensational headlines are no longer a key to sales either (Bureau of the Census, 1960). If there is a slow news day without physical drama, the paper, being a multiple appeal medium without time constraints, is still read for its other sections—comics, sports, stock returns, etc.

But the pressure of selection is greatly increased by the mechanical characteristics of the newspaper plant. Newspaper production is slow and cumbersome, unable to handle all the news of the day at one time. Consequently, as information begins to flow into the newsroom the editor must begin committing himself to choices from the very beginning, before he knows what his total universe of choices will be. Thus, "news" is determined more by what time in the publishing cycle it is received than by any other single factor (Van Horn, 1966).

If it is received early, when a great proportion of space remains to be filled, a news item has a maximum chance of being used. If it is received late, when little or no space remains, then it must be far more important than earlier items in order to be selected. If two items arrive at the same time, the decision is influenced by more subtle factors: the conventions of the corporation, the editor's perception of reality and of the readers' needs and desires, the values held by professionals around him, his consciousness of competition, and his personal idiosyncrasies (Buckalew, 1967; Tuchman, 1969). (Personal idiosyncrasy is a diminishing factor but it still survives. At one time the editor of the Kansas City *Star* was a man who intensely feared snakes and never permitted the word "snake" to appear in the *Star* while he was on duty. An editor of the Providence *Journal* hated dogs and the only time he permitted a photograph of a dog to appear in that newspaper during his days of leadership was when a collie bit an infant to death.*)

BUDGET AND OTHER ECONOMIC FACTORS

Budget usually determines the quantity of news received and reflects the value that the proprietor places on its quality. In the few places where there is

---

*Some unattributed observations are by the author on the basis of journalistic work and research in the mass media over a period of 28 years.

still face-to-face competition it is also a measure of getting more news faster than a rival, or of pre-empting a total service from a rival. If the budget permits a large quantity of information to reach the editor's desk it gives him two things: a broader view of the events of the day and a greater degree of choice, which require subtler discrimination.

Budget also makes a difference in the nature of news. A small staff operating on a minimal economy often does little more than process information provided by outside sources. These outside sources usually have special interests and take pains to make their own self-serving information available. This gives the paper little importance as an independent scanner of the social horizon; instead, it tends to make it the passive recipient of information originated by special interests.

Stringent budgets mean little or no investigative reporting or in-depth writing. This affects salaries so that talented professionals will not come to that organization or if they do they will not stay. And because there are no uniform standards of media performance and no reliable data on the relationship of news expenditures to profits and survival, budgets for presentation of news are extremely flexible.

There is another constraint for broadcasting that causes less difficulty for print: when an extraordinary live news event occurs it is necessary to decide whether to cover it completely and in real time. If the decision is made to televise it as it occurs, then a scheduled commercial program must be cancelled and its revenues lost, usually irretrievably. If the cancelled program is part of a series the sponsor will be further dissatisfied because the progress of the series has been broken for the habitual viewer. The breaking point in relations between Fred Friendly, in charge of news for CBS, and the network's management occurred when the network declined to cancel an entertainment program in order to carry live an important hearing of the Senate Foreign Relations Committee during the height of the controversy on the Vietnam war (Friendly, 1967).

News executives in broadcasting usually argue that in addition to their responsibility to bring the public important live news, cancelling entertainment programs to cover breaking news wins the loyalty of viewers who become confident that dramatic news will always be delivered to them as soon as possible. But ratings of such sudden changes are not usually made, and it is sometimes possible to prove a smaller audience for the live coverage of a political event, except for such stunning dramas as the assassination of President Kennedy. Public health may be grounds for replacing entertainment programs with live news, but corporate interests usually prevail despite extremely high profits for networks and their own stations.

This is a much easier problem for newspapers. Serious newspapers must occasionally decide to make extra space to accommodate extraordinary news. This can be done by compressing other news, dropping some advertising, or adding pages. None of these methods is extremely expensive and some cost nothing at all. Even the dropped advertising is usually recoverable simply by running it the next day. The cost of adding four pages is not massive, though few papers do it except under extraordinary circumstances.

The predominance of entertainment in broadcasting, both in proportion of total time and in corporate energy expended, is obvious. In daily newspapers, advertising may occupy more than 65 per cent of the total space but it strikes the consciousness of the reader less than television advertising and entertainment since the reader can easily scan and reject it. Furthermore, newspaper advertising and entertainment is less vivid. The ideological content is minor, too, although comic strips are increasingly social and political in nature, and editorial advertising is a growing form of community communication, albeit still small except during intense political campaigns. Nevertheless, newspaper executives believe that entertainment features are indispensable to economic success.

There has been a national controversy for some time over the practice of large papers buying the most popular features and, by contract with the supplying syndicate, pre-empting the feature's use in a large geographical area extending beyond the paper's own circulation zone. Called "territorial exclusivity," this practice has been attacked by smaller papers and is the subject of current litigation by the United States Department of Justice. The practice is significant as a measure of what proprietors feel is necessary for their success, though it is not clear how it actually affects income. It does affect the use of space, since syndicated and staff-originated entertainment features may occupy far more space than the news itself. The importance of entertainment content remains one of the received wisdoms of the trade that could benefit from objective study.

Some portions of newspapers match the commercial orientation of "news" on many smaller broadcasting stations. Special sections like real estate, business and finance, travel, and food, for example, are almost always industry-oriented, their editorial content handled outside the tenets of ethical news. Most professional journalists regard these sections as the least ethical and professional in printed journalism, with blurring between commercial promotion and news that would be considered corrupt in the rest of the news columns.

There is a social message in non-news matter. It is chiefly a message for uncritical mass-buying and materialism. But it has also been a major barrier to applying news standards to corporate activities. The impact of real-estate entrepreneurship on the pathology of cities has gone almost untouched in newspaper investigative reporting even though real-estate sections have been a standard feature of newspapers for decades. The same is true of automobiles. Although the used car salesman has been a standard stereotype of unscrupulous merchandising in American social discourse and humor, it was a taboo subject in newspapers until Ralph Nader made his appearance. The relation of tobacco to health also was a subdued subject even when newspapers gave spectacular treatment to other medical developments, including preliminary data on other causes of disease.

"Consumerism" is still considered a subversive word in commercial journalism circles. But in recent years there has been a marked change, partly because alternative sources have aided the consumer directly even to the disadvantage of merchants and manufacturers—books, magazines, courses—and partly because newspapers belatedly discovered that their readers responded positively.

In broadcasting, the impact of non-news—or entertainment—has been much more direct and more of a public issue. Here, too, there is a powerful message to buy and consume. Violence on television, a standard ingredient, has been a matter of controversy almost from the medium's start, raising the question whether it stimulates violence in society (Lange, Baker, and Ball, 1969). The Surgeon General's Report makes clear—though most news stories about the Report did not—that television violence has a significant influence on behavior.

Less noticeable and less studied is the impact of entertainment content on social values. Television, even more than print, is economically based on the need to collect a maximum audience, so it tends to stay away from material offensive to specific groups and from subjects of interest only to small portions of society. Despite years of attempts at new entertainment formulae, the sovereign attention-getters that are not offensive to social and political groups are sex and violence plus stereotypes of personalities and social situations. Sex and violence are primal themes of unending attraction. Stereotypical situations and personalities are instantly recognized and therefore accepted as legitimate and undisturbing.

Sponsors, in addition to putting intense skills into their commercials, concern themselves with the content of the programs they sponsor. Ten corporations through their sponsorship control the bulk of prime-time American television. Their concern about the social impact of their programming is illustrated by the set of guidelines established by one of the ten corporations, General Mills, for producers of their television programs:

> Where it seems fitting, the characters should reflect acceptance of the world situation in their thoughts and actions, although in dealing with war, our writers should minimize the 'horror' aspects. . . . There will be no material on any of our programs which could in any way further the concept of business as cold, ruthless, and lacking all sentiment and spiritual motivation [Bogart, 1973].

There has been insufficient study of such corporate concern, though they have been noted by Bogart and others.

LEGITIMACY

All influences on media content contribute toward an imponderable but real characteristic of news policy within journalistic institutions: conferring to particular subjects "legitimacy" for news treatment. There are almost limitless possibilities in reportable events in the world (and the universe). Most are eliminated because the news net has no contact with them and so does not "know" about them. But the net gets broader and more intricate with time, so the total knowable phenomena continue to increase. Most of these are eliminated because practicing journalists, wherever they may be, "know" that some events are not "news." This is a practical requirement of operations because communication channels, like space and time for public presentation, are limited. So most known events must be screened out of the channels or out of the final dissemination process.

But what determines which events are "legitimate" candidates for inclusion in the collection of information? The legitimacy of any category of events changes with time and place, but at any given moment almost the entire journalistic establishment accepts that, and accepts it to the degree that those subjects considered "illegitimate" are for all practical purposes not observed or thought to exist.

For example, for almost a hundred years after the Civil War there was a racial caste system in the United States and widespread involuntary servitude. But that was almost never reported in conventional news, including in the most enterprising daily journalism.

There has been semi-permanent poverty despite affluence since the start of the Industrial Revolution and markedly since the end of World War II; yet this, too, did not become a recognized subject for journalistic treatment until the early 1960s.

Even in the most accepted of conventions of local reporting—crime—there have been distinctions between "cheap murders" and "murders that make news." A "cheap" murder is the killing of someone of low status and often goes unreported. To be "news," a murder need not involve a person of prominence but one of middle-class or higher social status.

The "legitimacy" of some news as a candidate for publication is obviously the result of interaction between prevailing social standards and the media. White society was not sufficiently disturbed by the racial caste system to make it a political issue during most of the period after Reconstruction. Poverty was so taken for granted that it was almost invisible to the affluent until recently. The distinctions between crimes reportable as news did not change public perceptions until crime reached the middle class to such a point that the existence of crime anywhere affecting anyone became a measure of social stability and safety.

Yet this standard of reflecting what society takes for granted is contrary to another major element in deciding what becomes "news": novelty, change, or something society does not expect. The discovery of conditions and events not in common understanding is often considered a pioneering and exciting step by journalism. So there is more to the conferring of "legitimacy" than the prevailing standards of society, though that, too, is important. Neither is the arbitrary exclusion of some subjects from becoming "news" based on any rational measure of "reality." Lynchings and other brutal means of suppressing blacks were far worse during the period of non-coverage than when civil rights became an intensely "legitimate" subject.

Another element contributing to "legitimacy" is corporate self-interest as perceived by management of the newspaper or broadcasting station. "Consumerism" is no more needed now that it was when even the *New York Times* refused subscription advertising from *Consumers Union* because that magazine criticized by name goods advertised in the *Times* and other newspapers.

But the perception is more subtle than primitive economic self-interest. News executives and reporters are deeply involved, perceptive of social interest, social need, and their own role in society. This is a subject that historical studies might illuminate (Lowe, 1970).

The inchoate conception of legitimacy is illustrated in one of the more influential books affecting journalism, *The Image*, in which Daniel Boorstin (1962) popularized the term "pseudo-event," a phenomenon contrived solely to catch the attention of the media, and which, in the absence of the media, is cancelled or does not exist.

There is a large body of common assumption about producing pseudo-events as the population becomes more sophisticated about the media. But the implication of Boorstin and others who use his thesis has tended to be that the pseudo-event is inherently bad and that it is largely used by cynical groups manipulating the media.

Two things seem overlooked by this thesis. First, with the development of mass communication on a highly technological, impersonal basis, the so-called pseudo-event becomes necessary for entering the mass communication net. It is no longer possible to reach a significant portion of the community from a soapbox in the park or from the steps of the biggest church. The standard method is to use the mass media, and it would be strange if intelligent news sources wishing to transmit messages to the community did not evolve some method that would fit the technological and logistical conventions of the media. In that sense, the pseudo-event is a rational and necessary device.

Second, most criticism about the creation of pseudo-events has concerned groups that lack acceptable credentials for attention, that tend to be non-established. Yet pseudo-events contrived by socially accepted groups are readily covered and seen as natural and legitimate.

What if the President of the United States gave a news conference and nobody came? All press conferences are pseudo-events, held solely to enter the news net and meaningless otherwise. The conferences and releases of members of Congress, agency heads, governors, and mayors are considered "real" and not "pseudo." Cutting ribbons to open bridges and tunnels is now conducted almost entirely for the media. But demonstrations by low-status or un-recognized groups are criticized when covered if their purpose is plainly to attract the media.

FUTURE RESEARCH AND THE STUDY OF CHANGE

The general state of research into the central dynamics of the news process still consists of a few landmark studies and their detailed replications. Warren Breed's "Social Control in the Newsroom" (1955), Garvey's counter-part work in television (1971), and White's "gatekeeper" studies (1964) and their updating form the nucleus of such investigation. Another category of research concerns the interaction between journalistic and governmental de-cision-making: for example, Cohen (1963) on foreign policy. But both the social control studies and interaction work are only a beginning and attention to more basic and contemporaneous relations within news institutions is required.

The central function of journalism, like all information, is to permit a more valid view of "reality." This is a broad definition and includes that difficult word "reality." Nevertheless, how well the media fulfill this function is a basic measure of media performance. Studies should be initiated and pursued to determine performance on some basis other than easily quantified simple phenomena such as clear adversary community issues whose treatment by the media is judged by mathematical calculation of space and time allotted per side.

There are disparities between the professional journalist's view of "reality" as he perceives it and as he believes his public needs to see it or wishes to see it. In one form, this raises the question whether the professional journalist exercises professionalized standard criteria for selecting news based solely on some collective professional assessment of the scene or whether such an assessment legitimately needs to be moderated to meet the perceptions and desires of the audience. At one extreme there is the possibility of "cultural imperialism" by the professional journalist; at the other, pandering to the most superficial and generalized impulses of the public, regardless of the apparent importance of other matters. Not enough research has been done to reconcile these conflicting approaches.

More retrospective studies are needed on broad subjects so that, with the passage of time, there will be basic agreement on their salient points and a method to judge their treatment by the media. The Lippmann-Merz (1920) study of the *New York Times'* coverage of the Russian Revolution is an example of the kind of work needed, but with more contemporaneous events measured in terms of both presentation of salient events and the effectiveness of the media's communication with its audience.

Lacking in research so far is careful descriptive work on the evolution of the media and on a large population of the media. Most work is done on a single unit—a particular newspaper or broadcast station or special activity of a network. Or if there is a more generalized study it is done at a particular time. This leaves unclear the dynamics of change among the media as a whole.

There has been a rapid change within news institutions in the last decade. The received conventions that decade after decade automatically conditioned each novice journalist to comply with traditional values are being rejected and reformed. Standards of "legitimacy" are being questioned. The primacy of direction from above is being challenged from below. A different kind of novice professional has entered the field. And the alternative press has produced new journalistic forms and content: radio, television, books, and personal contact with experts in fields covered by journalism have replaced the daily newspaper as the daily bible of the outside world. All this has placed the standard media in the position of competing not only for the attention of the citizen but also for power to conceptualize distant reality.

The change has come about partly because the audience was ready for it. Since World War II the average American has become more cosmopolitan—through travel; television; job mobility; higher educational achievement; and the breakup of traditional family, neighborhood, and community ties. Public affairs have also achieved a higher place on the common public agenda. The growth of government influence on individual lives has led to the average citizen's deeper involvement in the political and economic life of his community and nation—concern about property taxes, concern about school curricula, concern about the influence of zoning boards on his neighborhood, of highway commission decisions on his driving, and of national policies on his employment and income.

It appeared to some observers that newspapers in the 1950s and early 1960s were out of touch with these changes in their audience and in their social environment. Television, a newer medium, tended to have younger executives and was less ingrained with an ancient body of tradition. On the other hand, this medium was less serious so the contemporaneous nature of broadcasting leadership was not as influential as it might otherwise have been, though it was plainly more communicative with younger audiences than print.

The New Journalist

Until this decade, a majority of newspapers were owned or controlled by small private groups, often a single family (Swayne, 1969). Leadership was by genetic accident with newspaper direction determined by the most promising or aggressive sons or sons-in-law (almost never daughters). But the elder who built the paper was usually a strong, tenacious man who continued leadership into his seventies and eighties. In the meantime, his sons, sons-in-law, or other heirs apparent grew old in subordinate positions and passive obedience. Eventually "the old man" died or became infirm, by which time the appointed heir was in his fifties, beyond his prime and still known to his staff as "the kid." Or else, the long reign of the founder permitted proliferation of progeny until many families were taking incomes out of the property and dividing inherited power, providing struggles for inheritance of leadership or unanimous apathy.

Whatever the causes, the 1950s were characterized by the passing of the elder proprietors of a generation of modern newspapers, instability of leadership, and the start of impersonal corporate accumulation of newspapers that was accelerated by diffusion of individual leadership. Today newspaper chains own two-thirds of all dailies and increasingly have conventional corporate standards for business and production management rather than traditional or idiosyncratic ones. They tend to change editorial operations slowly or not at all.

The largest factor of change has been the introduction of a new kind of professional journalist at the lower levels. Before World War II newspapering was one of those occupations that afforded working-class families—rarely women except during wartime or for limited special work—middle-class status or better. College educations were seldom required and were often a disadvantage at the point of employment. This produced some outstanding journalists who remain examples of the importance of personal qualities over formal training.

But it also produced a majority of journalists whose only perceptions of the outside world after they left junior or high school were what they saw and heard in their newsrooms. Typically, they began as teen-age copyboys, learning from their demi-gods in green eyeshades. If they were aggressive and intelligent they became cub reporters, usually spending their early months or years as a police reporter, at that time considered a major avenue to daily news and a beneficial introduction to news values and techniques. It also provided a simplistic view of society and a habit of close association with formal power which came to be seen as a natural reward of their occupation. It could lead to a healthy rejection of pomposity and pretention, but it also helped to produce the strong strain of anti-intellectualism that characterized American newsrooms for generations.

With the expansion of higher education and more sophisticated demands upon newspapers by their audiences, there was an influx of reporters from middle-class backgrounds with college educations. They brought a different view into the newsroom—conditioned by formal study and book knowledge of politics, social forces, and economics as opposed to the simplistic standards previously accepted on most papers. It created tension between the older, traditional leaders and the younger, more intellectually prepared novices.

Ironically, this tension was probably prevented from becoming explosive because the earlier college-educated journalists seemed not to be the most intellectually skilled and highly motivated of the college graduates. According to academic journalists, it is in the last fifteen years that academic journalism has changed from attracting students from the lower half of their classes to students from the upper half.*

Originally, skilled students regarded journalism as a low-status occupation. Those who did enter the trade were small in number and lacked the critical mass to challenge traditional assumptions; thus, they tended to perform as though they accepted the older, anti-intellectual patterns of "news" coverage. Learning by doing was still the chief method of entry so they learned how to write in the special pyramidal style of older journalism and to adopt the superficial cynicism of the traditional veteran.

The social revolution of the 1960s changed all this. The importance of social reform in American society affected large numbers of college youth and as they recognized the importance of the media as agents of change, more perceptive, highly motivated students began to appear regularly in the better journalism schools. The influx of the new students also brought turbulence, expressed in problems of "advocacy journalism" and the clash between older editors and younger reporters who challenged, and still challenge, assumptions of journalism.

The growth of professionalism among journalists, started earlier, continued in this same period. It was encouraged by a number of factors: the evolution of larger, more stable newspapers; the slow but steady maturation of broadcast news; greater demands of society upon public information; attraction of a more carefully prepared novice; the overlap of daily journalism with periodicals, journals, and books that placed journalism within the mainstream of intellectual and social change; and a sharp increase in pay and job security through unionization and competition for journalistic talent by other industries.

Professionalism has both aggravated and provided an escape for tensions between traditional and the newer social consciousness values of the news

*This information is based on interviews by the author.

media. It has aggravated tensions by providing a new degree of unity among working journalists in opposition to traditional, institutional constraints that they regarded as inadequate, unethical, or demeaning. There is a growing incidence of staffs openly challenging the policies of their superiors in news organizations. Staffs have, for example, attempted to buy advertising space for editorials counter to their own paper's position (sometimes granted by the paper, sometimes refused). It is one of the motivations behind the growth of local journalism reviews, usually published by reporters from local standard media and printing stories rejected by the standard media or critical of their policies.

Such challenges have led some papers to offer space on their editorial or "op-ed" pages for working journalists to write their subjective assessments of current issues. In a few news organizations, provision has been made for participation of professional staff in periodic reviews of news and editorial policy. But the tensions continue to grow in intensity and are not always peaceful or resolved. In some organizations, reporters are discharged for contributing to local journalism reviews and there are continuing crises of "loyalty" and conformity to institutional standards.

Government-Media Relations

It is difficult to discuss developments in government-media relations without acknowledging the complicating factor of recent government hostility toward the media. On the whole, urban professionals have rejected official pressures and have demanded that their organizations decline to cooperate with authorities in ways that tend to make the media arms of law enforcement or conforming organs of officialdom. The governmental attack has made professionals more conscious of their individual ethical responsibilities as differentiated from their responsibility solely to their organization. This is not wholly unjustified. Journalism corporations have often asked the government for special postal rates, exemption from anti-trust laws, and other privileges, and there is significant concern among working journalists that in a conflict between the institutional press and the government such considerations might outweigh journalistic independence and tempt corporations to cooperate with law-enforcement and other agencies of government in order to prevent harm to their corporate position.

Government attacks have taken the form of orchestrated denunciation of the media by the highest officials of the executive branch from 1969 to 1973, the threat of removal of broadcast licenses from stations that carried public affairs commentary offensive to the executive branch, the demand for political and news commentary scripts by the chairman of the Federal Communications Commission, intensified investigation by the Federal Bureau of Investigation and other intelligence arms of government of news media professionals considered hostile to the current political leadership, audits of income taxes of news media correspondents and columnists considered unsympathetic—all to a degree unprecedented in previous White House-media conflicts.

A number of broadcasting stations have quietly permitted law enforcement authorities to have their outtakes (film and tape eliminated by editing
and never aired), and some newspapers have done the same with photographic
negatives and reporters' notes and documents—without the approval, and
sometimes without the knowledge, of the individual journalist who first
gathered the material from his sources. While the media as a whole reject
official collusion on principle, there have been enough individual cases of quiet
or open assistance to intensify the motivation for professional separation of the
journalist from complete direction by his organization on matters dealing with
the press and government.

The conservative Republican attack on the media has aggravated the
endemic tension between conservative media leadership and working journalistic staffs. It is generally assumed (but not known with any scientific accuracy)
that most working journalists tend to be liberal Democrats. It is known—from
endorsements—that the overwhelming majority of publishers and station managers are Republicans. By attacking working journalists, the Nixon Administration, and before it to a lesser degree the Johnson Administration, has driven a
wedge between the two. Until the Watergate disclosures, accomplished by only
a handful of newspapers and journalists, the growing trend of independent
investigative reporting on national politics and political organizations was
threatened.

Objective studies of media coverage of public phenomena in which the
media have, or believe they have, a substantial corporate stake are needed. For
example, a history of media treatment of tobacco and health should be done in
the context of the simultaneous behavior of the media and other medical
reporting of preliminary indications of causes of well-known diseases. What is
particularly needed is insight, using the social sciences, into the evolution of the
"legitimacy" of such topics—from unawareness to rejection to open treatment.

Operating Practices

Because so much of the quality of journalism depends on economic
support it is curious that there has never been a systematic study attempting to
answer the haunting question of whether persistently high-quality news is more
profitable than low-quality or mediocre performance. There are problems of
definition of "quality" and that, by itself, should be a major research concern.
On the whole, however, research has avoided the subject of measurable criteria
of quality in journalism for discrete institutions. The subject can be approached
from a number of angles, some of which are comfortably quantitative.

Newspapers can be described by daily space devoted to serious news, size
and salary level of staff, types and quantities of stories. Broadcasting can be
judged in the same way, using time rather than space. Qualitative judgments
can be made by separate sets of panels whose collective personal judgments can
be compared according to common criteria for degree of agreement.

The causes of economic success are difficult, but not impossible, to
analyze. The impact of editorial and content changes must be measured over a

long period of time before anything like a clear consequence can be hypo-thesized. Economic influences—like the nature of average content, the growth pattern of the market in which the medium operates, and the relationship to competing media—have to be factored out to approach a thesis on cause-and-effect for quality news.

Legitimacy. An understanding of the dynamics in conferring "legitimacy" to categories of news will provide needed insight into how the media both create and reflect social forces. The early stages of school integration, civil rights, student rebellions, and ecology as prime public issues have reached sufficient maturation to permit studies of the methods by which they became "legitimate" subjects of news treatment and of the nature and consequences of media treatment.

For example, the Supreme Court decision of 1954 on school integration produced such a public impact that it automatically became a "legitimate" subject for reportage; however, subsequent media coverage of school integra-tion was not accompanied by equally discernible public phenomena to fully explain how various media reacted to the evolution of the issue and its current fading.

A study of birth control treatment and abortion would also provide insight into the interaction of the media and other public institutions, such as the church and legislatures; the conflicting perceptions of practitioners within the media; and the changes in power relationships of other institutions to which the media respond—all of which would illuminate the media as agents of change, if in fact they were.

Decision-Making. Richer studies are needed of the origin of perceptions of key individuals in decision-making in the media. Harold Isaac's *Scratches on Our Minds* (1958) demonstrated the inadequacy of prior and subsequent quantitative and simple research in this area. It showed that valuable and original insights can be gained by working in depth with a selection of persons most of whom have had subconscious emotional reactions to broad subjects (in Isaac's book, India and China) of which they were unaware but which had profound consequences on American attitudes. Too little modern psychological and psychiatric knowledge has been applied to the study of decision-making in the media.

There is needed, for example, a careful set of parallel studies of social perceptions of owners, publishers, editors, and various levels of working staffs. Until this is available, knowledge of the complicated interaction of these people to produce news absorbed by the public has to depend on reference to older studies such as Breed's (1955) or on individual and impressionistic reports.

Understanding the interaction of these actors in the scene would provide guidance in the struggle to keep professional journalism insulated from the increasing power of corporate trends in journalism. On the one hand, more and more news media companies are being absorbed in chains and conglomerates that not only increase impersonality but also raise the problem of journalism becoming a subsidiary or byproduct of much larger non-journalistic activity of the parent company. If a non-journalistic corporation is considered justified, as it is, in trying to positively influence media treatment of its activities, what happens when the same corporation owns the news medium it wishes to influence? On the other hand, the clear growth of professionalism—that is, an assumption of more or less standard ethics among a large body of working journalists—provides some counterweight to corporate journalism. There is a growth of the idea of "democracy in the newsroom"—participation by all practitioners in the news policy of their institution.

Exploratory studies are needed to determine, first, if there is a pattern of new relationships arising from corporate giantism in journalism and, second, the effectiveness and practicality of experiments in existence for purely professional influence, at a working level, on the major decisions that determine the total treatment of news.

Despite over a generation of intense controversy, the simple, factual data on social and political characteristics of practicing journalists is not yet known. It is assumed that most are now college-educated and liberal in political tendencies, but this is just beginning to emerge from preliminary data (Johnstone, Slawski and Bowman, 1972-1973).

There are problems of "herd journalism" and the disproportionate influence of a few prominent journalists in setting directions for their colleagues but this, too, is only impressionistic. We do not know from any serious data the effects of practitioners being heavily concentrated away from corporate leadership, as in Washington; or of large groups of professionals being mixed with corporate leadership, as in New York; or of varying mixes of size and relationship to corporate leadership in other parts of the country.

How do internal ambitions and rivalries within journalistic institutions affect the news? It seems clear that they do, but we do not know enough about the phenomenon. It is generally assumed that the evolution of local printed monopolies in 97 per cent of newspaper cities has diminished or eliminated the factor of competition. But the disappearance of a "common enemy" may merely have aggravated internal struggles. With the growth of large corporations extending far beyond a local unit, competition in both print and broadcast media is for promotion into the national hierarchy of the organization or for transfer to more prestigious units. The conflict between the pressure to increase circulation and the pressure to economize in order to maximize profits takes on a novel dimension when it becomes a strictly internal confrontation—without an external source, such as a local competitor, to use as a standard of comparison.

Forms of employee ownership or participation of ownership have had insufficient study. There are questions here that go beyond the comfortable assumption that workers are justifiably rewarded for their efforts, or that professionals exercise their control for the benefit of the news product. There are sufficient fragmentary data to justify careful examination of such issues as the following: Does an employee-owner become more or less tolerant politically? Does he or she become more or less generous in allocation of budgets for news? (In some places newly invested news employees have become opponents of anything but minimal expenditures on news gathering in order to increase their dividends.) How are daily and hourly decisions made when a large group has real power?

Technology. Research, or at least careful projections, on media organizational structures must be under new conditions of information gathering and dissemination. It is reasonable to assume that within five to fifteen years much of what is now the largest part of printed news organizations—production—will be eliminated by new technology. What will happen when news and editorial operations constitute not the present 10 per cent of budgets but perhaps 60 or 70 per cent? How will this affect the nature of leadership? In the light of giantism in news corporations, will the savings increase the exportation of local profits to diversified industrial development, or will it intensify the energies used in producing local news?

Relations with the Community

Media-community relations have been a major subject of concern for some time. Surface manifestations are local and national press councils, the slow but significant increase in "action line," and correction columns, the anxiety of some proprietors over public opinion polls that show substantial hostility toward the media, especially the printed media. What are the most effective feedback mechanisms for enabling news media to learn about their own communities, about undramatic but significant social change, about constituent needs and reactions, and about the efficacy of different information-diffusion techniques within their communities?

Metropolitan newspapers usually operate in the midst of non-white inner city populations while serving white suburbanites. It is not a tenable pattern but newspapers have not responded in any large-scale way to the problem. The status of minorities on news media staffs and the absence of women in anything but specialized and constricted positions are equally and increasingly troublesome matters. As the situation changes, new questions will arise: What is the social and psychological impact of granting new status to previously inhibited minorities on the staffs? Does their inclusion in the professional ranks change the newspaper's contents? If there is a change, is it related to the number or the position of such individuals involved in policy-making? Do the answers to these questions suggest how the news media can remain in touch with a changing society and at the same time become more highly professionalized and corporately stable?

There has been a steady rise in the last decade of small alternative news media, yet there is no good history of their growth and impact. If cable television achieves the status many wish for it—surplus multiple channels operated by a common carrier and open to all users—how will that change dissemination of information within the community? What will be its impact on existing professional institutions of news?

Research suggestions cannot be made without acknowledging the general resistance of the media to systematic study. This appears to be a combination of traditional sense of privacy from the time when newspapers were family enterprises; fear that information may be used by labor unions in negotiations with management; the atavistic reflex to deny information to competition; plus anxiety that any information or systematic plan to obtain information will be utilized by government to restrict, tax, or disturb existing patterns of the media.

Some of these fears are justified; others are based on genuine uncertainty about the effect of current moves. There is a significant move, for example, to provide more public access to the news media and right of reply enforced by law or court order (Barron, 1967). It addresses itself to a real problem but it also raises questions of freedom to publish and speak without restraint. Careful research into such problems and fears might bring a needed degree of factuality and knowledge to a field now characterized by vagueness and anxiety bordering on paranoia.

Another major reason for lack of research on so many fundamental matters has been fear on the part of investigators and their supporting institutions, fear of offending media operators, fear of public denunciation or of private political retaliation by the media. Excessive caution and prudence has not been beneficial to the public or to the media that desperately need some of these data but do not realize it.

Two optimistic impressions: More competent social science and other investigators are now available for media research; insofar as news media anxieties can be allayed by care and competence this should help. Also, the new breed of professional journalists—those more knowledgeable in social science techniques, less ingrained with inherited xenophobia when their own institution is involved, and more concerned with challenging traditional assumptions—are increasingly reaching positions of editorial power and can be expected to understand and sympathize with serious research into the dynamics and structures that control our news and public information.

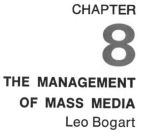

THE MANAGEMENT
OF MASS MEDIA
Leo Bogart

The subject of how media are managed is not merely of academic interest. It raises important questions in the domain of public policy. The mass media themselves have perhaps never before been subjects of such intense public discussion. The issues are varied: the completeness and fairness of news coverage; the public's right to access; the newsman's freedom from judicial interference; the lifting of established barriers to expressions that transgress social mores; and the role of government in setting postal rates and awarding broadcast franchises. The technology of media is undergoing tremendous and rapid changes. The ownership and financial structure of media are changing, too. These developments should spur research on the media system and on the people who run it.

The purpose here is to suggest topics of inquiry. Media management is first defined, then positioned within the larger framework of mass communication research. There is a brief overview of the existing sources of information. The research agenda is interwoven with observations, findings, and illustrations on: the characteristics, goals, and operating styles of media management; the functions of management in resolving operational conflicts and coping with pressures from the public, from advertisers, and from government; and the structure of media organizations, the termination and founding of media, and the management of new communication technology. Finally, some urgent policy research questions are isolated, and some suggestions on research strategy offered.

The study of media management is inseparable from the study of how media are organized, staffed, and operated. Management is the controlled exercise of power in the interests of an enterprise. Top management has the responsibility for setting and articulating the organization's objectives, planning its organizational structure and activities, budgeting and maintaining financial controls, obtaining the necessary funding or investment to initiate projects, and maintaining standards in current production. The mass media are unusual among production-oriented organizations in that some degree of power and influence over public information and taste is exercised by everyone who has any responsibility for creating or selecting content. Every newspaper reporter, magazine copy editor, or radio disc jockey has at least the potential power to reach an audience with his own version of what is worth being read, seen, or heard.

If management were defined merely in terms of the supervisory function, then every pressroom foreman, mailroom supervisor, or assistant night city editor would have to be placed in this category. In news organizations, decisions of critical importance must often be made at high speed under considerable pressure, with minimum opportunity for consultations and approvals; these decisions are often made by individuals who stand low in the formal hierarchy of power.

In most media organizations of any size and complexity, job functions are highly specialized. Students of the mass media are usually concerned with operations that have to do with editorial or programming content, and individuals working in these areas of the media are disproportionately more often the subjects of biographies, gossip, and press reports than their counterparts in such important media functions as engineering, production, purchasing, distribution and circulation, marketing and advertising. The reason for this appears to be self-evident. Those concerned with news, information, and entertainment may be no more powerful or talented than their colleagues in other parts of the organization, but their talents are more visible. They are more likely to be endowed with the perceptiveness and communication skills required to pass on their own observations to a larger public in the form of memoirs, speeches, and other personal writings. Moreover, their power is generally considered to be directly related to the influence that media bring to bear on the public's opinions, values, and tastes. The head of the subscription fulfillment department of a women's magazine may be more valuable to the company, and more highly compensated, than the fashion editor, but it is the fashion editor who without any question is picked as the more rewarding subject of study by most journalists and sociologists.

Many other important but comparatively neglected job functions are essential to media operations and ultimately influence the character of information and entertainment that is diffused. In most of the major mass media, these functions include the production, planning, sales, and promotion of advertising. They represent a significant part of the total body of communication and suffuse the whole mass media experience from the standpoint of the audience.

The character of print media is inseparable from the definition of their geographical territory and the social characteristics of their readers. But this definition is not merely determined by their content; it reflects promotional policy, price incentives, and other tools for building (or contracting) circulation to fit marketing specifications.

An understanding of the structure and technology of production and diffusion is essential to an appreciation of both the opportunities for creating audiences and the constraints on content. In this context come the peculiar problems of UHF television and FM radio, newsboy recruitment in urban ghettoes, and the effects of postal rate increases on little magazines.

In the case of motion pictures, books, and records, managerial decision-making on the part of producers, manufacturers, and publishers occurs in constant interaction with decision-making that occurs elsewhere throughout the whole system of distribution. There are patterns of interlocking ownership, constant movements of personnel from one side of the business to the other, and an intimate network of personal associations and professional as well as economic interests. Thus, a thorough exploration of these media leads us beyond the businesses of manufacturing books, films, and records and into the study of such institutions as general merchandise retailing, real estate, organized crime, and the live entertainment industry. It also brings us back to a more traditional preoccupation of mass communication research: the study of how organized influences are brought to bear on the tastemakers in the press and in broadcasting, whose criticisms, reviews, and publicity create and shape public awareness of particular books, films, and records.

Within every specialized sphere in every media operation, managerial controls are generally exercised with a high degree of autonomy. It is the task of general management to mediate the inevitable rivalries and conflicts among the specialists who make up the organization, and to step in when any one component runs into non-routine problems. This means that in many well-run media, general management is often divorced for extensive periods of time from any active decision-making role that directly involves communication content. Thus, "management" is largely exercised by individuals below the level of ultimate power. Consequently, their managerial actions are always subject to review and to the need to accommodate to parallel centers of secondary power within the same organization.

The news operations of a newspaper or a broadcasting station may normally be conducted with a high degree of independence, yet they are still subject to the control of a publisher or station manager. He, in turn, may be no more than a hired hand reporting to the management of a chain or group that may also have diversified business interests in rival media or even in other types of industry. And in at least some instances, this top management may consist of paid functionaries who hold office by the appointment of an absentee ownership or of an outside board of directors that meets only occasionally. (A board ordinarily follows the leadership of the management, but it is still capable of turning that management out if conditions demand it.)

It is difficult, therefore, to delineate precisely where management begins and ends in the mass media; it is almost impossible to make generalizations about media management that apply equally well to large organizations and to small ones, to single-media organizations and to conglomerates, and to all of the individual media which differ so greatly in their audience habits and compositions, in their technology and economic base, and in their history. Conclusions from past research, and recommendations for future research, must on the whole remain highly specific to the media they describe.

The term "media" emerged from the world of marketing and advertising. In that context it has been used to designate vehicles of commercial communication that can be classified, ranked, and compared on a common basis in terms of total audience and advertising cost efficiency, with only secondary concern for their unique communication properties. The social scientist may find it more difficult to lump all forms of mass communication into the same conceptual framework. Only for certain very limited purposes can we ask questions that are equally applicable to the *New York Review of Books*, Twentieth Century Fox, and public access cable television. Perhaps there is some common ground between the president of the National Broadcasting Company and the editor of an underground newspaper in Memphis, but the theoretical generalizations from such disparate cases must necessarily be limited in scope.

Each medium has its own peculiar communication properties and its own characteristic audiences; it also has its own unique internal economic structure, its own competitive system, and its own unique mix of requirements in talent and skill and capital. In the United States and other democratic countries, the federally franchised and regulated broadcast media face unique controls and self-imposed internal restraints.

Not only is there considerable ambiguity in the definition of "management" within media organizations; a large and growing share of media content is developed by independent suppliers outside the major media organizations, especially in television. Syndicates, independent producers, "packagers," and similar entrepreneurs have their own internal managerial problems and control structures which interact with those of the broadcasting industry.

There are also powerful controls exerted upon the media from outside, by business associations, trade unions, professional groups of media operators and specialists, government regulatory agencies, advertisers, and advertising agencies. While officials of such external organizations are not by any means part of media management, their influence can be so decisive that they must be included as appropriate subjects of research into the practices of media management.

THE LITERATURE ON MEDIA MANAGEMENT

The study of media management has received less attention from social scientists than the study of content and audiences. There is, nonetheless, substantial relevant writing on the subject. Not all of them scholarly, the works range from analyses of media economics to polemics, biographies, and novels. There is a vast historical literature on the press, to which studies of film and broadcasting are steadily being added.

A great deal of valuable documentation, of public curiosity and journalistic interest, has appeared in the form of reportage on specific incidents of media decision-making and mismanagement; gossip about personality clashes; interviews with leading media personalities; and other accounts—often subjective and opinionated in tone—of management selection, power struggles, achievements and failures.

Most existing sociological studies deal with only one medium or another, and most deal with only one aspect of that medium. Comprehensive sociological descriptions of a medium have been attempted in Jarvie's (1970) book on the movies and in works by Glessing (1970), and Leamer (1972) and Lewis (1972) on the "underground" press. Such sociologists as Park (1922 and 1925) and Lee (1947) pioneered the examination of newspapermen, their job roles, their values, and their judgments. Park, as a reporter turned social scientist, was preoccupied with the nature of news and the formation and shifting of popular interests. In the past four decades, there have been a variety of studies of newsmen, using interviews, field observation, and experimental techniques. Some of these studies have been made from the perspective of occupational sociology (Rosten, 1941; Kruglak, 1955; Yu, 1964; and Bogart, 1968); others have more directly focused on patterns of power and influence (Nimmo, 1964); still others have looked at news operations from the standpoint of institutional structure. Tunstall (1971), for example, described how British specialist correspondents interact with their professional associates, their editors, and their news sources.

Another type of sociological research has used the case history method to describe how a particular news organization functions. Breed (1955) examined how newsroom judgments are made in the heat of daily newspaper production. His study has stimulated considerable similar research, such as Weaver's (1968) dissertation on the news operations of a metropolitan New York newspaper. Decision-making in the production of network television news has been researched by Gans (1966), and more recently by Epstein (1973) and Warner (1969a and 1971). The same subject has been illuminated from a distinctly personal and non-scholarly perspective by a working television newsman (MacNeil, 1968).

Studies similar to those conducted among newsmen have been done among several other occupational subgroups in the media world. Early studies of the Hollywood film-making community in its heyday were contributed both by Rosten (1941), a sociologist, and by an anthropoligist (Powdermaker, 1950). In the same tradition are Cantor's (1971) studies of television producers.

From time to time other surveys of specific media occupational groups are conducted for a very limited purpose, such as salary studies. Many of these surveys are small in scale and conducted unscientifically, but nonetheless they can shed some historical light on the evolution of media organizations and their internal practices. Such research is not usually reported in the academic literature, though it may be briefly summarized in the trade press. When conducted by volunteers untrained in research procedures, these media surveys sometimes lead to erroneous conclusions; for instance, they may fail to distinguish between respondents in positions of great power and influence and those with similar titles but minor roles.

Still other studies are never revealed to the public, or are revealed only in part. For example, a survey conducted in 1967 included much valuable information about news judgments, salaries, educational backgrounds, and reading habits of newspaper managing editors and telegraph editors. However, many of the findings were considered unflattering by the sponsoring organization—the Associated Press Managing Editors—and so they were never released in full, in spite of their potential scholarly and practical interest. (A more recent study of ethical problems in editorial management has been published by the same organization, in spite of its sensitive nature.* A notable study of the popular music industry was conducted two decades ago by Columbia University's Bureau of Applied Social Research but only a selected part of the findings were ever reported (McPhee, Ennis, and Meyersohn, 1953).

Economic studies represent another essential resource for the understanding of media management practices. Baumol and Bowen's (1966) study of the economics of the performing arts does not deal with the mass media at all, but it is an excellent model of the type of useful analysis that relates the structure and functioning of cultural institutions to their economic underpinnings.

Not as comprehensive, but highly useful, are studies of the ownership of the press (Nixon, 1968; 1971) and other media. Such analyses, especially when they permit comparisons through time, are excellent starting points for empirical research on the relationships between media owners and their hired managers. Several recent reports have undertaken to assess the effects of media cross-ownership and competition on profits and advertising rates. Some found an association between joint newspaper and television ownership and higher advertising rates (Rosse, Owen, and Grey, 1970); others disputed that analysis (Lago and Osborne, 1971).

Evidence on how competition affects the quality of editorial or programming performance is highly inconsistent, and this important subject cries out for much more definitive research. Litwin and Wroth (1969) concluded that media with concentrated ownership covered the news in greater depth because they had more resources. This was contradicted by Levin (1971), who found that television stations owned by newspapers carried less locally originated programming. Anderson (1971-1972) found no difference in the news sources and practices of television stations owned by newspapers and others, but found that the newspaper-owned stations departed more often from norms of objectivity. Grotta (1970), in a study of 104 newspapers, found that when competition gave way to single ownership, the price to the consumer went up without any increase in editorial quality. No changes were found when newspapers went from independent to chain ownership. Rarick and Hartman (1966) found that competitive papers produced more sensational and human interest material, but also more local news and less boiler-plate. Findings such as these have received interesting annotation and commentary in congressional hearings on the Newspaper Preservation Act and in Federal Communications Commission (F.C.C.) hearings on media cross-ownership rules.

---

*This survey of 210 managing editors found that two-thirds would accept free trips. Ten per cent said they assigned reporters to write publicity in the news columns as a condition for the sale of advertising, and ten per cent also acknowledged that advertisers were treated differently from non-advertisers in the news columns [*Editor and Publisher*, Nov. 18, 1972].

This kind of story is only a lead to the real research that should be done. Who is venal, under what circumstances, and with what consequences for the paper and the public? The opportunity for such research is hardly confined to only one medium. (Among 123 farm broadcasters surveyed by Wolfe [1970], 95 per cent were personally involved in the sale of their programs to commercial sponsors. Wolfe inferred that the farm broadcasters' intimate relation to his audience is merely instrumental to the sale of commercial time.)

The Rand Corporation study of media economics, summarized by Bagdikian (1971), provides important data on internal costs. The financial operations of the media are also illuminated by annual reports of publicly held media corporations, analyses of financial performance by brokerage firms (notably Dirks and Co.), and periodic trade press reports of typical operating budgets.

For print and broadcasting, editorial and programming practices are inseparable from distribution and advertising patterns. There have been occasional economic analyses of media rate structures, such as Ferguson's (1963) study of the local-national rate differential in the daily newspaper industry. The impending growth of cable television will bring about tremendous changes in the financial structure of broadcasting. A number of studies have been made of the economics of cablecasting (Land, 1968; Sloan Commission, 1971).

Apart from academic studies by sociologists and economists, there exists an enormous body of journalistic literature on the subject of media management, offering many useful data and interesting insights. This includes such popular works on television as those by Mayer (1972) and Brown (1971); and continuing reportage in *Variety*, *Broadcasting*, *Editor and Publisher*, *Television/Radio Age*, *Media Decisions*, and other trade publications, as well as in the business press and in popular magazines.

Major problems in media operations are often uncovered in investigative reports that are published in politically oriented magazines, "underground" (radical) weeklies, gossip sheets such as the *Gallagher Report* or the *Media Industry Newsletter*, and (in recent years) journalism reviews. Such articles are usually handled in muckraking or polemic style. While they do not necessarily meet the test of acceptability as evidence, they are invaluable as statements of hypotheses or definitions of problems that deserve more dispassionate social research. Even trivial incidents of this kind are worth exploring.

Valuable writings on media management are also found in biographies and topical exposes. Like the Hollywood stars they created, motion picture moguls from David Griffith to Louis B. Mayer have excited the interest of biographers (Freud, 1970; Zierold, 1969). Lords of the press (Seldes, 1938) have also been a perennial topic, with giants such as William Randolph Hearst (Carlson, 1936; Swanson, 1964; O'Loughlin, 1970) and Henry Luce (Jessup, 1969; Swanberg, 1972) repeatedly the subjects. Irreverent works (Lundberg, 1936); sympathetic life histories (Kendrick, 1969); and official biographies of, for example, Edward Scripps, James Copley, David Sarnoff (Lyons, 1960), and William M. Gaines (Jacobs, 1972) all shed light on managerial styles and motivations. Stern's (1969) study of Palmer Hoyt's career as editor-publisher of the *Denver Post* offers a rare sociological case history of the impact of a strong individual personality (and self-conscious agent of change) upon a news organization. Similarly useful are personal reminiscences, whether mellow (Catledge, 1971) or bitter (Lindstrom, 1960).

The advertising business has yielded autobiographical confessions from such varied personalities as David Ogilvy (1963), Jerry Della Femina (1970), and George Lois (1972). Advertising tycoons and their agencies have, from time to time, been the subject of rich and often fascinating revelations in business publications. (See, for example, *Fortune's* article on Marion Harper,

Jr. [Wise, 1968] and occasional articles in *Barron's*, *Forbes*, and the *Wall Street Journal*.) Much of this material carries important insights into how the media operate, and into the premises that their clients accept.

Another source of data are media company histories—some authorized, like Berger's (1951) view of the *New York Times*; others unauthorized (Talese, 1969). Directly pertinent are case histories of significant crises in media management: Friendly's (1967) *Due to Circumstances Beyond our Control* reports on the events that led to his resignation from C.B.S.; Ungar's (1972) *The Papers and The Papers* deals with the press coverage of the Pentagon Papers case; and Hersh's (1972) *Cover Up* reports (among other things) the apathy of media management to the story of the My Lai massacre.

Case histories are sometimes produced in a fictional format. Fictionalized treatment has been a rich source of description and insight into the human relationships and conflicts through which occupational roles manifest themselves. White's (1961) *The View from the Fortieth Floor* portrayed the death of *Collier's* Magazine; similar romans à clef (Foreman, 1959; Miller and Evans, 1964) have described the life and death of television series.

CHARACTERISTICS AND STYLES OF MEDIA MANAGEMENT

Since there is a large body of literature on media management, a review of what has already been studied automatically suggests an inventory of subjects for research.

What do we want to know about the people who run the media? First of all, it is important to understand who they are, and to what extent they can be characterized, or at least typologized, medium by medium. What distinguishes an innovator or an impresario from a corporate bureaucrat? How do media managers define their personal goals and objectives and those of the enterprises they run? In what ways do they believe that their own definitions are different from those they ascribe to their peers and competitors? What are media managers' sources of general information? What are their political beliefs, social prejudices, patterns of personal association, outside civic and business interests, private assets, and personal media habits?

Media elites have close interpersonal relationships with political elites, cultural elites, and the elites of other types of business. In many instances, their members are, or consider themselves to be, part of these other circles. There appears to be no existing sociometric research into such personal relationships, which could be combined with studies of residence patterns, club memberships, and outside community and charitable interests. It may be difficult to differentiate involvements pursued consciously from either or both sides in pursuit of business advantage from those that merely reflect the social class positions of the participants. Walter Lippmann has observed that newsmen have a continuing dependence upon their sources and that this inevitably imposes limitations on their reportage. (In this connection, see Blumler's [1969] study of the relations between British politicians and the producers of a public affairs television program.)

Both the formal and informal relationships between media management and government officials deserve scrutiny, especially in the federally regulated broadcasting industry. Federal Communications Commissioner Nicholas Johnson (1973) speaks of

> the desire on the part of the Commissioners, themselves, either to be reappointed or to be employed by the industry. Either of which would tend to promote the same kind of response on their parts as the business at hand. The same principle applies to the staff, many of whom may regard the F.C.C. as a stepping stone to a more lucrative job in the industry. . . . Another problem is the constant socialization—the lunching together, the parties, and just the camaraderie of friends who then find it quite difficult to take actions adverse to each other.

Attention must also be given to the political structure and paid staffs of membership organizations such as the Associated Press and the Magazine Publishers Association. Leadership in these organizations can be translated into economic advantage, and vice versa.

To study who enters management in a field that offers opportunity for upward mobility, we may have to begin by considering how the media are staffed and the criteria by which programming and editorial personnel are recruited and promoted into the ranks of decision makers. Judgments of individual ability and skill are undoubtedly tempered by congeniality of temperament, social background, or political considerations.*

The career histories of media executives characteristically reveal transformations of role and self-concept also worth studying. Specialists become generalists as they ascend the hierarchy. As they are moved from department to department and from function to function, they acquire new skills and often a new outlook. Even when they remain bracketed within a specialty, their contacts with other specialists increase as their positions acquire wider scope, and this raises their understanding of rival departments in the same enterprise.

Employee and executive turnover within media organizations should lend itself readily to quantitative analysis. Journalism schools periodically survey their graduates to see where their careers have led them. Clearly, there are different mobility patterns of personnel within different types of media enterprises. Within what geographical frame does this normally occur, and with what consequences for the sharing of information and ideas? How do members of media management move across different sections or specialties of the business? Movement may perceived as a conscious effort to broaden

---

*The findings of studies done to date appear somewhat banal. For example, managers of public television stations were questioned by McIntyre (1971) as to what made for successful performance. Their replies stressed general managerial skills and academic training in broadcasting. Radio and television executives questioned by Higbee (1970) preponderantly felt that a college education was essential for employment in the industry. About half felt that a major in broadcasting was desirable, though there was also considerable criticism of academic courses in the subject.

skills or simply considered to be part of a conventional policy of promotion from within.

A media executive's loyalty to his profession or to the industry as a whole may sometimes overcome his immediate business self-interest. Conflicts of this kind can arise in connection with the enforcement of industry codes (such as that of the National Association of Broadcasters). A professional association (for example, the American Society of Newspaper Editors) may command a greater sense of allegiance than an employer, and an executive may be much more concerned about maintaining the esteem of his reference group than about personal advancement. Episodes involving such conflict or personal crises are especially worthy of study. What is the history of attempts by various media specialists to develop a professional identity and to establish codes of ethics and standards? What are the significant reference groups for different media managements? How do these reference groups change as individual managers go through their typical career cycles?

As educators and professional standards in journalism and broadcasting are upgraded, the typical values of media managers' should reflect these higher standards. But what standards of quality do media managers set for themselves? Rhea (1970) questioned the managements of ten television stations in large cities and ten in small ones. He found that general managers did not perform up to their own ideal conception of their role and did not differ much from departmental managers one level down. How do media executives rate individual vehicles within their medium in terms of their own standards? (Foote [1970] studied this for educational television.) How do they explain variations in the quality of media performance?

There is evidence that media managers distinguish between their own personal tastes in media content and those that they attribute to the mass public. Hollywood television producers interviewed by Cantor (1971), for example, tended to watch only news and sportscasts in addition to their own shows and samplings of competitive series at the start of the season. They considered their own output "at too low a level" for their own taste. One who never watched his own show said, "This kind of drama does not appeal to me." (See also, Elving's [1970] study of FM station managers' attitudes toward FM radio.)

How do the decision-makers vary in their perceptions of public taste and in their philosophy of how to reconcile it with their own? Do they see themselves as leaders or followers of mass taste and opinion (Gerbner, 1972)? To what extent do they consciously plan to impose tastes or to influence opinions? When is this done on principle, and when for profit? (A notice of a summit conference of the popular-music industry held in New York in April, 1973, suggests that the promotion of country music reflects a conscious effort to find a new sound as a popular substitute for rock to fit a changed political climate.)

There are wealthy patrons for media just as for the performing and literary arts: publishers issue notable books to achieve esteem rather than profit; foundations, such as Russell Sage and Bollingen, and many university presses expect their publications to show a loss; Huntington Hartford subsidized *Show* magazine at considerable expense. (He may have been genuinely convinced that this was a viable investment; or he merely may have wanted a personal vehicle to bolster his own identity and taste.) But commercially successful media have also been started or turned to promote personal interests. How different is the use of a medium to serve political ambition or ideology from the notorious subvention of French newspapers by munitions firms at the time of the Third Republic?

Media managers must reconcile their political beliefs with their self-interests when they are confronted, as they recently were, with major critical policy questions that involve an Administration they support and elements in their own business. Such anomalies have arisen, for instance, on the issue of newsmen's immunity, the proposed curtailment of network time, the control of the Public Broadcasting System, and the publication of the Pentagon Papers.

To what extent is there an exact congruence between the personal views of media owners or top managements and the editorial positions taken by their media? Few media executives have clearly formed opinions on all the issues upon which their editorial writers must render judgments. When, and on what kinds of issues, do publishers and station owners take on the opinions of their hired editorial writers rather than vice versa? (Newspapers owned by the same chain sometimes support different presidential candidates. In single-ownership markets with both morning and evening newspapers, two out of five have separate editors, and presumably separate news operations. In many instances, they also have distinct editorial views.)

A participant observation study of news organizations by Warner (1971) found that there is a greater scope for deviance, especially in television, on matters that have not been clearly defined by policy. The less the editor knows about a subject, the more opportunity the working newsman has to structure the output to conform to his own goals. He is more likely to do that if he himself initiates the story and if his professional status is high. Deviance from organization policy is more likely to be tolerated when working conditions require a collaborative effort, as in television news coverage.

What are the upper limits of disagreement that different managements are willing to tolerate, and what accounts for the differences in philosophy between more and less permissive managements? Incongruities between editorial policies and personal belief may be a cause of disagreement or conflict within the media organizations themselves. Cremer (1971) describes two types of television news directors: one perceives the newsroom to be free from management constraints; the other feels misunderstood and interfered with by management. The typical station general manager views himself as supportive of the news department; news directors understand that the manager feels this way, regardless of how they themselves see him.

To what extent do the personal backgrounds and individual lifestyles of media managements affect the decisions they make? The range between autocratic and democratic styles of management may be somewhat different in the media than in other types of business. Bennett (1970) studied the managers and employees of twenty-one radio and television stations and found that employees invariably saw the manager as more autocratic then he saw himself.

W. A. Smith (1972) stresses the importance of the individual television producer's personality. He interviewed twenty-one persons involved in the production of the "Bronson" television series. Most had been hired through personal acquaintance with the individuals doing the hiring. The producers pursued their objectives without regard to program or audience research or to the desires of the studio and the network. Both the success and failure of the series were attributed to the leading actor. The personal qualities of those involved in the production were responsible for their power and authority.

Managements of media that are dynamic and expansive differ from those of cautious and conservative media. Are there any parallels between managerial style and policy outlook? Madden (1971) suggests that the personality of those in authority may have an important influence on the content of the media that reach the public. Among twenty-eight editors of the *Philadelphia Inquirer*, those who ranked low on the F-scale of authoritarianism gave bigger play to stories of protest demonstrations than did more authoritarian editors. Madden concluded that "relatively trivial details about hair, dress, and demeanor can measurably affect the display of news in a newspaper."

The study of managerial style must examine the different strategies used to cope with competitors, new production techniques, and subordinates in organizations that are in transition from personal control to impersonal bureaucracy. Henry Luce reminded newcomers to his staff, "I am the boss; I can hire, and I can fire." This blunt style of expression may have seemed appropriate to him at a time when the combination of public ownership and a second generation of active management had dimmed the luster of his founding-father role.

People who own media, in whole or in significant part, are not necessarily involved in their day-to-day management. In battles over ownership, such as the extended litigation over S. I. Newhouse's efforts to buy control of the *Denver Post*, members of an original family of owners may be trotted out to lend an appearance of legitimacy to one side or the other, but the professional management takes on the real burden of the battle. It is instructive to consider the activities of the members of the Bok family during the last days of the *Saturday Evening Post*, when they belatedly emerged to wring their hands at Board of Directors' meetings (Friedrich, 1970).

Normally, there is always some point at which even the most permissive or indifferent absentee owner asserts his residual property rights: when his income, equity, or cherished beliefs are threatened. Thus, Chairman William Paley has periodically intruded into operational affairs at C.B.S., as when he decided to cancel the television showing of David Rabe's play, *Sticks and Bones*, on the evening when prisoners of war first returned from Vietnam. Such instances of owner intervention may represent a valuable subject of research, one that no study of the organization and functioning of media can ignore. These rare occurrences serve as reminders of where ultimate power lies.

THE MANAGEMENT OF CONFLICTING VALUES

Within the hierarchy of media management, there are specialized areas ruled by their own appropriate systems of work rules, goals, and standards. To follow the conventional wisdom, these areas may be grouped crudely under two major headings. First, there are those that follow the general pattern accepted in business: to maintain the organization, to keep it out of trouble, to make a profit by prudent spending and effective selling, and to grow and prosper. In the media business, this means pleasing the public in order, where applicable, to please advertisers. The medium's output is a product for sale. Second are those that may be described as self-expressive, creative, professional; they involve discovery, revelation, persuasion.*

The result of this dichotomy need not necessarily be bad. A study of the creative operations in British television (Windlesham, 1969) suggests that there is an inevitable conflict between program producers and general management, but that the resulting dynamic tension offsets orthodoxy, complacency, and routine. Media that are founded to advance a political philosophy or deviant lifestyle are sometimes transformed into enormously profitable enterprises. Thus, the history of a publication like *Rolling Stone* would reveal fascinating transformations in the orientation, interests, living habits, and social contacts of its founders.

Profit-centered goals are usually ascribed to people on "the business side," including those in sales and production; creative goals to those responsible for content. But in practice, this clearcut division does not exist. Cantor (1971) has shown that producers, who typically have a previous work history as writers, are necessarily placed, for business reasons, in a position of reshaping and rewriting the work of their own hired writers (with whom they typically have close social connections).

The balancing of organizational and cultural needs in the production of television programs has been studied by Elliott and Chaney (1969) and Lewis (1969-1970). Lewis surveyed program decision-makers at 521 commercial television stations and isolated eight factors to explain their decisions: feedback from viewers, commitments to the F.C.C. and its regulations, ratings, feedback and comments from critics and other media, opinions of production and operations managers and news directors, personal "instinct," background and experience, sponsors' opinions and advertising sales potential, and trends in viewing and program balance.

Ongoing operations require close coordination of specialized functions. Mature members of an established media organization normally communicate across the gap, and thus assimilate some of one another's values. People on the editorial or programming staff are ordinarily realistic about the practical demands of the medium as a business that requires an income and a production mechanism. Similarly, those on the business side usually recognize the importance of maintaining public credibility and acceptance of the content.

---

*It is only fair to acknowledge that in domains of the operation that are not directly concerned with content, there are also goals that pertain to the exercise of craftsmanship. For a promotion man or an engineer, excellence of performance may be its own reward, apart from the hope of advancement. But craftsmanship is consistent with both the profit and creative orientations, and is not really relevant to the conflict of values that interests us here.

Of course, the incompatibility of business and creative values may never erupt into overt conflict, and yet hinder performance. For instance, Brooks (1970) interviewed 100 employees of radio and television stations in eight cities to find out how they would handle controversial news stories. He found that the technical and business components of the organization conflicted with the artistic and professional ones. Suppliers, advertisers, and market conditions were found to exert considerable influence on programming decisions.

In minor media, conflicts between the proponents of these two orientations are resolved outside of public view. But in media that are highly significant because of their audience size or their history, such conflicts are newsworthy, and the resulting public review and commentary can result in dramatic showdowns. Although the positions of the opposing orientations are apt to be projected to the world at large as though they represent diametrically opposed values, they are more likely perceived by management as disputes of judgment over means rather than ends.

Three such episodes are illustrative: Fred Friendly's resignation from C.B.S. after the television network's new president—allegedly acting on orders of Frank Stanton—insisted on broadcasting a rerun of "The Lucy Show" rather than carrying live Senate hearings on the Vietnam War; the resignation of Willie Morris, editor of *Harper's*, after his publisher sought to get him to change the publication to meet the challenge of declining readership (Fischer, 1968); and the dismissal of the legal counsel for the *New York Times* after the firm had warned against publication of the Pentagon Papers.

The latter instance illustrates the fact that the demands of business are not always triumphant when they conflict with professional judgment or the creative imperative. The Friendly case notwithstanding, broadcasting networks frequently broadcast live news events at a considerable loss of commercial revenue, and usually with a substantial loss of their audiences. (However, Epstein [1973] argues that the loss of revenue is much exaggerated, since the networks save the costs of producing entertainment shows and recover commercial spots through "make-goods.") Love (1969) interviewed 90 newsmen on the handling of air time after the assassination of President Kennedy. She found that at such a moment of crisis the networks subordinated their commercial objectives to maintain the collective values of the nation. Network executives responded as citizens and as controllers of communications rather than as businessmen. On the local level, instinctive decisions on how to handle the assassination helped to reaffirm social norms and values.

It might be especially instructive to study marginal cases of proposed preemptions of network time to determine how and by whom the decisions to proceed or not to proceed are reached. The decision to broadcast the fateful Army-McCarthy hearings live was made by a middle-echelon executive at C.B.S. who announced it on his own initiative, thereby putting his superiors in a position where they would be making news if they overrode his judgment. Had the question whether to preempt regular programming been bucked upstairs, history might have been different.

It is important to examine instances in which—with or without external pressure—top management interferes with editorial or programming decisions that are normally handled routinely by specialists. What occasions or triggers such interference? Decisions to intervene may be made after prior questioning or discussion, or they may be presented as arbitrary orders. What techniques are used to communicate and justify such intervention to the staff? What determines the nature of the reaction?

Although newsmen work under varied conditions and hold a variety of journalistic philosophies, there does appear to be a high degree of congruence in their news judgments (Buckalew, 1969). One indication of the strength of independent standards of editorial professionalism is the remarkable similarity in editorial mix among newspapers in different parts of the country and in different circulation size groups. (The evidence is in an as yet unpublished study of content in a national sample of newspapers.) The business decisions of media managements customarily manifest a respect for professional standards. Under what conditions, and for what motives, are these standards disregarded or flouted?

The growth of professionalism, or at least the growth of interest in the concept of professionalism, reflects the changing relationship between media and educational institutions from the standpoint of manpower recruitment and training, financial endowment, and intellectual stimulation and criticism. A somewhat related function can be ascribed to press reviews and press councils (Murray, 1972; Balk, 1973). What types of incidents or transgressions provide subjects of criticism, commentary, and grievance proceedings?

The professional autonomy of network television news operations is affirmed by Warner (1969a), who concludes that the criteria for news selection are: importance to the public, the number of people affected, audience interest, dramatic quality, freshness and timeliness, and political balance. Gelles (1971) points out that the television newsman's concern with objectivity often leads him to create a balance, even if one does not really exist. Epstein's (1973) study of NBC news arrives at similar criteria. He stresses the constraints imposed upon the decision-makers by the medium's format, economics, and technical requirements.

Breed's (1952) oft-cited study suggests that reporters and editors gradually incorporate a newspaper management's editorial outlook and that this unconsciously guides their handling of the news. Garvey (1971) examined the attitudes of news staff members and managers at three television stations. His evidence supports Breed's thesis that staff members absorb the viewpoint of management over a period of years of work in a newsroom and that hiring practices have little effect on maintaining policy. But Garvey found that acceptance of the management outlook declined among those with the longest employment and the greater prior experience in broadcast news.

In a study of reporters for two daily newspapers in a southeastern city, Sigelman (1973, p. 149) concluded that job applicants tend to gravitate toward the paper with which they are politically most sympathetic. The reporter gradually assimilates the policy bias of the newspaper for which he works, simply by virtue of his membership in the organization. "Bias is the product not of a simple policy imposition—policy avoidance calculus, but of a far more complex and subtle organizational process. . . . [T]he key to understanding bias lies not in conspiracies, not in conflict, but in cooperation and shared satisfactions." The ways in which this happens "preserve for the reporter the institutional methodology of objective reporting."

How widespread is the process of absorbing management values? To what extent is it resisted? Flegel and Chaffee (1971) questioned 33 reporters on the two daily newspapers in Madison, Wisconsin. On both papers—one conservative and one liberal—reporters were found to be more strongly directed by their own opinions than by those of their editors and readers. Reporters tended to ignore external pressures, but not their private convictions.

Several studies have shown that working newsmen tend to be liberals and Democrats; by contrast, media owners are predominantly Republicans. How are these conflicts of opinion mediated and resolved? To what extent do the attitudes of staff members affect senior executives? Efforts, successful and unsuccessful, by reporters to express opposition to a newspaper's editorial policies through paid advertisements would make especially revealing case histories. How does management respond in such episodes? To what extent, and under what circumstances, are individual or collective opinions of staff members incorporated into editorial policy?

There are wide differences among media in the extent to which an outlet is provided for viewpoints not in conformity with those of the management. A parallel may be drawn between internal conflicts on political issues and disagreements on matters of taste. In the popular music industry, for example, there have been debates over lyrics carrying thinly disguised references to sex or drugs. Who takes what position in such discussions, and how have the arguments been resolved?

Another subject for research is the position and power of trade unions in the various media. Managements respond differently to a strike or the threat of a shutdown; their various strategies of opposition and accommodation have equally varied consequences (Raskin, 1965a and b; Kelber and Schlesinger, 1967).

Union leadership has often played a role in restricting technological change within a medium. Some craft unions, such as the Screen Writers Guild, may have fostered a sense of occupational identity for a group. The Newspaper Guild, broadened from its original base of newsmen (Leab, 1970) to include clerks and advertising salesmen, may have raised labor's bread-and-butter collective bargaining concerns to a higher priority than journalistic interests. What is the result in terms of management's ability to transmit its goals within an organization, job mobility, and the social stratification of the work force? How are management practices affected by the presence of powerful craft unions in shops that are totally organized on either the production or editorial (or programming) side, or both?

HANDLING AUDIENCES AND ADVERTISERS

In shaping media content, management is guided or limited by the need to maintain income by maintaining the audience. What conceptions (and misconceptions) do media managers have of their audiences, and how are they formed

(Snider, 1967; Atwood, 1970; Wilkins, 1971; Cantor, 1971 and 1972)? Cantor (1972) interviewed twenty producers of children's animated cartoons to see how they managed to please both the viewing audience and the buyers of their films. The producers were found to have a limited perception of the audience: they regarded program effects as the responsibility of network officials and parents and viewed their own production activities as business enterprises rather than as art or educational forms.

Film makers and book publishers may regard changes in the cultural mores as an external force to which they must respond; in unusual cases, they consider themselves conscious agents of change in the culture. If they see themselves as agents of change, how do they devise their strategy? What makes it sometimes successful and sometimes not?

Research is widely used as a basis for management decisions in some media organizations, and is unknown in others. Executives responsible for content are often suspicious of research, or consider it appropriate only for the promotion of advertising. Under what circumstances are research findings about audience interests and desires accepted, rejected, or reinterpreted to suit prior preconceptions?

Media managements tend to cater to existing tastes, either of the mass or of the particular target audience to whom they address themselves. What leads them, at least occasionally, to create new tastes? Hirsch (1971) found Michigan teenagers indifferent to the lyrics of familiar hit songs. He concluded that the "revolution" in the content of popular songs can be better explained "as a reflection of musicians' personal values and economic pressures on the radio and recording industries rather than as a response to consumer attitudes and preferences." Johnson (1973) likens those who select radio music to gate-keepers for other types of information. He found them to be highly subjective and vague in describing audience goals and musical standards. Records were selected on the basis of their sales, according to personal taste, and on intuition about audience preferences.

Venturesomeness in book publishing and the popular music industry, which are independent of advertisers, may be more common than in the commercial media. How does this reflect the economic demands of business competition among different companies with their separate stables of authors or composers? The high-budget promotion of sensational low-budget books and films differs from normal sales and distribution practices in these industries. The economic risks involved in these deviant types of ventures should be compared with those of the more conventional kind.

Little magazines (Hoffman, 1946) and the radical "underground" press often carry on a perilous existence, since those who manage them give the expression of ideas precedence over the operation's needs as a business enterprise. Elite media can keep going on charity or as a byproduct of political commitment, but mass media can hardly survive without a solid economic base.

Media management must constantly compare the economic return from mass audiences yielding a small per capita revenue with that from smaller audiences producing a higher rate of return. Such managerial decisions may carry significant consequences for the culture. People are willing to pay more to satisfy tastes that depart from the norm, in the direction of either elite culture or the socially unacceptable. Television industry spokesman have argued that a pay TV system with very limited audiences may be much more profitable than commercial television and thus drive out mass entertainment. (Blue movies are already being transmitted on pay cable TV into hotel rooms.)

When film distributors and theater owners switch from family entertainment to the more profitable "adult" films, they convert popular tastes as they create an audience for the new products that they are distributing. What determines the duration of such artificially induced shifts in taste (like the promotion of "country music," already mentioned)?

There must be a difference in the character of management and the willingness to assume risk between those media that require substantial capital investment in a production plant and those that essentially involve the discovery and coordination of talent and can be operated on a shoestring. Ownership passed from generation to generation is more likely to be encountered when large capital investment is important. As in other types of enterprise, the profit motive creates pressures for continual expansion, and further accumulation of profits reinforces these pressures by finding its way into new channels of investment. But as businesses grow, their production requirements create a need for greater amounts of capital, which eventually must be raised from the public, and thus lead to a diffusion of ownership. This process is encouraged by the system of inheritance taxes, which require media heirs to raise large amounts of cash when they come into their own.

In what ways is the political content of media determined by their profit orientation? It is generally assumed that commercial media are constrained in their expression by the limited tolerance of their conservative advertisers, and that all media tend to reflect the conservatism of the businessmen who own and manage them. These propositions deserve more systematic investigation than they have received. It has been suggested (Wolf, 1971) that marginal or vulnerable economic health in a media enterprise is likely to be associated with political conservatism. Is the unsuccessful or failing enterprise more likely to lower its standards of professional excellence and integrity to please advertisers, as Bowers (1967) reports?

How and when do advertisers become involved in influencing, directing, or censoring media content? Under what circumstances is this done consciously and deliberately, and with what consequences? To what extent are influences exerted by informal, indirect, oblique discussion and social contact or common participation in civic affairs? Specific instances of advertiser intervention deserve examination. Through what process is the decision made to intervene, both on the part of those who wish to exert influence from outside and by their advocates within the media organization? What steps are taken by members of management and staff to rebuff or accept such intervention? (Bowers [1967] found business office intervention most likely to take place on close-to-home matters affecting local advertisers, and least likely to occur with respect to broad public issues.)

A report on the National Food Editors' Conference (Karp, 1972) not only made direct charges of improper influence by advertisers, but also raised the much broader question of whether newspapers—or the media generally—provide adequate coverage of consumer affairs. Growing public interest in consumer protection suggests that a reevaluation of existing editorial practices would be timely. How is consumer news reporting currently being handled? What accounts for policy differences among similar newspapers and magazines—in editorial budgets, volume of original writing (as opposed to publicity handouts), extent of product testing, and degree of integrity in the face of advertiser pressure? When, and to what extent, are articles published that advertisers consider offensive, and what forms of influence are used to prevent this, with what results within the media organization? When existing practices are under fire, what determines management's willingness to modify them, or its insistence on standing pat?

Consumer affairs represent only one area in which media must adapt themselves to changing public interests, either through the modification of existing practices or the establishment of new enterprises. Advertiser demand and resistance play an important part in determining the rate and success of such adaptation, and media management's techniques for handling such pressure is a prime subject for research.

POLITICAL RELATIONSHIPS

In publicly supported media, such as educational and public broadcasting, the traditional conflicts between creative and commercial values are replaced by a new kind of conflict between creativity and political constraints. This is in many respects merely a continuation of the old struggle: management is faced with the problem of maintaining the loyalty and enthusiasm of the professional staff without antagonizing the providers of essential funds. But apart from this temporizing aspect, there may also be naked political control objectives. In this connection, it would be relevant to study the managerial crises that took place in the Public Broadcasting System when the second Nixon administration sought to change its political character by shifting power from the network to more conservative and timid local stations. (This case history should be compared with the operations of publicly supported broadcasting systems in other democratic countries, and with a similar crisis faced in 1968 by the French broadcasting system [O.R.T.F.]).

Commercial media are not immune to the necessities of maintaining a satisfactory relationship with the political powers-that-be. The freedom guaranteed by the First Amendment is far from absolute. Broadcasting is regulated, and even the press is subject to certain government controls in its production and distribution functions, and occasionally in its content. (Wage and price controls, postal rates, libel and obscenity laws all represent restrictions on absolute freedom).

The Nixon administration's attack on the television networks and on the "eastern establishment" press may represent no more than a recent dramatic episode in the continuing adversary relationship between media and government in the United States. This relationship represents a major topic of inquiry that transcends the scope of this paper.

The suppression of art and popular music styles in Fascist and Communist dictatorships demonstrates that no mass medium is devoid of political aspects;

even so, there are obvious distinctions to be drawn between media in which an important component of content is represented by information with a high political charge and media whose contents are produced and assembled primarily for their diversionary or entertainment appeal.

The conservative, pro-Republican orientation of most American newspapers is widely taken for granted. A study of 17 Michigan dailies and 9 weeklies conducted before the 1966 election revealed that although 23 of the 26 papers denied that they were editorially aligned with either party, 20 endorsed the Republican candidate for governor and 18 the Republican candidates for the Senate. Most papers attempted to be nonpartisan in their news columns, but in nearly every case the Republican candidate got the headlines (Bishop and Brown, 1968).

Although the box scores of editorial presidential preferences are toted up every four years, there has been no comparable compilation of the positions taken by newspapers (or for that matter, by radio and television stations) on the innumerable local issues not ordinarily linked to national partisanship. Wilde's (1969) study of news decisions made at the *Chicago Sun Times* concludes that "investigations of slum landlords, tax assessors, and machine politics" are avoided because it is contrary to the interests of "capitalist control." Can this gloomy conclusion withstand sharp scrutiny? Hvistendahl (1970) questioned 43 Iowa weekly editors. Contrary to his original supposition, those who seemed closer to the "local power structure" behaved more aggressively than others in their investigation of news sources. This is a crucial subject for more research, and the answers are apt to be complex. Fedler (1973), in a study of Minneapolis media, found that aggressive minorities received more attention than comparable "established" groups.

Media differ in their forcefulness or pusillanimity of editorial expression on matters that affect the political and economic powers-that-be in their constituencies. What factors—organizational, financial, and psychological— enhance or suppress the willingness to take a forceful stand, and a forceful stand on behalf of an unpopular cause? Wolf (1971) studied public affairs programming on commercial television stations in the fifty largest United States markets from 1966 to 1968. He found that network-affiliated stations were more likely to editorialize and did so on more controversial topics than the unaffiliated. There was considerable diversity in the rate of rejection of network programs (typically partisan documentaries) by individual affiliates. Group-owned stations were no more likely to editorialize than single-ownership stations, but they appeared to devote less air time to public affairs and news programs.

In this connection, it would be instructive to study the actions taken by media companies whose financial interests are threatened by the proposal before the F.C.C. to prohibit multiple-ownership of newspapers and broadcasting stations in the same market. What kinds of studies, deliberations, negotiations, and lobbying occurred in response to this proposal? How did these responses change after it appeared that the proposal was unlikely to be implemented? What would be the probable consequences if this were again to become a lively issue?

A different area of inquiry relates to the suppression of news at government request or in deference to the public interest. The *New York Times'* voluntary censorship of its correspondents' reports on the impending Bay of Pigs invasion is the classic example. Local news media have cooperated with government authorities at times of crisis in order to avoid exacerbating public emotions by revealing the extent of disorder. What do such voluntary news blackouts imply for the traditional function of the press to publish objective reports of what is happening without regard to the social consequences? At what level does such gatekeeping occur, and under what circumstances is there a break in the common front? What are the divisions of opinion and practice among newsmen and media managers with regard to this problem?

Paletz and Dunn (1969) suggest that voluntary blackouts reflect the alliance of the press with "the wielders of community power." They examined the news coverage of Winston-Salem newspapers at a time of racial disorders in 1967 and concluded that news was deliberately handled in such a way as to curb violence and calm the community. A more complex, though not contradictory report, emerges from Flanery's (1971) study of coverage by the four local newspapers of the Chicago civil disorders of April and August, 1968. From interviews with over 200 newsmen, he concluded that all four papers consistently played up violence by demonstrators and rioters but interpreted police violence as normal and necessary and therefore underplayed it. When police violence was reported, rewrite men in a number of instances rejected it as undocumented, exaggerated, or not newsworthy.

Yet another aspect of media-government relations is involved in the regulation (and self-regulation) of content that is offensive to the sensibilities of the majority, or a significant minority, of the public. In recent years, there have been dramatic shifts in media standards with respect to sex and obscenity. In the book publishing and film industries, these changes have been linked to the issue of freedom of speech and thus given political overtones. For example, at a recent meeting between newspaper executives and officials of the motion picture industry, the latter pleaded for a relaxation of restrictions on advertising X-rated films on the grounds that this represented an abridgment of the First Amendment.

The 1973 Supreme Court decision permitting local rulings on pornography opened up a new set of questions: How do the film and book industries cope with this changed situation—by appealing the ruling, by waging a fight on local fronts within the framework of the ruling, by changing their output?

THE STRUCTURE OF MEDIA ORGANIZATIONS

What is the nature and structure of the institutional web that ties together diverse and often competing organizations in a large and fragmented media industry? To answer this question requires study of the functions and internal politics of trade and professional associations and their conventions and meetings; the trade and technological press, university departments of communication, broadcasting, and journalism; and brokers and suppliers (of equipment, newsprint, and services) who purvey information and often act as go-betweens. The role of newspaper syndicates, film producers, and program "packagers" also deserves study. How do these suppliers develop and promote their output? Under what conditions can they be innovative, rather than followers, of established formulas?

What are the objective characteristics of media organizations that are rated high or low in quality of performance? For example, what differences exist between comparable media organizations that are characterized by high and low rates of factual or typographical error? How are errors corrected, both for public consumption and in terms of internal critiquing and discipline? What review or adjudication procedures are used to cope with grievances, criticisms, and suggestions from the staff or the public?

Power is distributed so widely in large media organizations that it is very difficult to draw a line beyond which the exercise of managerial prerogatives begins. It is also hard to distinguish between the exercise of ownership rights and other forms of control. And media organization may have separate components and staffs that operate autonomously in their editorial policies (like the morning and evening newspapers in Minneapolis and Richmond), yet corporate owners, explicitly or tacitly, may set limits on the independence of these individual managements.

In enterprises with interests in competing media, what managerial strategies and structures are used to maintain common organizational objectives and yet retain a sense of staff dedication to the separate and irreconcilably competitive objectives of each component? Organizations restricted to a single medium often differ in the quality and morale of employees and managers, and in the autonomy they provide those responsible for content. What accounts for such differences? It should be possible to characterize differences in managerial philosophy and style between media owned by public corporations and those that are family owned or dominated.

Swayne (1969) examined changes in the ownership of 437 metropolitan newspapers between 1950 and 1967. By 1967, three-fourths of the papers were owned by families, but there were 49 fewer than in 1950. Group ownership accounted for 62.4 per cent of circulation in 1967, compared with 39.9 per cent in 1950. My own analysis of the 251 dailies with circulations over 50,000 in 1973 shows that 184, with 73 per cent of the aggregate circulation, are still under private ownership. Moreover, 42 of the 67 papers owned by public corporations, with over two-thirds of the circulation, are still managed or effectively controlled by members of the original owning family. But of the newspapers that are privately owned, about a fifth of the circulation is represented by papers that are run by a professional management. The implications of this transition affect broadcasting as well, since a substantial proportion of the radio and television stations in major and middle-sized markets are newspaper-affiliated.

Thus, in large media enterprises, professional management increasingly replaces the owner managements of the past. The values, goals, motivations, tastes, and political instincts of these professional managements undoubtedly differ from those of their owner predecessors. (Such largely staff-owned newspapers as the *Milwaukee Journal* and the *Kansas City Star* should be studied to see whether and how their managerial styles or operational procedures differ from those of similar newspapers.) It can be argued that each medium has its own distinctive economic base, production technique, and mix of content, which produce a characteristic set of management objectives and values. Does this override the question of whether or not management is combined with ownership?

THE DEATH AND BIRTH OF MEDIA

Failing media are often kept going by their owners long after their survival has become totally indefensible in business terms. Apart from their financial resources, what kinds of men are susceptible to sentiment, ideology, or a sense of historical mission? And what kinds of situations produce managements with cash-register minds, immune to such emotions?

The most revealing description of media failure is to be found in the memoirs of those who helped to inter the *Saturday Evening Post* and in White's (1961) fictional account of the death of *Collier's*. Such reports, valuable as they are, must be taken not as history but as documentation for historians to evaluate and interpret. It would be invaluable, and not at all impossible, to review with John Veronis and Nicholas Charney the story of their triumphant promotion of *Psychology Today* and their fiasco with the *Saturday Review*; or to set similar post-mortems from film and television producers who have had both failures and successes with the identical script and production formulas. "Underground" newspapers' meteorically brief life-cycles also deserve some attention.

Fresh autopsies of deceased media are apt to be written from a strongly personal vantage point, and rarely express the opinions of those who were faced with the crucial (and unsuccessful) decisions. An exception may be found in the self-justifying reminiscences of Matthew Culligan (1970) and Martin Ackerman (1970) regarding their experiences at Curtis Publishing. A reporter's harsh account of the events that led to the closing of the *Newark News* (Reeves, 1972) contrasts vividly with the former publisher's impassioned rejoinder (in a letter to the *Columbia Journalism Review*, March-April, 1973), which exhibits the kind of inside knowledge that would only have been revealed in a gesture of self-defense. Studies of the deaths of important media are not merely of academic interest; they reveal something about the operations of media that are alive and apparently healthy, and they presumably can teach lessons that may avert repetitions of the experience. To get the most comprehensive and objective view of such an episode (if done after the fact rather than through participant observation) would require extended interviews with all the parties involved—including management, employees, union leaders, advertisers, and readers. Since these individuals disperse quickly, the time to conduct such research is immediately after the event. The same applies to studies of critical labor negotiations and disputes.

Just as the anatomy of media failure is worthy of research, so are the secrets of media success. The decision to launch an enterprise is no less instructive than the decision to kill it. Yet I have not encountered any research by social scientists on how a media organization is built from an original idea into a going enterprise, even though there is much relevant information in biographies of media tycoons and in corporate histories. There are also useful journalistic accounts of the origins of such successful magazines as *New York*, *Sports Illustrated*, and *Psychology Today*. These should be supplemented by more systematic study. For example, it would be invaluable to conduct a continuing study of the steps underway at this writing to establish a new metropolitan afternoon paper in New York and a new UHF television station on Long Island. This is an atypical research opportunity, but in magazines and in broadcasting, new media enterprises are constantly being announced in the trade press. A study has been made to determine the characteristics of weekly papers that successfully change to daily publication (Stone, 1972). This should be supplemented by empirical research to determine how the decision was made and what actions were taken to implement it.

What differences, if any, are there in the initiating processes for new media that have essentially money-making objectives and others started for ideological or noneconomic reasons? (In recent years, a number of newspapers have been launched because of political disagreement with an established monopoly, for example, in Phoenix, Minneapolis, and Atlanta. They might have been more successful if they had been founded strictly as profit-making ventures, rather than as political voices.)

In more general terms, there is need for study of how investment decisions are arrived at—both within established media organizations and in their dealings with the financial community. What determines whether profits are reinvested in an established media business; invested in related, comparable, or some other media; or invested in totally different enterprises?

MANAGING TECHNOLOGICAL CHANGE

How does technological change alter the format or content of media? New technology makes possible the decentralized production of newspapers, which in turn makes it easier to publish zonal editions shaped to meet the changing requirements of retail advertisers and rounded out with local news and feature material. How is the decision made to go this route? Who presses for change? Who resists it?

Similar questions might be asked about zonal editions of magazines or editions delivered to specified lists of subscribers. These innovations are made possible by computer technology, which permits zip code districts to be classified into demographic groupings, presumably corresponding to advertiser interests. To what extent does new technology impose its own logic upon an existing production system, and to what extent is the technology merely summoned forth to meed media managements' changed perception of advertiser or reader demands?

The special engineering problems that have beset UHF television from the very start have made entrepreneurship in this business much more risky than it is for the largely profitable VHF stations. What has prompted continuing ventures in UHF? How have entrepreneurs establishing new UHF stations sought to learn from the lessons of their predecessors?

The evolution of photocomposition and offset printing has facilitated the emergence of low-budget publications that appeal to sectional or minority tastes. It has aided the rise of the radical or "underground" press. It has also stimulated the establishment of local community newspapers. The neighborhood press has long been part of the urban scene. (Its socially cohesive function has been studied by Janowitz [1952]). In new suburban areas, free offset "penny savers" or "shoppers" have also appeared on the scene in large numbers. Their nonexistent or minimal editorial budgets make it possible for them to strongly undercut the advertising rates of the conventional established press, thereby posing an economic threat. However, these same papers have sometimes shifted from a free to a paid circulation base, at the same time increasing their editorial content and becoming indistinguishable from other weeklies. It would be instructive to examine instances of such transformation, as well as the competitive responses of the existing media.

The evolution of new media such as cable TV presents good opportunities for policy research. What kinds of individual entrepreneurs and established businesses ventured into these businesses, and at what stages? What changes have occurred in the competitive position of small, local entrepreneurs and large cable operating systems? Subjects for study include: the scramble for franchises; the dealings of cable operators with local government bodies, leading to a criminal conviction in one instance; the solicitation of subscribers; the opening-up of channels to public access; and the development of independent local programming. These issues should be examined both for specific cases on the local level and for their larger implications on the national scale for this major new form in communication.

Journalistic accounts and economic analyses have provided a rather complete picture of the transformation of book publishing in the post-war period. New technology—computerized typesetting, photocopying, and microfilm retrieval systems—has changed the economics of publishing and is expected to have even greater implications in the future. The huge growth of school and college enrollment and of the national educational investment has multiplied the size of the text book market. With the rise of paperbacks has come an expansion of book distribution channels. Publishing houses have gone through a process of merging with or being acquired by large conglomerate corporations. The latter development, as is well known, has significantly altered the author-publisher relationship and may have had consequences in the content and character of what is published. But I know of no study that has tackled the organization and marketing of the book publishing industry in sociological terms.

How did the motion picture industry make the transition from conventional 35 millimeter black and white cinematography to wide-screen color, to combat television's inroads into its audience? What did this involve in terms of production techniques and budgets, theater construction, story selection and casting?

The motion picture industry's increased dependence upon the television networks has produced tremendous changes in its ownership and organization.

The separation of the studios from the theaters by government anti-trust action in 1950 has transformed the power structure of the industry. It has led to the absorption of the studios by industrial conglomerates and has subordinated the entertainment aspects of theaters to their real-estate interests. The processes of change in the management of the film industry are still sufficiently recent to warrant first-hand sociological study. The divestiture of studios from theaters is a good illustration of how the policies and plans of media organizations may be drastically affected by government actions that cannot necessarily be anticipated.

Entrepreneurial decisions in the media may be dependent to a substantial degree upon prior investment decisions made by manufacturing firms. David Sarnoff of RCA made an enormous financial commitment to the manufacture and promotion of color television on the assumption that there would be a large long-term benefit for his company if the market could be expanded by keeping prices down. Broadcasters then had to decide whether and when to invest in equipment and color production; they ultimately profited from the enhanced appeal of their medium to advertisers. NBC's ownership by RCA made this situation more complex than usual, but it still represents a good case history of adaptation to technological change.

SOME PRIORITY SUBJECTS FOR RESEARCH

Empirical research on the management of media will find stimulation, support, and analytical explication in a number of different bodies of social science theory: organization theory, the study of management, the sociology of occupations and professions, role and attitudinal congruity theory, theories of personality, conflict resolution, socialization, the study of elites and of community power structure, pricing theory, etc. However, only occasional studies (Tunstall, 1971) consciously organize data in terms of a theoretical superstructure.

It is to be expected that social, economic, and psychological theory will continue to pose some important problems for research on media management. But now and in the immediate future, specific subjects for empirical research are more likely to arise from important and unresolved policy issues in the media. Several illustrations may be given. In each instance, media management faces interesting dilemmas, decisions, or strategic planning problems.

1. How will print media, faced with strong rate competition from broadcasting, manage to shift a larger share of the burden of economic support from advertisers to readers?

2. How can print media seek government subsidy—in the form of postal rates that do not reflect the actual expenses they create for the Postal Service—and at the same time retain total freedom from government intervention?

3. To avoid external censorship, what self-imposed limitations should media accept on their subject matter, language, or imagery, without aborting their own freedom of expression?

4. What will happen to media organizations if they are forbidden to own newspapers and broadcasting stations within the same market? If the divestiture of such properties is ordered by the F.C.C. (as has been proposed), how should the exchange or transfer of ownerships be arranged?

5. How can public broadcasting operations be maintained free of interference from the federal bureaucracy or local politicians? How can the autonomy of local station managements be preserved while maintaining the high level of creative input that is only possible with the resources of a national system?

6. How can the transition from wireless to cable television be made in an orderly way, with minimum exploitation of the public, with maximum choice of programming for the viewer, and maximum access by those who wish to communicate? What new institutions will have to be developed if diffusion systems become a public utility separated from the production of programming? How will these change further as cable TV phases into a more comprehensive home communications system with a feedback mechanism?

These questions merely illustrate the types of practical problems for which the study of media managements can provide guidance.

HINTS FOR THE MEDIA MANAGEMENT RESEARCHER

In the United States, much of the existing research on media audiences, content, and effects has been supported, directly or indirectly, by the media themselves, as a byproduct of their competitive commercial interests. By contrast, research on media management, structure, organization, staffing, and operations must largely look to independent sources of financial assistance. Fortunately, this type of research rarely requires the kind of massive and costly data collection necessary for audience research; it can sometimes be done best by a lone investigator, who immerses himself in the ongoing activities of a media organization, wins the confidence of its personnel, and unobtrusively establishes himself as part of the scenery over a period of time during which he can carry out observation and informal interviewing. Foundation encouragement of research in this area should therefore emphasize independent scholarship rather than survey projects conducted by large task forces.

The most productive research program would concentrate on individual case histories of specific media organizations, rather than on the search for generalizations through comprehensive surveys of *all* media. Yet it *is* possible to think in terms of an over-all media system. The total effects of mass communication are impossible to dissect by source. Moreover, there is an intermeshing of ownership interests and information resources among media. Most important, there is considerable mobility on the part of talented individuals who move from one mass media institution to another, creating: a common vocabulary; an interdependence of salary scales; a common set of interests, fads, and preoccupations; and a sense of participating in the creation of the common culture. (This very process is itself worth studying.)

Mass media in the United States include a vast and heterogeneous array of institutions. But because their audiences are highly concentrated, a meaningful analysis of media organizations must begin with those comparatively few that account for a high proportion of the public's total exposure. The study of a "typical" newspaper, magazine, or broadcasting station leads to less interesting generalizations than an equivalent study of a newspaper like the *New York Times* or the *Washington Post*, a mass magazine like *Reader's Digest*, or a television network, none of which is in any sense representative of its medium.

The people who run such major media organizations are super-elites, notoriously difficult for social scientists to study first-hand. They tend to be exceptionally able and intelligent people who have a strong sense of privacy. They are adept at dissembling, being keenly aware of any disparity between their personal beliefs and the consequences of actions taken on the job. The researcher is intrigued by organizational stresses and conflicts that reflect struggles for power and ambiguities of role on the part of individuals torn between material interests and nonmaterial values. But such conflicts often elude research because they are perceived by the participants—and by the trade press and the general web of gossip—as personality clashes rather than as expressions of larger, impersonal social forces. The right to personal privacy is apt to be invoked against the intrusion of an outside observer, even on institutional matters in which the individual does not count.

Although top executives of media organizations are apt to be reluctant to speak out candidly on the delicate personnel and financial matters they must handle on their jobs, this is less likely to be true of men who have recently retired or moved elsewhere. They may be more accessible to interviewers and also more willing to produce inside knowledge on the handling of critical situations.

It is difficult to conduct a true participant observation study of a medium's failure, since anyone in a real position to be fully informed is apt to be too deeply involved to maintain his detachment. For the same reasons, it is difficult to be a good participant observer of a medium's conception, gestation, and birth. Also, those responsible for running an organization are normally loathe to reveal confidences after their efforts have failed; they are often just as reluctant to tip their hand to the competition if they have been successful. But it is precisely at times of crisis and while memories are fresh that the most valuable information can be gathered.

Rewarding opportunities for research are revealed in instances of public dispute or criticism involving media operations. They generally occur when there is a conflict of principle among members of the organization or when the management departs from accepted norms or standards of practice.

This study of media management has reviewed the literature and presented conclusions and suggestions from a strictly American perspective. It goes without saying that it is highly desirable to conduct parallel research on mass media management in other countries that have contrasting systems of media ownership and structure.

9

IMPLICATIONS OF NEW
INFORMATION TECHNOLOGY
Edwin B. Parker

This chapter will not attempt to describe the trends taking place in information technology or the social and policy implications of those trends. Those tasks have been attempted elsewhere (Parker, 1973a, 1973c; Parker and Dunn, 1972). The focus here is new directions in communication research that seem important to pursue because of those trends. The discussion is organized into four sections: social history, policy research, techniques research, and economics of information.

The topic is approached from a general system theory perspective in which the universe can be dichotomized into matter-energy on the one hand and information on the other (Miller, 1965). Matter and energy hardly need definition; the concept of conversion of matter into energy (burning coal or gasoline to obtain heat or motion; creating nuclear reactions on the basis of Einstein's famous $E = MC^2$ equation) is also familiar. Information is defined as pattern or organization of matter and/or energy. The transmission of information requires energy, whether it be sound waves produced by the human voice, electromagentic energy required to broadcast television, or mechanical energy required to transport a book or newspaper from one place to another. The storage of information requires matter or energy: the message may be stored on paper, on microfilm, or in human brain cells. Duplication of information requires putting a similar pattern on many "markers," for example, printing multiple copies of a magazine or newspaper. Since information is pattern or organization, there must be some minimal amount of matter or energy (the marker) on which the information is stored or transmitted. The marker may be large or small, requiring differing amounts of matter or energy, without changing the information it carries (microfilm, for example, requires less matter than printed paper for the same information content). Information technology, then, is the matter-energy arrangements for storing, transmitting, duplicating, or processing information.

Information technology is distinguished from technique in the sense used by Jacques Ellul (1964). Technique is the knowledge of how to produce a desired effect, whether through manipulation of matter-energy or through manipulation of information itself (as in propaganda messages). Technique is thus information, rather than matter-energy, even though it may manifest itself in the manipulation of matter and energy. Nevertheless, one of the implications of changes in information technology is that new techniques must be learned to utilize it. Use of printing technology requires literacy; effective use of computers for information processing may require computer programming skills (computer literacy).

McLuhan (1964), with his slogan, "The medium is the message," reminds us that major social consequences follow from changes in the matter-energy arrangements for storing or transmitting information, partly because changes in the technology lead to different messages being sent and to changes in who can send and receive them. With the introduction of a new medium for storage of information, such as printing, the pattern of use of a previous medium, for example, the human brain, shifts somewhat. We depend more on external lists and notes to ourselves than on our own memories, and we depend more on printed history and news than on the memories of old men and travelling ballad singers (McLuhan, 1962).

The focus here is new or changing information technology. This is consistent with the social science research strategy of deviant case analysis or examining variance. In stable situations, the relevant variables are confounded; it is when things begin to change that we often get an insight into the function and significance of previously stable components. Changes in information technology can be examined either as a dependent variable of social science interest (what are the causal factors in our culture leading to changes in information technology?) or as an independent variable (what social effects follow from changes in information technology?).

From the perspective of the larger society, examining the major social impacts or trends that follow from changes in information technology is most significant, although we ought not focus too narrowly on the media of traditional interest to mass communication research. Print and broadcast media are undergoing technological change, but the major social impact of changes in information technology is likely to follow from changes in computer information-processing or office copying machines.

The greatest social impact is likely to follow from the media undergoing the greatest change. The key change that influences how widely new information technology diffuses through the society seems to be the reduction of the amount of matter-energy required to transmit or store information. Major reductions in the unit cost of the matter-energy component of information storage and transmission can lead to wide diffusion and major social impact. The computer information utility* is still some years away, but the unit costs of computer information processing are dropping faster than costs of conven-

---

*An "information utility" may be conceived of as a communication system that enables a member of a mass audience to interact directly with a central computer. The system may also include such elements as television displays, other communication lines, and data storage devices.

tional media and hence deserve careful examination (Sackman and Boehm, 1972).

SOCIAL HISTORY OF COMMUNICATION

Major changes in the information technology utilized by any society amount to a significant change in its culture. The diffusion of television or computer information systems throughout a society is not a variable like those in communication experiments, such as manipulating order of presentation in a propaganda message. Changes in information technology permeate the whole society. Rarely does the pattern of diffusion permit a definitive experimental analysis in the tradition of tightly controlled experiments. The diffusion of television, office copying machines, and computers, to cite just three examples, are cultural events that are difficult to replicate within a single culture. The diffusion happens only once and the early adopters are systematically different from late adopters in significant respects. Differences between users and non-users of the technology are more likely to be the result of initial differences leading to different times of adoption than effects attributable to the new technology. Direct comparison of different societies at different levels of technological development does not provide a completely satisfactory measure of effects because it was major initial differences in culture that led to the development and introduction of new information technology in one culture before others.

The phenomena of interest are in many ways more suited to historical research techniques than to techniques of experimental psychology. The kind of historical scholarship that is most needed is more difficult than developing chronologies of the introduction and diffusion of technology, more difficult than analyzing the information content stored in or transmitted by the information technology at different periods, and more difficult than writing biographies of key people involved with the technologies. What is needed is historical scholarship that attempts to interpret the general social history of the culture as it is influenced by changes in information technology. This will require a good deal of sifting of evidence and careful logical analysis to develop reasonable tests of alternative explanations for the social changes taking place.

One excellent example of such a study is Eisenstein's (1969) analysis of the "problem of the Renaissance." The historical problem puzzling Eisenstein was why one particular medieval revival of learning began a social chain reaction that we now describe as the Renaissance, while earlier medieval revivals were similar in many respects but seemed to sustain their revivals for shorter periods and only at the expense of lowering the level of learning or scholarship in other subjects or geographical areas. That particular revival, the Renaissance, began a cumulative process of growth of knowledge that is still continuing. In Eisenstein's instructive analysis, printing technology facilitated the process by reducing the unit cost of storing and transmitting information.

Studies· of the social history of communication in earlier periods should serve to set present and continuing changes in information technology in better historical perspective. We may underestimate the magnitude of the social changes that have been taking place in the last half of the twentieth century if we only observe change on a year-to-year basis. We seem to be in the midst of a revolution in information technology that, in the space of less than half a century, may result in greater change than that attributed to the invention of printing technology. Harold Innis, the Canadian economic historian, in *The Bias of Communication* (1951) and *Empire and Communication* (1950), made an excellent start in the direction of providing solid economic and social histories of cultural change as influenced by information technology. His works were a major factor in stimulating the creative thinking of McLuhan; unfortunately, they did not lead to a generation of scholars continuing the tradition of economic and social history that he began.

The social history of information technology is likely to be enriched by the introduction of explicit theorizing and quantitative analysis in addition to the traditional tools of historiography. An excellent example is a recent paper by N. Katzman (1973) in which he examined implications of new information technology for widening or narrowing the gap between the information-rich and the information-poor. He cites several historical examples indicating that the long-range effect of each new change in information technology, once it is fully diffused through a culture, may be a levelling one. When everyone has access to television, for example, the gap between the information-rich and the information-poor may perhaps be less than before the introduction of the new technology. But during the period of diffusion of information technology, the gap between the advantaged and disadvantaged always widens.

Katzman cites literacy data from nineteenth-century Italy as one of his examples indicating that during the period of diffusion, male literacy rates grew much faster than female literacy rates, widening the advantage men had over women. He reanalyzes data on children's learning from "Sesame Street," demonstrating that some programs intended to benefit the disadvantaged may permit even greater gains by the initially advantaged and unintentionally widen the cultural gap, even while increasing the absolute level of the initially disadvantaged.

His analysis makes it clear that while each innovation in information technology may provide a levelling or democratizing influence when fully diffused, the constant historical progression of one new technology after another may always leave the disadvantaged farther behind. This reasoning—that the poor have access to the old media while the rich have the new—is the basis of some radical opposition to the development of cable television (Strasser, 1971). Katzman has provided careful scholarship bringing the historical evidence to bear on that assumption.

Examples of first-rate social history of communication are all too few. This is an area of scholarship through which our understanding of the role of information technology in society could be greatly enriched if more excellent scholars were attracted and supported to engage in historical research.

POLICY RESEARCH

The motivating questions behind much communication research are often normative. In addition to the scientific motives of creating knowledge or better understanding for its own sake, there are strong motives to understand the effects of information technology (and information content) on society for public policy purposes. For example, studies of the effects of television on children (Schramm, Lyle, and Parker, 1961; Surgeon General's Scientific Advisory Committee, 1972) were undertaken with either implicit or explicit consideration of the public policy potential of research results. The key questions are not just those concerning effects; they concern what public policy should be if different effects are desired.

Concern with the social effects of new technology has generally led to an increase in the research activities now called technology assessment. The assessment of information technology may be particularly significant because of the potentially far-reaching effects of changes in access to information on redistribution of political and economic power. Conceptualizing the problem as one of technology assessment may reduce the chances of conducting research that can be effective for policy purposes (Parker, 1973d). The problem is the wide discrepancy in political and economic power between technology developers and technology assessors. The real issue may not be the technology itself, but rather the institutions that capture or grow up around the new technology. Questions of institutional control of information technology should be added to the questions of assessment of technology qua technology if key policy questions are to be answered. The institutional structure controlling the technology will largely determine which segments of society benefit from (or are harmed by) the technology.

The sooner we study each new information technology, the greater the chance of being able to use the research results to influence policy in a meaningful way. Studies of the effects of television broadcasting on children, conducted in the late 1950s and 1960s, had little chance of influencing the nature of television and its effects on children because the institutional and economic structure of broadcasting had been set in place more than three decades earlier.

United States policy on domestic communication satellites is now set in place and is unlikely to change in the near future, despite the fact that the first such satellite has yet to be launched. By contrast, policy questions concerning the role of cable television are largely answered, even though cable construction in major cities is only just beginning. Cable policy questions are more open to renegotiation than satellite policy questions because of the number of unresolved questions, but not nearly as open as they were prior to the issuance of the Federal Communications Commission's new cable rules in 1972.

Policies on computer communications networks that will play a major role in society in the 1980s are still open to influence, but few communication researchers are examining questions of the potential social impact of alternative policies. One of the barriers to such research is that it is often necessary to have a considerable understanding of the technology and its economics before meaningful hypotheses about potential social effects can be formulated, let alone tested. Few social scientists concerned with social effects of communication have the necessary background in technology and economics.

One implication is that we need more interdisciplinary research—not only research in which behavioral scientists collaborate with economists and engineers but also the sort in which technical, economic, and behavioral research skills are combined in one researcher so that creative syntheses are more likely to emerge. Even untested speculation about potential social effects may be useful in guiding policy and future research if it is based on knowledge of the technology and other similar social effects (Parker, 1973b).

An important question to be faced in policy research concerns who is the client for the research. It may not be possible to draw a sharp dividing line between policy research and policy advocacy because social value questions are very much involved in the choice of policy problems studied and policy alternatives examined. So-called impartial or value-free research conducted for one particular client, such as the Department of Defense or a large corporation, is likely to serve the interests of the client, if only through the choice of questions studied. If the whole framework of policy research and analysis assumes a centralized authority that can implement policy recommendations, then the whole research effort is biased in the direction of central control, rather than decentralized or distributed decision-making power, and thus may beg the key policy question to be faced as new information technology is introduced into society.

If the policy researcher declines to use the knowledge gathered in policy research, he may be merely giving up the field to stronger political forces, thereby indicating that his motives were really directed to basic knowledge questions rather than to social policy. Or his neutral stance may allow his results to be used by others for purposes he may not approve. Or it may be merely a policy advocacy gambit, an attempt to garner greater support for the value-assumptions hidden in the choice of research problem through claims of scientific neutrality.

To be socially useful, policy researchers may have to engage actively in policy advocacy. Explicit statement of value premises may be a more intellectually honest way to approach policy research than avoidance of value questions. It may be necessary to spend as much time explicitly analyzing value positions as ensuring that the impartiality of the empirical research cannot be faulted by people with differing value positions.

One kind of communication policy research that is needed is sociological and economic analysis of the major institutional forces shaping the new information technology. Studies of IBM, RCA, Bell Telephone, and Teleprompter, for example, may lead to more useful evidence on future trends of information technology and their social impact than studies of the technologies they utilize. Studies of how these corporate forces in fact influence the structure of society may be more effective than studies that try to determine which policy would be most beneficial for society if only there were some benevolent force sufficiently powerful to implement it.

The key policy question that must be faced in the course of developing new information technology concerns the centralization or decentralization of control. Since the publication of George Orwell's *Nineteen Eighty-Four* (1949), we have been alerted to the dangers of a centrally controlled communication system. As the innovations in information technology proceed in the direction of making that kind of information control technically and economically possible, we need to guard against the possibility of drifting toward such control in the name of economy and efficiency. The result is anathema to the democratic and decentralized political power premises on which our society is built. Centralized computer data banks and monopoly control over cable television channels are not peripheral to the functioning of society; they go to the heart of our political assumptions (Sackman and Nie, 1970).

TECHNIQUES RESEARCH

Much of communication research has been concerned with questions of how to use existing information technology effectively. Studies of propaganda and persuasion have focused on the most effective way to use face-to-face, print-mediated, or broadcast-mediated communication to bring about changes in audience attitude; experimentation with instructional television (or other instructional media) has studied how to most effectively utilize existing media to meet instructional goals; and studies of communication and national development have been concerned with how to utilize existing media for nation-building and economic growth.

As new information technologies become available, a whole new program of research is required to learn techniques for their effective utilization. By the 1980s, the combination of broadband cable television channels and computer information retrieval systems may make it technically and economically possible to have on-demand access to any local, state, or federal public documents. There will still be gatekeepers—newsmen and editors—to select and interpret information, but it may also be feasible for individuals to indicate to the computer the gatekeeping specifications or selection criteria for things to be brought to their attention. And individuals may be able to browse more directly through public documents. Research on computer information retrieval techniques is needed in the 1970s to make that application of information technology more likely in the 1980s.

Technology will make possible many kinds of man-machine interactions for storage, transmission, manipulation, and retrieval of information. Engineers and computer scientists alone will not be able to develop the kind of information systems that will be satisfying to large numbers of users. Behavioral science knowledge of human information processing and use of communication media, plus behavioral science research skills, will be needed to develop computer systems responsive to user needs (Parker, 1970a; Parker and Paisley, 1966).

The instructional potential of cable television will be considerable, especially if the two-way cable transmission capability required by the Federal

Communications Commission is in fact installed in major cities. Digital response televised instruction will be possible, with thousands of students seeing the same television presentation while making their responses on a digital response pad, much like a touch-tone telephone or a typewriter keyboard. Instead of exclusively one-way instruction, students can be asked to actively practice appropriate responses or to respond to multiple choice questions. Aggregate responses can be made available to instructors in real time, for optimal modification of the presentation. Individual responses can be retained for input to a computer-managed instruction system based on mailing supplementary material (remedial or enrichment) tailored to the particular level of knowledge of each student. Through such a system, educational opportunity can be economically provided for everyone regardless of age, sex, number of young children, etc. It can be likened to making "Sesame Street" a two-way street in which children respond to teaching about letters and numbers by hitting the appropriate button on their home device, acquiring active practice as well as passive viewing. Television itself was available as a communication medium for some time before we learned to use it as effectively for instruction as the producers of "Sesame Street." Much research and development will be needed to effectively use the radically different media that computer-information systems and two-way cable television make possible.

Technology changes are lowering the costs of the electronic and computer media. Half-inch videotape permits community groups to originate programming on cable television at reasonable costs (Kletter and Rucker, 1972). With "broadcast quality" two-inch videotape, such media use would be economically prohibitive. Community radio stations in remote Indian or Eskimo communities or in urban low-cost housing developments are becoming viable propositions. Small ethnic groups or interest groups can program their own radio channel on cable television more cheaply than by video-cablecasting.

Just as writing was once a skill reserved for a few scribes, but later became near-universal (in North America and Europe at least), so audio and video media may no longer be the exclusive province of professionals. The growing use of audio cassettes provides one example of this trend. Eventually, use of computers will not be the exclusive right of a particular priesthood of scribes (the computer programmers) but will be a general skill. Computer literacy and audio-video media literacy may become important skills for acquiring equal opportunity in the information-dependent society we are creating.

Much research remains to be done on the use of small or low-cost electronic media for community development in industrial societies and national development in Third-World countries. Use of media for personal development may be much more significant for community development than present uses of mass media, which require large capital investment and of necessity treat people as passive audiences rather than as active participants in a development process.

ECONOMICS OF INFORMATION

Recent and future changes in information technology consist of innovations that reduce the matter-energy costs of information. As a result of lowering unit costs of storing or processing information, the demand for and the supply of information products continues to increase. The elasticity of demand appears to be such that lowering costs increases the percentage of the gross national product (GNP) that goes into information activities.

Diebold (1973) argues that we are now beginning the third phase of the 200-year-old industrial revolution, which will be increasingly concerned with the production and distribution of information. He argues that the first century of the industrial revolution was dominated by Great Britain. By mismanagement and inertia Britain lost out to the United States in what he calls the second or "Henry Ford" stage of the industrial revolution. He suggests that Japan, or possibly Europe, may overtake the United States as a major economic power in the next century if the United States continues to keep its economic focus on production of goods instead of on production and distribution of information.

Machlup (1962) concluded that by 1958 production and distribution of information already accounted for 29 per cent of the GNP in the United States. He also concluded that the information segment of the economy was growing at the rate of approximately 10 per cent per year, approximately double that of the economy as a whole. Drucker argues: "Knowledge, during the last few decades, has become the central capital, the cost center, and the crucial resource of the economy" (1969, p. xi).

A recent Japanese "white paper" recommends a major, centrally planned development of what they call "the information society." It proposes a five-year national investment of 1,000 billion yen ($3.2 billion) to sustain an annual growth rate of GNP in excess of 10 per cent; by contrast, there would be a 7 per cent growth rate if they followed the United States-style laissez-faire policy of information investment (Japan Computer Usage Development Institute, 1972).

A recent Congressional Report, "American Productivity: Key to Economic Strength and National Survival" also recommends investment in an expanded communication infrastructure. That report says, "Although a skeleton national computer net exists . . . , expansion of such a net into a full-fledged computer utility . . . could bring vast productivity gains at low costs." (U.S. Congress, 1972, p. 6).

Concern about the role of information in economic growth is increasing at a time when some segments of society are beginning to question the economic growth ethic that has long permeated our society. The pressures for conservation of energy, recycling materials, zero-population growth, and a generally balanced ecology—still small but growing—may only appear to be directly counter to the strong economic growth ethic. Since it is matter and energy that must be conserved in a balanced ecology, economic growth based on an increasing percentage of information activities (as opposed to production and distribution of material goods) may be consistent with a balanced ecology. By reducing the matter-energy costs of information processing and increasingly substituting information for energy (by working more intelligently with new techniques rather than working harder with previously known techniques), it may be possible to reconcile economic growth and balanced ecology.

Also to be reckoned with is the continuing demand for more equitable distribution of the resources and opportunities of society. Efforts to help the economically and culturally disadvantaged, in particular to provide open access to post-secondary education, are likely to continue. Politically, it may be more difficult to redistribute wealth in a society that is not undergoing economic growth than in one that is. In the latter case, economic gaps could be closed by appropriate distribution of new wealth to the disadvantaged without taking (or taking as much) from the advantaged. Unfortunately, economic growth may lead instead to a widening of the gap between rich and poor. Even though the poor are better off, the rich may get even richer as a result of economic policies designed to create incentives for those with wealth to invest in areas of economic growth potential.

The concept of equal opportunity implies an equitable distribution of information. Even if the wealth of matter and energy remain unequally distributed, equal opportunity means that everyone in society has the information necessary to compete. If knowledge is the major factor in economic growth, then a society that allows every child and every adult to learn and to produce as much new knowledge as he is capable of should be wealthier—especially if wealth is measured in terms of quality of life, and not just in quantities of matter and energy. If every child has equal access to the information resources of the society, unequal distribution of wealth may still result from rewarding those who make the most of that opportunity. But the resulting unequal distribution need not perpetuate itself from one generation to another, creating dysfunctional social tensions.

These are complex issues of macroeconomics that lead to questioning some of the assumptions of economic theory. The economics of information is a difficult and insufficiently developed area within economics. When the bulk of our economy was based on agriculture and manufacturing, with information only a small component, it was reasonable to develop and utilize an economic theory that dealt primarily with the production and distribution of matter and energy, even though it created many anomolies in the economics of information. Now that production and distribution of information is both a very large and the fastest growing segment of the economy, a major program of research into the economics of information seems called for. Thus, economic research may be the most significant direction for communication research resulting from changes in information technology. And the changes in information technology may make the economics of information the most significant new direction for research in economics.

Many specific problem areas and questions within the economics of information have been discussed by Lamberton (1971). One important question is how to arrive at optimal social investment in the production of information—for example, expenditures on scientific research. Patent law, copyright law, and trade secret law all attempt to make information an appropriable commodity in the hope that, by so doing, sufficient private incentives will be created to lead to expenditures on the production of knowledge. But there is increasing dissatisfaction with these legal attempts to patch up an area in which free-enterprise competition clearly fails to create sufficient incentives (Goldstein, 1973). Government expenditures on science and technology are one response, but how can one calculate a level of expenditure that leads to optimal social return on the investment? Similarly, government expenditures on the distribution of knowledge—e.g., for education—are assumed necessary, even by free-enterprise economist Milton Friedman (1962), because too little would be expended on education otherwise. The optimal amounts of such investment constitute an interesting problem in the economics of information.

The amount of investment that is optimal and the kind that is likely to be most efficient are issues that need to be examined concurrently. For example, government funds used as a leverage to stimulate greater private investment might be more efficient use of government funds than direct government operation of information enterprises. To date, research and development activities have been geared mostly to productivity gains in the agricultural and manufacturing sectors of society. Now that the information sector of society is larger than the agricultural and manufacturing sectors combined (assuming Machlup's definitions of the information sector), government investment geared to productivity gains in the information sector might be more efficient, especially since that is a sector with serious private sector underinvestment.

Many of the problems in the economics of information stem from the fact that information is not like a commodity that only one person or group at a time can possess. Information can be shared with others, while the original possessor keeps it himself. In some cases, the original possessor may make the largest economic return if he keeps the information secret; in other cases, he will need to share it with many others to obtain an economic return. The optimal amount of distribution of information may differ vastly, depending on the perspective—whether of society as a whole or of an individual possessor. No longer is the problem one of a zero-sum game in which what one gains another loses. Instead, information leads to non-zero-sum games in which collective strategies may lead to a much higher total return on investment, but individual attempts to maximize return may reduce the total to be shared to much less than what is theoretically possible.* Current economic theory tends to assume competition rather than cooperation as the appropriate mode. That assumption may not be the best for information economics.

According to current economic theory, optimum investment is reached under conditions of perfect information for all decision-makers. But that begs the question of how much economic resources should be expended on obtaining the information. The statistics of decision-making under uncertainty may provide some guidelines for individual decision-makers but they do not solve the problem of an optimum for society. Spence (1972) has shown that there are many points of equilibrium with respect to information expenditure. The amount an individual needs to spend on information is a function of how much others are spending on information. We may have stable underinvestment

---

*In game theory terms, a zero-sum game is one in which the total amount of valued resources is fixed such that the sum of the gains and losses of all the players is zero. A non-zero-sum game is one in which the sum of the gains and losses can be different from zero. Hence each player's gain is not necessarily at the expense of other players.

(from the perspective of a social optimum) in which additional information expenditures seem unnecessary because others are not making that investment either. On the other hand, we may have serious escalation of information expenditures in which individuals need to spend more on information because their competitors do, even though the total expenditure is higher than would be socially optimum.

The lack of appropriate data for analysis makes it difficult to investigate these questions of economic theory. The national income statistics of the United States Department of Commerce are highly unsatisfactory for scholars attempting to work on the economics of information because the data are not aggregated to facilitate analysis of the information component of the economy. Much empirical work needs to be done with economic statistics concurrently with economic theorizing or the theorizing may prove sterile.

INTERDISCIPLINARY RESEARCH

Four general areas of significant and promising directions for communication research have been discussed. Most needed is interdisciplinary research, requiring combinations of talents different from those found within a single academic discipline. The kind of research needed in the social history of communication requires not just the best of current techniques in historiography, but also an understanding of communication technology and an ability to handle quantitative data analysis in a sophisticated way.

The areas of policy research that need investigation require not only the blending of skills from different disciplines (including engineering, economics, social psychology, and political science), but also the rethinking of the relationship between examining knowledge questions and value questions. Effective policy research may require as much attention to making the researcher's value assumptions explicit as it does to making the knowledge assumptions explicit. A blending of policy research and policy advocacy may be necessary for the former to be effective. Such a blending may not interfere with the impartiality and credibility of empirical research if the value questions are handled explicitly. In this way, the possibly more serious problem of implicit value assumptions being hidden in so-called objective policy research may be avoided.

The development of techniques for effective use of new communication media may constitute the area in which the most research is needed. This is an area in which the activities are more applied than basic research (closer to the development end of the research and development continuum). The traditional skills of behavioral science researchers may be most useful here, although to be effective they must be combined in interdisciplinary projects sometimes including engineers, economists, and computer scientists.

The economics of information may require the most research. It may also be the area least in need of interdisciplinary research. To a non-economist, the problems seem clearly to fall within the scope of the discipline of economics. Nevertheless, the problems may need to be posed for economists by those who have been more directly concerned with the social and political role of information in society. Since satisfactory resolution of these questions may require a significant shift in the current set of assumptions of economic theory—i.e., a shift of paradigm (Kuhn, 1962)—it may be necessary for scholars less socialized into the current discipline of economics to learn the necessary skills to tackle the problems without the same deeply ingrained commitment to previous economic assumptions.

10

SOME PRIORITY AREAS
FOR FUTURE RESEARCH
W. Phillips Davison
Frederick T. C. Yu

In this concluding chapter we shall try to do three things: outline some basic questions that we feel communication research should attack if it is to become a more coherent and more useful body of knowledge, highlight a number of research directions in individual sub-areas of the field, and make a few observations about ways in which communication research might become more fruitful scientifically and more valuable socially.

CENTRAL QUESTIONS FOR RESEARCH

The following five groups of priority questions for future research address problems that are mentioned in several of the foregoing chapters or that came up repeatedly during the Arden House discussions. Thus, they represent concerns that are fairly widely shared among communication researchers, although not necessarily granted priority status. The problems cut across the areas into which we have subdivided the field, but their solution will depend on advances within the individual areas. All of them bear on a single question: What kinds of knowledge are necessary if societies are to make rational decisions regarding the organization and operation of the mass media?

These five question complexes may be summarized as follows: What social and individual needs can the mass media help to satisfy? What is the preferred relationship, for each society, between mass communication and interpersonal channels? What types of media and content are best suited to what kinds of tasks? How can standards of mass media performance be defined? How can the media confer the greatest benefits at the lowest cost?

The first question might borrow its formulation from Jeremy Bentham: How can the mass media promote the greatest good for the greatest number? It can no more be answered definitively than could the questions of political philosophy with which Bentham struggled. Nevertheless, communication research can carry us toward increasingly apposite approximate solutions by specifying with more precision the needs of individuals and groups and the ways in which mass communication can help satisfy them. Since, however, the space available on any spectrum of the mass media is limited, and since human capacity for attention is limited (even though we may not know the limits in either case), the satisfaction of one need may entail slighting another. This means that researchers should move toward the difficult task of estimating the relative importance of the various functions served by the media for groups and individuals, and calculating the implications of using media space and time for one purpose rather than another.

It makes little sense to continue to call for more of everything that might be desirable: more coverage of international affairs, more attention to environmental issues, more access to the media for individuals and groups, more high-quality entertainment. Somehow a balance among these various categories of material must be achieved, and communication researchers may be able to help define the kind of balance most likely to serve specified individual and social values.

Two variables are involved in a calculus of this type—both of them difficult to measure: How important is the need, and how well does mass communication satisfy it? In addition, attention should be given to content that is either dysfunctional for any part of the audience or appears to serve no functions at all. Researchers will perform a useful service if they can identify kinds of content that can or should be eliminated. Media systems, also, may be dysfunctional for a given society, or for parts of it. As John Robinson (1972b, p. 83) has observed, the mass media "may have been responsible for creating even larger divisions of opinion in our society than would have been the case without the media." Tichenor, Donohue and Olien (1970) have noted that an increase in publicly available information may widen the "knowledge gap"—the difference in the level of information possessed by more educated and less educated groups.

The second group of priority questions concerns the interface between mass communication and person-to-person communication, and the extent to which one type of communication can be substituted for another. Are there tasks now taken care of by face-to-face communication that could be performed in whole or in part by mass communication? Or should certain functions now served by the mass media be returned to traditional channels? Translating these questions into everyday terms, one might ask: Can some of the purposes of school integration be served by linking various schools together on television, as well as by busing children or building larger schools? Would social and individual needs be better satisfied if some types of entertainment were supplied by neighborhood actors and musicians rather than by the mass media?

Ways in which person-to-person and mass communication channels supplement and reinforce each other should also be considered. Organizations such as the United States Information Agency have long grappled with the problem of how much emphasis to place on individual contacts and how much on providing information via the mass media. The debate has often been carried on in the context of the elite versus the mass audience, but it has become clear that the different channels can supplement each other even when the audience is held constant. A United States Information Agency official has predicted that "the growth of information available through advanced communications technology will increase rather than diminish the need for interaction between individuals and small groups" (Schneider, 1973). He recommends, for instance, televised transoceanic press conferences with two-way hookups that would enable journalists in the United States and other countries to participate. In educational settings it is clear that a classroom explanation will often make subsequent reading or viewing more meaningful to students; reading or viewing can also make subsequent classroom discussions more productive. Ways in which the various communication channels can be mutually supporting in other settings should be explored.

The third complex of questions also concerns decisions about the most useful mix of channels. What mass media and what types of content are most suited to what kinds of tasks? What division of labor should there be among the media? We know that people go to certain kinds of sources for certain types of information. For instance, it has been found that the print media tend to serve as sources for science and helath knowledge, while electronic channels are more likely to be used as sources for information about political campaigns (Wade and Schramm, 1969). Further investigation should tell us more about the strengths and weaknesses of individual channels.

There has been a tendency for some observers to regard the various mass media as competing with each other. This may be true with regard to the advertising dollar, where a loss for one medium may be a gain for another, but it does not seem a useful perspective for social scientists. The more important questions are: Which one does which type of job best? How can different channels supplement each other?

In considering the "media mix" that would be most appropriate for a given task, researchers should guard against the temptation to focus their attention on the "glamour" media. As Menzel (1971) has pointed out, there are channels that occupy a position somewhere between those usually thought of as "mass" and those considered person-to-person (for example, a corps of salesmen all delivering similar messages to large numbers of prospects). In addition, the specialized mass media and house organs may often be overlooked. Yet these less massive channels may, in the aggregate, reach more individuals or inform them more adequately than can mass magazines, radio, newspapers, or television.

If both needs and a division of labor between mass and person-to-person channels are specified, and if the correct mix of mass media and media content is established, there will still be a fourth complex of questions: How can standards of media performance be defined? How can they be achieved by the institutions that produce and disseminate communications? How can the performance of those institutions be monitored?

The first question, with regard to specification of standards, can be answered in terms of the degree to which a given medium is performing the role it plays best in the satisfaction of individual and social needs. The criterion for a good newspaper, or for a superior television schedule, can be established only to the extent that researchers have been able to deal with the first three complexes of questions mentioned here. And the answers will, of course, vary according to the system of values used.

The extent to which these standards can be achieved will depend upon the level of competence and artistry of media personnel and the range of resources—technological and otherwise—at their disposal. Researchers may be able to assist media performance through work on journalism education, news and entertainment infrastructure, and the utilization of technology.

How to monitor media performance and how corrective action might be taken when desirable are related questions on which media sociologists may be able to shed some light. It is perhaps unrealistic to expect communication researchers to work out a comprehensive accounting system to assess media performance—something similar to the systems we use for measuring economic achievement. Nevertheless, this is a direction in which researchers should work. We should be able to develop indicators that, at the least, will give the public a more accurate reading than is presently available on the state of the mass media at any given time.

The kinds of action that might be taken to raise mass communication standards when they fall below critical levels will depend on the values of each society. Under political systems that place a high value on freedom of the media from government interference, researchers might place emphasis on such subjects as methods of self-regulation, effects of competition, and ways in which audience members can bring pressure on institutions that disseminate information and entertainment.

Carey (1973) has suggested that media standards may be raised if there can be developed a "tradition of sustained, systematic, and intellectually sound criticism of the press." He is not talking about press councils, ombudsmen, and journalism reviews, although all these avenues should be explored. To him, democracy and the concept of criticism are inseparable. He sees as one goal of the press the cultivation of a critical community—a community that will examine both the idiom used by journalists to portray the world and the kind of world that this idiom brings into existence. He notes that we have no history of the way journalists have chosen to portray events during the past three hundred years; "in fact . . . we not only don't have it, we haven't even conceived it." How this tradition of criticism might be established, together with a historical foundation for it, is another important question for researchers.

A final complex of questions concerns cost. The subject of media economics came up repeatedly at the Arden House conference, and it became clear that researchers have given relatively little attention to it. How can the resources devoted to information and entertainment be allocated most rationally? How can the greatest benefits be achieved at the lowest cost? Do economic factors sometimes work at cross-purposes with the satisfaction of needs? It appears probable that *Look*, *Colliers*, *The Saturday Evening Post*, and some of the other mass magazines that have disappeared were serving a useful function so far as subscribers were concerned—and certainly so far as some journalists and fiction-writers were concerned. But they failed to attract enough advertising to enable them to survive. Does this suggest that new economic bases for mass media should be explored?

Not only money but also the allocation of personnel and skill is involved. According to news reports, at the launching of the second skylab in 1973 there were "only" eight hundred reporters present. Is this the best use of scarce journalistic manpower? What other assignments might have been given to a portion of the lonely eight hundred?

The subject of media economics is studded with fascinating anomalies. Business firms pay a stiff price for advertising space and time. Yet professional sports, more profitable than many of the businesses that advertise, receive free coverage, even though news about a new product may be more valuable to more people than information about the outcome of a money-making sporting event. Our political system is dependent upon information provided by the mass media, yet there is great resistance to the use of tax money for the support of news organizations. There are reasons for all these anomalies, some of them good ones. But the reasons should be reexamined, and alternative systems of resource allocation should be considered. Communication research should give greater emphasis to media economics.

RESEARCH DIRECTIONS IN INDIVIDUAL SUB-AREAS

Each of the foregoing chapters has suggested a number of questions for research in the area with which it deals. We will highlight a few of those suggestions and outline some additional questions in each area that seem to us worthy of more attention than they have received thus far.

Uses and Gratifications (Chapter 2). In addition to studying the ways in which individuals utilize incoming communications and the effects that result from this utilization, it is desirable to learn more about the extent to which the mass media can help satisfy the individual's need to communicate. Very little work has been done on this. We have accumulated a fair stockpile of knowledge about the uses to which people put the mass communications available to them, but we are relatively ignorant of the gratifications people feel when they are able to express themselves through the mass media or when they feel that the media are speaking for them.

It is evident that, in a person-to-person situation, many individuals derive intense gratifications from speaking, from receiving attention. Can the mass media provide a surrogate for the face-to-face audience? Can they give people the feeling that they are participating in a public dialogue? Mass media are characterized as institutions that enable the "one" to speak to the "many." Should they be structured so as to give greater opportunity for the "many" to speak to the "one," or to each other?

This question arises in many contexts. One of them is public acceptance of policy decisions. As MacRae (1970, p. 208) observes, "No matter how technically correct a social or political decision may be, it will be supported more readily if those affected have taken some part in it or been consulted about it." Similarly, Stamm (1972, pp. 285-286) points out that the literature on environmental protection has for the most part ignored the wish of local citizens "that government officials and agencies be informed about their criteria for change." He regards this as a "serious oversight of research on environmental communication, and of mass communication research in general." Members of minority groups have complained that the mass media too frequently talk about them, regarding them as objects to be described, rather than giving them an opportunity to present their own views (Hill *et al.*, 1969).

Satisfaction of expressive needs is certainly necessary in the case of the artist; it may also provide some of the journalist's motivation. When asked why so many journalists were willing to stay on year after year in poorly paying jobs, a wire-service executive replied, "Because of their need to communicate." But how widely are such needs shared, how intensely are they felt, in what contexts are they experienced, and what can the mass media do to help satisfy them? Answers to these questions would be relevant to decisions affecting the quality of life in almost any society.

Socialization (Chapter 3). Regarding the role that the mass media play, or might play, in the socialization of the individual, three research areas appear particularly important: the degree to which the media supplement or influence primary-group channels of communication that the individual is exposed to early in life, the importance of mass communication in molding values and behavior patterns that may not be the subject of primary-group communication, and the influence of the media in socializing or resocializing individuals after adolescence.

Hyman (in this volume) has touched upon the extent to which print and electronic communications may interact with primary-group channels. The way parents address the infant or behave in his presence may be influenced by the baby-care book they consult or the program on child-rearing they watch. We know that person-to-person communication is of overriding importance in early socialization, but we are still relatively ignorant when it comes to specifying the ways in which the mass media may influence these intimate channels.

What is the role of mass communication when it comes to shaping values and behavior patterns for which the primary group offers no models? This question arises in connection with efforts to instill a love for reading in youngsters from households in which the adults are illiterate. It is also relevant to mass education efforts in developing societies, where children must somehow learn behavior patterns other than those present in the traditional culture. If we knew more of the answers to this question, might they facilitate a great leap forward? Or would we learn that the mass media are relatively powerless in such situations, and that available resources might be better used elsewhere?

Socialization in later life is another subject that is of importance to rapidly changing societies. It is also relevant for penology or almost any kind of retraining. To what extent are the mass media useful in teaching old dogs new tricks? The question has arisen in connection with discussions of Soviet and Chinese efforts to create a "new man" (Bauer, 1952; Yu, 1964), but little is known about the success of those efforts or about ways the media might be used for resocialization in other contexts. So far, science fiction writers have given the subject more attention than social scientists.

Communication and Organizations (Chapters 4 and 5). The role played by the mass media in various forms of social organization has been so little explored that almost any progress would be significant. The basic problem is to identify the functions performed for collectivities by the mass media, evaluate how well organizational needs are satisfied by given communication patterns, and suggest ways in which these needs might be satisfied better.

If one were to select for special attention one aspect of this complex of questions, it might be the way in which mass communication facilitates (or inhibits) accommodation among different groups. This problem goes beyond the study of conflict resolution, whether within or among national states and other organizations (UNESCO, 1969; Davison, 1974b). It has to do also with the division of labor among groups of varying types, the way they harmonize (or fail to harmonize), their goals, and the manner in which smaller groups and organizations come together to form larger ones. Most collectivities are made up of smaller social units—as nations may be composed of tribes and tribes composed of families—and the degree and rationality of accommodation among these constituent groups has a great deal to do with the quality of life. Anything the mass media might do to promote better accommodation would be of significant social benefit.

Government and the Media (Chapter 6). The first task for researchers concerned with democratic polities is to free themselves from the slogans and shibboleths that obscure the study of media-government relations. "Freedom of the press," "The people's right to know," "Press and government are natural antagonists"—these slogans may serve a purpose in popular discourse but they are too vague for use in the literature of social science. And it is not easy to define them more precisely.

For instance, "Freedom of the press" might be interpreted as the right of journalists to pursue their calling according to their own best professional standards, without outside interference. But who determines when professional standards have been violated, and what should be done then? "The people's right to know" may refer to the obligation of the media to make available information that will help to satisfy the needs of individuals and groups. But what happens when information that is functional for some consumers of the press is dysfunctional for others? The "natural antagonist" thesis contains a modest kernel of truth insofar as governments given limited powers are discomfited when attention is called to areas in which they have overstepped their boundaries. But the thesis obscures the much more significant mutual dependence between press and government.

Progress toward specifying preferred media-government relationships is likely to be more rapid if one looks first at the ways in which mass communications can best serve individuals and groups within society. Most people would like to have an efficient government; they would also like an honest one, and one that stays within the limits imposed by the values of society. The problem becomes one of finding a formula that balances the communication requirements of government as an organization (the need to disseminate instructions, receive information relevant to decision-making, etc.) against the need of individuals and groups to protect themselves against government excesses and pursue a wide variety of individual goals. We cannot, for example, evaluate the desirability of allowing the government to withhold certain types of information until we know both the degree to which stripping away this privacy would undermine government efficiency and the degree to which enforcing it would damage other interests of those in the society.

A very practical sub-question to which communication researchers might devote more attention is the extent to which a government in a democracy can function efficiently while using public channels of information. Most governments parallel public channels with a network of internal channels, some of them closely guarded. These are enormously expensive. If internal channels could be reduced and secrecy limited, savings to the society would be appreciable.

Media Sociology (Chapters 7, 8 and 9). Mention of innovation in government brings up the question of innovation in the mass media. Bogart and Bagdikian (in this volume) have described some of the factors that make innovation difficult—e.g., the conservatism of most media managers and the inherited professional conventions governing journalists. The question therefore arises: If researchers can specify ways in which mass communication could serve the needs of individuals and groups more effectively, how can the mass media be prevailed upon to make the desired adjustments?

Researchers do not have the influence to persuade media managers to embark on costly experiments—unless they can hold out reasonable hopes of increased profits; nor are they likely to prevail upon journalists to alter their working style. Nevertheless, researchers can learn more about the ways in which changes in media structure and media practice have come about in the past; they can also outline alternatives for future change that are likely to be least painful. As pointed out by Parker (in this volume), changes are in any case bound to come as a result of developments in communication technology. It is therefore incumbent upon the researcher to study the implications of the new technology for the communication process and make recommendations before structural and behavioral patterns have become set.

One aspect of innovation in mass communication that deserves particular attention concerns the ways in which the media get the information they process and present to the consumer. More useful information presupposes, among other things, better sources of information. It is therefore important to study the news infrastructure—the institutions through which information is made available to the press. How might these institutions do a better job? What new institutions should be added to the infrastructure?

More than news, in a conventional sense, is involved. The entertainment content of the media is also derived from an extensive infrastructure. And the quality of the entertainment presented depends in part on the accessibility of artists and materials. Researchers should ask not only how government and corporations might be persuaded to make more useful information available to the press, but also how television might be persuaded to tap a wider range of writers and artists.

We are all part of the infrastructure of the mass media, just as we collectively constitute their audience. Researchers have given attention to ways in which members of an audience can help to bring about improvements in mass communication—by demanding them (Rivers and Schramm, 1969). Perhaps we should also study ways in which we might help to improve mass media performance by providing the media—individually and through the groups to which we belong—with better information and entertainment materials.

SOME GENERAL OBSERVATIONS

Communication researchers should make greater efforts to ensure that their investigations, whether directed toward the solution of practical problems or inspired by scientific curiosity, contribute to a central body of theory. This is not a novel injunction, but it bears repeating in view of the increasing demands placed on researchers by government and other decision-making bodies.

One UNESCO report (1972) lists the first two tasks of communication research as supplying basic data and general findings to policy makers, and helping planners to elaborate alternatives. A student of communication in Asia has expressed much the same thought: "The important thing is for communication research to be fully harnessed to serve the ends of development" (Feliciano, 1973). Pressures for applied research come from those concerned with alleviating poverty, meeting the needs of developing countries, improving race relations, resolving conflicts in both national and international arenas, advertising and marketing, and many other subjects. Those making such demands usually assume tacitly the existence of a body of theory and research techniques that can be applied to any problem involving communication.

It is true that some partial theories and some research techniques are available, but not nearly enough. If students are able to extend this body of theory and techniques they can be of greater assistance in answering a wider range of questions. Issues involving communication will change as world conditions change; those that have priority today are likely to be of secondary importance tomorrow. But basic conceptual and research tools have a longer shelf life. If they can be improved, they will be available to solve problems that are imminent and possibly even more pressing than those already facing us. In this respect, communication research does not differ from research in any of the sciences. All have practical utility only to the extent that they have developed an adequate base of generalizable knowledge on which to draw.

But communication research, along with some other branches of social science, does not always have to make a distinction between basic and applied research. Those in this field of study do not have to choose between curing the king's pneumonia and working with their test tubes in the laboratory, or between helping a mentally deranged patient and running rats through a maze. To a large extent, the laboratory of communication research is the functioning society. Basic knowledge is acquired in the process of working on real problems. The researcher is likely to construct new theory and techniques while he is in the process of helping a developing society to use mass communication in education, or while searching for ways to resolve international conflicts or sell soap. He does, it is true, rely on certain concepts elaborated by psychologists and others who may do much of their basic research in artificial environments, and he may himself return to the laboratory on occasion, but major advances in understanding mass communication have come through studying significant problems in the real world.

The search for generalizations that will apply to an increasingly broad range of problems involves analyzing and comparing studies that deal with a wide variety of specific questions. In this respect, mass communication research has been wanting. There have been a fair number of cross-national comparisons but few efforts to compare findings from different functional areas. For instance, the role of communication in national development might be compared with the ways in which the mass media can be used to help urban ghetto residents break out of the poverty cycle (Dervin and Greenberg, 1972). The parallel between research on race relations and on international communication has been noted, but it has not yet led to an appreciable body of generalizations applying to both areas. An exception, perhaps, is the field of persuasion, where studies of election propaganda and advertising have tended to merge into a body of middle-range theory. Nevertheless, a great deal of additional effort should be devoted to teasing out regularities from the now substantial body of empirical studies and field observations.

A corollary is that, in choosing problems for investigation and in designing research, greater efforts should be made to build upon existing knowledge. In connection with this project, we reviewed a substantial quantity of the recent literature on mass communication. It was discouraging to note how little of it had any theoretical referent at all. Historical studies of publicists and media, in particular, often consisted of raw description, barren of any generalization that would contribute to an understanding of communication at other times and places. Some historical accounts, it is true, seemed to speak to recurrent issues. To name only one, Ames' (1972) article on the subsidized press in Washington between 1819 and 1846 notes the limited influence of subsidies on the editorial policies of the newspapers concerned. It can thus be arrayed alongside investigations that indicate the importance of economic factors in influencing editorial policy and those that relegate economic factors to a secondary role. Analysis of this body of literature may eventually enable us to generalize more fruitfully about the relationship between the mass media and their economic bases of support. Academic personnel who advise on master's essays and doctoral dissertations could speed up the process of building mass communication theory if they were more rigorous in insisting that research done under their supervision should be generalizable to situations other than the one studied.

Another observation arising from the present project is that American students of mass communication should give more attention to research done abroad. We are tending to become parochial. At one time, we could assume that most research on mass communication was done in the United States, or was at least published in English. This was certainly the case in the late 1940s when Schramm (1948) compiled his "One Hundred Titles for Further Reading" in the field of mass communication. But it is no longer true. We have been fortunate in this undertaking to have the collaboration of two scholars from Israel and one from England. Perusal of the references in their chapter shows that a large proportion of the studies they cite, and many of the most important ones, were made in Western Europe. We have been impressed by the volume of mass communication research published in Japan, much of it not available in English (Kato, 1973). Valuable material can be found in journals published in Eastern Europe, Latin America, and elsewhere. American scholars cannot take it for granted that the research of foreign scholars will be brought to their attention; they will have to make an effort to get it. Further, the problem is asymmetrical: most communication researchers in other countries read English, while most American researchers are lamentably deficient in their command of foreign languages.

Access to research done in other societies is particularly important when it comes to theory building. Not only is it desirable to know which regularities persist in a variety of political and cultural contexts, but some countries offer more favorable settings for certain types of research than others. A division of labor is involved. For example, it has been possible for researchers in Eastern Europe to study types of publicity campaigns that are rare in the United States, Western Europe, or Japan. One such campaign had as its purpose persuading builders to adopt higher standards in housing construction; it partially succeeded (Brěcka, 1972). Similarly, scholars in some countries have the opportunity of studying the impact of new media as they are introduced; others may observe the relationship between mass communication and a variety of political systems. International cooperation and comparison are necessary if this research is to contribute to a common body of theory.

As one means of reducing the parochialism of American scholars we suggest the establishment of a journal devoted to translations or abridgements of selected research reports originally published in languages other than English. Abstracts (sometimes in French, German, Spanish and Russian, in addition to English) currently carried by many journals are a welcome gesture toward international scholarship, but they are inadequate.

Another suggestion of a general nature is that mass communication researchers should give more attention to the design of new media systems and the restructuring of old ones. Work thus far has tended to emphasize the implications and applications of existing media; possibilities for change should be explored more exhaustively.

Students in the area should work toward a level of competence at which they could specify the relationship between mass communication and the satisfaction of individual and social needs. In addition to understanding the implications of current media performance, they should be able to suggest new patterns that would increase the capabilities of the mass media to contribute to desired values. Rather than limiting themselves to the study of the impact of new media as they are introduced, they should make it possible for society to direct new technologies. This is not to imply that communication researchers should be the decision-makers when it comes to the introduction of new systems or the restructuring of old ones, but they should make it possible for decisions to be implemented with a greater knowledge of the probable consequences.

In order to specify the implications of alternative designs of media systems, it is necessary to draw simultaneously on all branches of mass communication research. A recommendation or observation that takes only individual needs and uses into account, and ignores the functions and dysfunctions of mass media for collectivities, is likely to be of limited utility. It is also important to examine alternative mass communication systems from the point of view of media sociology: Where will the information they carry come from? What forces will determine the actual nature of their content? The difficulty of focusing and bringing to bear a whole body of knowledge—particularly when it is currently so widely diffused and poorly interrelated—is one reason students of communication have had so little influence on the structure of media systems. Hitherto, practitioners have been able to offer more useful advice.

When one considers a few of the major questions about mass communication currently facing decision-makers, it becomes apparent that many branches of research can contribute to the answers. What kind of a mass communication net does a developing society require in order to satisfy certain values? What standards should govern the licensing of cable television? How should public broadcasting be structured? Questions such as these can be dealt with adequately only in the light of what is known about their implications for individuals, collectivities, and the operation of the media themselves.

Progress has been made in drawing together communication studies that are applicable to certain problem areas. One researcher, for example, has identified 273 such studies in a guide to "social, psychological, and communication variables explored in family planning research" (Rosario, 1973). If a higher level of generalization can be achieved, more propositions can be expected to apply to more problem areas, and it should be unnecessary to prepare compendiums of this magnitude that apply to specific fields.

Mass communication researchers have the responsibility not only to mobilize their own findings so that they can be applied to a wide variety of problems, but also to formulate questions for the consideration of students in other disciplines. Just as we have tended to study communication institutions that have already been developed through the enterprise of others, we have ordinarily taken a passive role with regard to research in psychology, sociology, and other fields that contribute to understanding of the communication process. The practice has been to go to the library in order to find out what the historians have done, rather than to levy requests on the historians—or other specialists—for research of a particular type. Our colleagues in other fields have concerns of their own and they may not heed our requests, but it is more likely that a question will be answered if it is asked.

This volume does not concern itself directly with the knowledge that we would like to draw from other disciplines but cannot—either because it does not exist or because we cannot find it. But it is not difficult to give examples of the kinds of questions that might be asked. For example, can those who specialize in comparative linguistics tell us how much meaning is changed when a text is translated from one language to another? The answer would be relevant to the consideration of alternative structures for international television, and many other aspects of international communication. Can physiologists provide an approximation of the physical capacity of the brain for information storage? This datum would be useful in connection with the problem of information overload, which is often raised in an era when mass media are proliferating. It has long been accepted that students of communication should borrow from other fields, but we have usually borrowed what already has been in stock. We should work more systematically to prepare grocery lists for submission to various potential suppliers.

In some cases, it may be necessary for communication researchers themselves to enter other disciplines in pursuit of needed knowledge. As Parker points out (Chapter 9 in this volume), a specialist in another field may be so wedded to a given way of examining a problem that he is unable to adapt to a new set of terms. "Since satisfactory resolution of the questions [about mass communications] may require a significant shift in the current set of assumptions . . . it may be necessary for scholars not so socialized . . . to learn the necessary skills to tackle the problems."

Whether or not students of communication attempt to qualify themselves in other disciplines, it is clear that a wide variety of skills will be necessary if the major research questions facing us are to be attacked successfully. Some of these problems will require massive efforts by teams of researchers; others might be better dealt with by single individuals whose competence extends to several of the social sciences, or who are skilled both in the communication arts and in one or more academic fields.

New research techniques will be needed in some cases. We have not considered research methods a major focus of this volume although they are touched upon in some of the individual chapters. Our hope is that by specifying problems we will stimulate thought about the methods and designs that might be used to solve them. And, of course, we hope to stimulate further thought about better ways of defining the principal problems, too.

AFTERWORD: ANOTHER VIEW
OF RESEARCH PRIORITIES
Forrest P. Chisman

I approach the problem of priorities in mass communication research as a foundation executive concerned with the field broadly, rather than as an academic researcher who specializes in certain aspects of it. This, I believe, gives me a bird's-eye view of problems in the field, although I am often not sure whether the bird is an eagle or an ostrich. Also, I can take no personal credit for some of my ideas on the subject. I have queried a great number of communication researchers about their priorities and have participated in a number of conferences on mass communication, including the Arden House conference that led to this volume. Some of my conclusions spring from an attempt to synthesize the most common answers to my questions and the various viewpoints to which I have been exposed; other observations represent personal opinions about the kinds of research that would be most helpful.

A number of recent reviews of mass communication research, particularly research with a psychological emphasis, have noted that it is evolving in three important directions. The first is toward a decreasing emphasis on the isolated individual as a recipient of mass communications and an increasing emphasis on the influence of the social and interpersonal context within which he makes use of communications. Hence, we have the growing school of "co-orientation" research.

Concurrent with this development is an increasing emphasis on the individual as an active participant in determining the effects of mass communications upon him, and a decreasing emphasis upon models of human behavior that depict him as passive or depict his psychology as mechanized in a fairly rigid sense. The "uses and gratifications" approach to research (represented in this volume by the chapter by Katz, Blumler, and Gurevitch) has stressed these points and has enjoyed considerable vogue in recent years.

Finally, there is decreasing emphasis on the study of mass communications' effects on individual attitudes and opinions, and increasing attention to the ways in which mass communications affect the information environment in which individuals and groups form their attitudes and opinions. Hence, we have a growing body of research on the "agenda-setting functions" of mass communications in the political sphere.

All of these trends are healthy and should be encouraged. I would, however, like to suggest five other perspectives that are in many ways extensions of those just noted, and which, if accepted, might add to their effectiveness. First, if it is important to study the ways mass media influence knowledge and information, as well as attitudes, it may also be significant to broaden our perspective to include social sentiments, such as trust, outrage, piety, respect. This suggestion is made by Herbert Hyman in this volume, and it deserves very careful attention. The sentiments have been neglected generally by psychologists in recent years. It may well be that here, in one of the most culturally determined facets of individual psychology, we can find the major influence of the media, which are, after all, our primary sources of popular culture today.

Second, while acknowledging that most studies show the effect of mass communications on attitudes, particularly political attitudes, to be small, I am not sure that we should give up on attitudinal research. Looking for the moment only at studies of political attitudes, I think it is fair to say that the more fine-grained the research has been—that is, the more it has taken into account a great number of psychological variables—the greater significance attitudes have seemed to have in explaining individual behavior. Most research on the effects of mass communications has not been very fine-grained in this sense.

Perhaps what we need are more investigations of how people react to the media based on in-depth interviews. Such studies might attempt to show how the media bring about changes in major attitudes by small increments, or how communications affect attitudes that do not seem directly related to the explicit content of the media message. For example, broad attitudes, such as respect for political authority, may be affected by editorials about the Watergate affair; specific attitudes toward political parties or personalities may not be. Research that examines a fairly large array of each individual's attitudes in some detail and relates them to other aspects of his personality is likely to come up with new insights about the effects of the media on attitudes.

Third, just as I believe that communication research should become more fine-grained, I think it should also become more broad-gauged. Particularly, more attempts should be made to study all aspects of a particular communication system simultaneously. For example, rather than only studying the effects of political campaign propaganda on members of the general public, it would be valuable to examine the effects of certain pieces of propaganda, their content, and the ways in which they were produced, on the intentions and expectations of the politicians who produced them. This would throw effects research into a dramatically different perspective, if for no other reason than because it would lend great importance to the study of situations in which communications have no audience effects whatsoever. Findings about the reasons why politicians spend millions of dollars on political propaganda that has no influence may become highly significant.

A broad-gauged approach might make it possible to set up new typologies of communications systems. One might find, for example, that public information systems about health care, accident prevention, and civil defense are similar in revealing respects. Such a perspective is useful precisely because it stresses that communication is an important activity in our society regardless of its results, and that communication can be explained and understood as a social phenomenon only if one views it as a total system. A broad-gauged approach is also more likely to lead to policy-relevant findings, since it takes into account more of the factors relevant to mass communication.

Fourth, there has been too little research comparing the capabilities and utilities of different kinds of communication systems. For example, we should know more about what print journalism, as opposed to television journalism, can accomplish. Or, to use a familiar phrase, what mix of media is likely to make information campaigns succeed? These questions have been nibbled at for many years by advertisers and others, with some success, but more efforts along these lines are needed before we can truly say that we have a working understanding of media trade-offs, or of how to use the media more effectively in particular situations.

Finally, there is a need for more policy-relevant research of all types in the mass communication field—for research that can provide a basis for decisions by government or others about communications systems. This is, to some extent, special pleading on my part because much of my time is taken up with concerns about public policy regarding mass communication. Nevertheless, it is relevant that I, and most people who have this perspective, find little research to guide us and few individuals prepared to engage in such research. The Surgeon General's report on television and social behavior was an important step forward in this respect, even if it has led some critics to point out some of the pitfalls as well as the advantages of policy-relevant research.

All of the research perspectives mentioned above have potential relevance for public policy, but it requires a particular point of view and, perhaps, hubris on the part of the researcher to steer them in this direction. To take but one small example of how far researchers are from adopting this point of view, I have searched in vain for over nine months to find social scientists prepared to make a significant contribution toward identifying the kinds of social service programming that would be most appropriate for cable television. Despite the significance of this question for the future of the cable industry, the social science research community appears unwilling, whether because of lack of interest or lack of the necessary tools, to come to grips with it.

In addition to the example just mentioned, a number of other fruitful areas for policy-relevant research come to mind. To mention but a few of these: we know far too little about the effects of racial or sex-role stereotyping in the mass media or even about the degree to which either occurs; despite repeated cries for the employment of more minority group members in journalism organizations, we do not know whether their inclusion has a significant impact on the way in which news is reported to or received by the public.

There are, of course, hopeful examples of policy-relevant research. One of these is the research recently conducted by William Melody (1973) for Action for Children's Television. This study evaluated various courses of action that the Federal Communications Commission might take in phasing out advertising from children's television. It concluded that there is a good possibility that commercial advertisements could be removed without serious financial harm to the networks. But examples of policy-relevant research of this type are all too rare. From my point of view, it is vital that both the necessary interest and tools be generated in the coming years or social science will deserve the accusation that it can only observe society, rather than help bring about improvements in it.

All five of the above suggestions involve changes in the intellectual point of view of communication researchers. In addition, the last three suggestions (to investigate broad-gauged communications systems, trade-offs between different media, and policy-relevant issues) probably require a change in the structure of communication research procedures and institutions.

If we are going to fully comprehend some of the most significant questions in the field of communication research, then we must have more team research and, especially, more interdisciplinary efforts. There is simply no way in which communication systems can be studied by the individual psychological investigator and his research team unless such efforts are joined with those of sociologists of various schools, economists, and, in some cases, political scientists. The job is simply too big and the range of skills required too large.

Few institutions today have the ability to mobilize such research teams easily. Universities that have schools of communication do not, on the whole, seem to do this job much better than universities that house communication researchers in departments of psychology or sociology. We badly need to reexamine the kinds of intellectual resources that should be placed in continuing proximity to each other in universities and other research institutions if we are to move ahead in the field of communication studies.

Reexamining the combination of skills that should be brought together in communication research is only one way in which we must change our perspectives. We must also reexamine ways of employing available skills in order to make progress in high priority areas of this field. In particular, there is a need for more short- and long-term research than is presently being conducted.

The importance of "firehouse research" on fairly short-lived phenomena such as the Kennedy assassination or the Watergate hearings, which may have great and lasting effects, has been stressed repeatedly by researchers such as Kurt and Gladys Lang, but there are regrettably few examples of such work. Likewise, many social scientists have insisted that it is particularly important to acquire longitudinal data, since there is reason to believe that most effects of communication and most factors determining these effects are long-term—yet there have been practically no studies of communication effects over periods longer than one year. Funding sources probably deserve part of the blame for the lack of "firehouse" and longitudinal studies, but their responses may to some extent be modified if the research community insists more vigorously on the importance of such work and creates the kinds of organizational structures needed to carry it out.

Everything discussed so far relates in one way or another to studies of the psychological effects of mass communications and, indeed, psychology has for some time been the queen discipline of communication research. There are, of course, many other areas in the field that should be studied and for which psychology may not be as relevant: the economics of new and emerging media, their technological alternatives, and the legal issues that they raise—all these are of great significance. However, we appear to be making more progress in these areas than in the study of the psychology and sociology of the media. As a result, I have confined my remarks here to the latter areas.

I should like to make a final comment on the future of mass communication research. It has often struck me that this field is remarkable for its lack of broad theorizing. Where are the elder statesmen, the philosophers of the communications field? Innis, McLuhan, Lasswell, and a few others might be mentioned, but the roster is certainly small and new names have not been added to it in recent years. Philosophers in any field are important forces for development. They can open up new perspectives and re-route us from trips down blind alleys. More important, they can explain to us and to society what is perhaps the most important question facing us: What do we know about mass communication, and why is it important?

BIBLIOGRAPHY

Ackerman, M. S. 1970. *The Curtis affair*. Los Angeles, Nash.

Adelman, I. and C. T. Morris. 1971. A factor analysis of the interrelationship between social and political variables and per capita gross national product. In *Macro-quantitative analysis*, eds. J. V. Gillespie and B. A. Nesvold. Beverly Hills, Calif., Sage.

Alberoni, F. 1972. The powerless elite: theory and sociological research on the phenomenon of the stars. In *Sociology of mass communication*, ed. D. McQuail. Harmondsworth, England, Penguin.

Alker, H. R., Jr. 1966. Causal inference and political analysis. In *Mathematical applications in political science*, ed. J. Bernd. Dallas, Southern Methodist University Press.

Almond, G. A. and S. Verba. 1963. *The civic culture*. Princeton, N.J., Princeton University Press.

American Newspaper Publishers Association. 1970. *News Research Bulletin* No. 9.

Ames, W. E. 1972. Federal patronage and the Washington D.C. Press. *Journalism Quarterly* 49.

Anderson, J. A. 1971-72. The alliance of broadcast stations and newspapers: the problem of information control. *Journal of Broadcasting* 6.

Argyris, C. 1974. *Behind the front page*. San Francisco, Jossey Bass.

Arnheim, R. 1944. The world of the daytime serial. In *Radio research, 1942-43*, eds. P. F. Lazarsfeld and F. Stanton. New York, Duell, Sloan and Pearce.

Atkin, C. K. 1971. How imbalanced campaign coverage affects audience exposure patterns. *Journalism Quarterly* 48.

_____. 1972. Anticipated communication and mass media information-seeking. *Public Opinion Quarterly* 36.

Atwood, L. E. 1970. How newsmen and readers perceive each others' story preferences. *Journalism Quarterly* 47.

Bagdikian, B. H. 1964. Case history: Wilmington's "independent" newspapers of the Du Ponts. *Columbia Journalism Review* 3.

————. 1966. Houston listens to the ghost of Jesse Jones. *Atlantic Monthly* 218.

————. 1971. *The information machines*. New York, Harper and Row.

————. 1972. How liberal is the press? *Columbia Journalism Review* 10.

Bagrow, L. 1964. *History of cartography*. Cambridge, Mass., Harvard University Press.

Bailey, G. 1972. Rough justice on a Saigon street. *Journalism Quarterly* 49.

Bailyn, L. 1959. Mass media and children. *Psychological Monographs* 471.

Baker, R. T. 1972. Subpoenaing newsmen. *Columbia Journalism Review* 10.

Bakewell, J. and N. Garnham. 1970. *The new priesthood: television today*. London, Allen Lane.

Baldwin, J. 1960. Mass communication and the creative artist: some personal notes. *Daedalus* 89.

Bales, R. F. 1950. *Interaction process analysis*. Cambridge, Mass., Addison-Wesley.

Balk, A. 1971. Minnesota launches a press council. *Columbia Journalism Review* 10.

————. 1973. Background paper. In *A free and responsive press*. Task Force Report for a National News Council. New York, The Twentieth Century Fund.

Barron, J. 1967. Access to the press—a new first amendment right. *Harvard Law Review* 80.

Bauer, R. A. 1952. *The new man in Soviet psychology*. Cambridge, Mass., Harvard University Press.

————, I. de S. Pool, and L. A. Dexter. 1963. *American business and public policy*. New York, Atherton.

————. 1964. The obstinate audience. *American Psychologist* 19.

Baumol, W. J. and W. C. Bowen. 1966. *Performing arts: the economic dilemma*. New York, The Twentieth Century Fund.

Becker, H. S. and A. L. Strauss. 1957. Careers, personality and adult socialization. *American Journal of Sociology* 62.

Becker, J. and D. A. Fuchs. 1967. How two major California dailies covered Reagan vs. Brown. *Journalism Quarterly* 44.

Bennett, E. 1970. Manager perceptions of differences in high and low creative personnel in broadcasting stations—some dimensions. Ph.D. dissertation, Michigan State University.

Berelson, B. 1949. What "missing the newspaper" means. In *Communications research, 1948-9*, eds. P. F. Lazarsfeld and F. N. Stanton. New York, Harper.

————, P. F. Lazarsfeld, and W. N. McPhee. 1954. *Voting*. Chicago, University of Chicago Press.

————. 1959. The state of communication research. *Public Opinion Quarterly* 23.

Berger, Meyer. 1951. *Story of the New York Times, eighteen fifty-one to nineteen fifty-one*. New York, Simon and Schuster.

Berger, Morroe. 1962. *The Arab world today*. New York, Doubleday.

Berkowitz, L. 1962. *Aggression: a social psychological analysis*. New York, McGraw-Hill.

————. 1972. Social norms, feelings, and other factors affecting helping and altruism. *Advances in Experimental Psychology* 6.

Bishop, R. L. and R. L. Brown. 1968. Michigan newspaper bias in the 1966 campaign. *Journalism Quarterly* 45.

Blasi, V. n.d. *Press subpoenas.* Reporters' Committee for Freedom of the Press (duplicated paper).

Blume, N. and S. Lyons. 1968. The monopoly newspaper in a local election. *Journalism Quarterly* 45.

Blumler, J. G. and D. McQuail. 1968. *Television in politics: its uses and influence*. London, Faber and Faber.

————. 1969. Producers' attitudes towards television coverage of an election campaign: a case study. *Sociological Review Monograph* 13.

————, J. R. Brown, and D. McQuail. 1970. The social origins of the gratifications associated with television viewing. University of Leeds (duplicated paper).

————, and A. J. Ewbank. 1970. Trade unionists, the mass media, and unofficial strikes. *British Journal of Industrial Relations* 8.

_____. 1972. Information and democracy: the perspective of the governed. *Il Politico* 37.

Bobrow, D. B. 1972. Transfer of meaning across national boundaries. In *Communication in international politics*, ed. R. L. Merritt. Urbana, Ill., University of Illinois Press.

Bogart, L. 1965. The mass media and the blue-collar worker. In *Blue-collar world: studies in the American worker*, eds. A. Bennett and W. Gomberg. Englewood Cliffs, N.J., Prentice-Hall.

_____. 1968. The overseas newsman: a 1967 profile study. *Journalism Quarterly* 45.

_____. 1972. Negro and white media exposure: new evidence. *Journalism Quarterly* 49.

_____. 1972-73. Warning: the Surgeon General has determined that TV violence is moderately dangerous to your child's mental health. *Public Opinion Quarterly* 36.

_____. 1973. *The age of television—a study of viewing habits*. New York, Ungar.

Bogue, D. 1962. Recommendations for a sociologically correct family planning program in India. In *Research in family planning*, ed. C. Kiser. Princeton, N.J., Princeton University Press.

Boorstin, D. J. 1962. *The image or what happened to the American dream*. New York, Atheneum.

Bower, R. T. 1973. *Television and the public*. New York, Holt.

Bowers, D. R. 1967. A report on activity by publishers in directing newsroom decisions. *Journalism Quarterly* 44.

Bradburn, N. and D. Berlew. 1961. Need for achievement and English economic growth. *Economic Development and Cultural Change* 10.

Brěcka, S. 1972. Effectiveness of propagandist activity. *Otazky Zurnalistiky (Bratislava)* 4.

Breed, W. 1952. The newspaperman, news, and society. Ph.D. dissertation, Columbia University.

_____. 1955. Social control in the newsroom: a functional analysis. *Social Forces* 33.

Brooks, J. G. 1969. *American syndicalism: the IWW*. New York, AMS Press.

Brooks, J. M. 1970. A sociological study of commercial broadcast organizations. Ph.D. dissertation, Ohio State University.

Brown, D. E. 1970. The San Francisco Press in two presidential elections. Ph.D. dissertation, University of Missouri.

Brown, L. 1970. *Communicating facts and ideas in business*. Englewood Cliffs, N.J., Prentice-Hall.

———. 1971. *Television: the business behind the box*. New York, Harcourt, Brace.

Brown, L. A. 1949. *The story of maps*. Boston, Little, Brown.

Brunner, R. D. and G. D. Brewer. 1971. *Organized complexity*. New York, Free Press.

Buckalew, J. K. 1967. *The television news editor as a gatekeeper*. Iowa City, Iowa, University of Iowa Press.

———. 1969. A Q-analysis of television news editors' decisions. *Journalism Quarterly* 46.

Bureau of the Census. 1960. Household delivery of daily and Sunday newspapers. *Current population reports, population characteristics*, Series P-20.

Cable Television Advisory Committee. 1972. *Report of the Advisory Committee on Cable Communications to the Metropolitan Council*. Minneapolis, Minn., Metropolitan Council of the Twin Cities Area.

Cantor, M. G. 1971. *The Hollywood TV producer: his work and his audience*. New York, Basic Books.

———. 1972. The role of the producer in choosing children's television content. In *Television and social behavior*, ed. G. A. Comstock and E. A. Rubinstein. Washington, D.C., National Institute of Mental Health.

Carey, J. W. 1969. The communications revolution and the professional communicator. *Sociological Review Monograph* 13.

———. 1973. Journalism schools must contribute to the development of a systematic evaluation and public criticism of the newspaper press. In *Working papers for newspaper journalists in the seventies and beyond*. Washington, D.C., ANPA (duplicated paper).

Carl, L. M. 1968. Editorial cartoons fail to reach many readers. *Journalism Quarterly* 45.

Carlson, O. and E. S. Bates. 1936. *Hearst, lord of San Simeon*. New York, Viking.

Carrell, Bob, Jr. 1969. The mass media as gatekeepers in respect to advertising. Ph.D. dissertation, University of Illinois.

Cater, D. 1959. *The fourth branch of government*. Boston, Houghton Mifflin.

_____. 1972. The politics of public TV. *Columbia Journalism Review* 11.

Catledge, T. 1971. *My life and the Times*. New York, Harper and Row.

Cazeneuve, J. 1972. *La société de l'ubiquité*. Paris, Denoel.

_____. 1973. La télévision et la condition humaine. Lecture prepared for the International Symposium on Communication and the Human Condition, Barcelona.

Chaffee, S. H. 1972. The interpersonal context of mass communication. In *Current perspectives in mass communication research*, eds. F. G. Kline and P. J. Tichenor. Beverly Hills, Calif., Sage.

Child, I., E. H. Potter, and E. Levine. 1946. Children's textbooks and personality development: an exploration in the social psychology of education. *Psychological Monograph* 60.

Chin, A. S. 1948. Some problems of Chinese youth in transition. *American Journal of Sociology* 54.

_____. 1966. *Modern Chinese fiction and family relations*. Mass., MIT, Center for International Studies.

Clark, W. C. 1968. The impact of mass communication in America. *Annals of the American Academy of Political and Social Science* 378.

Clarke, P. 1971. Children's response to entertainment: effects of co-orientation on information-seeking. *American Behavioral Scientist* 14.

Cohen, B. C. 1963. *The press and foreign policy*. Princeton, N.J., Princeton University Press.

Cole, M. 1962. *The story of Fabian socialism*. Stanford, Calif., Stanford University Press.

Comanor, W. S. and B. M. Mitchell. 1971. Cable television and the impact of regulation. *Bell Journal of Economics and Management Science* 2.

Commission on Freedom of the Press. 1947. *A free and responsible press.* Chicago, University of Chicago Press.

Cooley, C. H. 1956. *Social organization.* Glencoe, Ill., Free Press.

Cott, S. 1971. The function of television in the presidential election campaign of 1968. Ph.D. dissertation, Columbia University.

Crandall, R. W. 1972. FCC regulation, monopsony, and network television program costs. *Bell Journal of Economics and Management Science* 3.

Cremer, C. F. 1971. The gatekeeper and authority: television news director/general manager dimensions of association. Ph.D. dissertation, University of Iowa.

Crossman, R. 1969. The politics of television. In *Panther record* 7. London, Panther.

Culligan, M. 1970. *The Curtis-Culligan story.* New York, Crown.

Dahlan, M. A. 1967. Anonymous disclosure of government information as a form of political communication. Ph.D. dissertation, University of Illinois.

Dahlgren, P. 1972. Television in the socialization process: structures and programming of the Swedish Broadcasting Corporation. In *Television and social behavior*, Volume I: *Media content and control*, eds. G. A. Comstock and E. A. Rubinstein. Rockville, Md., National Institute of Mental Health.

Darnell, D. K. 1971. Toward a reconceptualization of communication. *Journal of Communication* 21.

Daugherty, W. E. and M. Janowitz (comp.). 1958. *A psychological warfare casebook.* Baltimore, Johns Hopkins University Press.

Davis, K. 1940. Extreme social isolation of a child. *American Journal of Sociology* 45.

Davison, W. P. 1956. Political significance of recognition via mass media—an illustration from the Berlin Blockade. *Public Opinion Quarterly* 20.

————. 1974a. Mass media and international negotiation. *Public Opinion Quarterly* 38.

————. 1974b. *Mass Communication and conflict resolution.* New York, Praeger.

Dawson, P. A. and J. E. Zinser. 1971. Broadcast expenditures and electoral outcomes in the 1970 congressional election. *Public Opinion Quarterly* 35.

DeCharmes, R. and G. Moeller. 1962. Values expressed in American children's readers: 1800-1950. *Journal of Abnormal and Social Psychology* 64.

Della Femina, J. 1970. *From those wonderful folks who gave you Pearl Harbor.* New York, Simon and Schuster.

Dembo, R. 1972. Life style and media use among English working-class youths. *Gazette* 18.

De Mott, J. E. 1971. A content analysis of newspaper stories described as "interpretative." Ph.D. dissertation, Northwestern University.

Dervin, B. and B. S. Greenberg. 1972. The communication environment of the urban poor. In *Current perspectives in mass communication research*, eds. F. G. Kline and P. J. Tichenor. Beverly Hills, Calif., Sage.

Deutsch, K. W. 1953. *Nationalism and social communication.* Cambridge, Mass., MIT Press.

Diebold, J. 1973. Business, government and science: the need for a fresh look. *Foreign Affairs* 51.

Donohcw, L. 1967. Newspaper gatekeepers and forces in the news channel. *Public Opinion Quarterly* 31.

Doob, L. 1950. Goebbels' principles of propaganda. *Public Opinion Quarterly* 14.

Dreyer, E. C. 1971-72. Media use and electoral choices. *Public Opinion Quarterly* 35.

Drucker, P. 1969. *The age of discontinuity.* New York, Harper and Row.

Dunn, D. D. 1967. Interaction between the press and Wisconsin state officials. Ph.D. dissertation, University of Wisconsin.

————. 1972. *Financing presidential campaigns.* Washington, D.C., Brookings Institute.

Duscha, J. 1971. Public TV. *Columbia Journalism Review* 10.

Edelstein, A. 1973. An alternative approach to the study of source effects in mass communication. *Studies of Broadcasting* 9.

Eisenstadt, S. N. 1955. Communication systems and social structure. *Public Opinion Quarterly* 19.

Eisenstein, E. L. 1969. The advent of printing and the problem of the Renaissance. *Past & Present* 45.

Ellens, J. H. 1970. Program format in religious television, a history and analysis of program format in nationally distributed denominational religious television broadcasting in the United States of America: 1950-1970. Ph.D. dissertation, Wayne State University.

Elliott, P. and D. Chaney. 1969. A sociological framework for the study of television production. *Sociological Review Monograph* 13.

Ellul, J. 1964. *The technological society*. New York, Knopf.

Elving, B. F. 1970. A study of attitudes toward FM radio among managers of commercial and educational FM stations. Ph.D. dissertation, Syracuse University.

Emery, F. E. 1959. Psychological effects of the Western film. *Human Relations* 12.

Emmett, B. P. 1968-69. A new role for research in broadcasting. *Public Opinion Quarterly* 32.

Enzenberger, H. M. 1972. Constituents of a theory of the media. In *Sociology of mass communication*, ed. D. McQuail. Harmondsworth, England, Penguin.

Epstein, E. J. 1973. *News from nowhere, television and the news*. New York, Random House.

Erskine, H. G. 1970. The polls: is war a mistake. *Public Opinion Quarterly* 34.

————. 1972-73. The polls, pacifism and the generation gap. *Public Opinion Quarterly* 36.

Eversole, P. 1971. Concentration of ownership in the communicatio.ls industry. *Journalism Quarterly* 42.

Fagen, R. R. (ed.) 1964. *Cuba: the political content of adult education*. Stanford, Calif., Stanford University Press.

Failing Newspaper Act, The. 1967. Part I: Hearings before the Subcommittee on Anti-trust and Monopoly of the Committee on the Judiciary, U.S. Senate, 90th Congress.

Fairlie, H. 1973. How we knew what we were doing when we went into Vietnam. *Washington Monthly* 5.

Fedler, F. E. 1971. Access to the mass media. Ph.D. dissertation, University of Minnesota.

_____. 1973. The media and minority groups: a study of adequacy of access. *Journalism Quarterly* 50.

Feliciano, G. D. 1973. An overview of communication research in Asia. *Papers of the East-West Communication Institute*, East-West Center, Honolulu.

Ferguson, J. M. 1963. *The advertising rate structure in the daily newspaper industry*. Englewood Cliffs, N.J., Prentice-Hall.

Festinger, L. and N. Maccoby. 1964. On resistance to persuasive communica tion. *Journal of Abnormal and Social Psychology* 60.

_____. et al. 1956. *When prophecy fails*. Minneapolis, University of Minnesota Press.

Fischer, J. May, 1968. The perils of publishing. *Harper's*.

Flanery J. A. 1971. Chicago newspapers' coverage of the city's major civil disorders of 1968. Ph.D. dissertation, Northwestern University.

Flavell, J. H. 1968. *The development of role-taking and communication skills in children*. New York, Wiley.

Flegel, R. C. and S. H. Chaffee. 1971. Influences of editors, readers, and personal opinions on reporters. *Journalism Quarterly* 48.

Foote, A. E. 1970. Managerial style, hierarchical control and decision making in public television stations. Ph.D. dissertation, Ohio State University.

Forer, R. 1955. The impact of a radio program on adolescents. *Public Opinion Quarterly* 19.

Foreman, R. 1959. *The hot half-hour*. London, Angus and Robertson.

Forrester, J. W. 1969. *Urban dynamics*. Cambridge, Mass., MIT Press.

Frankel, M. 1971. The "state secrets" myth. *Columbia Journalism Review* 10.

Freeman, E. 1936. *Social psychology*. New York, Holt.

Freidson, E. 1953. The relation of the social situation of contact to the media in mass communication. *Public Opinion Quarterly* 17.

Freud, P. 1970. *The movie moguls; an informal history of the Hollywood tycoons*. Chicago, H. Regnery.

Friedman, M. 1962. *Capitalism and freedom*. Chicago, University of Chicago Press.

Friedrich, C. 1950. *The new image of the common man*. Boston, Beacon Press.

Friedrich, O. 1970. *Decline and fall*. New York, Harper and Row.

Friel, C. 1968. The influence of television in the political career of Richard M. Nixon, 1946-62. Ph.D. dissertation, New York University.

Friendly, F. W. 1967. *Due to circumstances beyond our control*. New York, Random House.

_____. 1970-71. TV at the turning point. *Columbia Journalism Review* 9.

_____. 1972. Justice White and reporter Caldwell. *Columbia Journalism Review* 11.

Fromm, E. 1941. *Escape from freedom*. New York, Farrar and Rinehart.

Furu, T. 1971. *The function of television for children and adolescents*. Tokyo, Sophia University.

Gans, H. 1957. The creator-audience relationship in the mass media. In *Mass culture: the popular arts in America*, eds. B. Rosenberg and D. M. White. Glencoe, Ill., Free Press.

_____. 1966. The shaping of mass media content: a study of the news. Unpublished paper delivered before the American Sociological Association.

_____. January 11, 1970. How well does TV present the news. *New York Times Magazine*.

_____. 1972. The famine in mass communication research. *American Journal of Sociology* 78.

Garvey, D. E., Jr. 1971. Social control in the television newsroom. Ph.D. dissertation, Stanford University.

Gelles, R. J. 1971. The television news interview: a case study of the construction and presentation of social reality. Ph.D. dissertation, University of New Hampshire.

Gelmis, J. 1970. *The film director as superstar*. Garden City, New York, Doubleday.

George, A. L. 1959. *Propaganda analysis*. Evanston, Ill., Row, Peterson.

Gerbner, G. n.d. Images across culture: teachers in mass fiction and drama. Annenberg School, University of Pennsylvania.

———. 1972. The structure and process of television program content regulation in the United States. In *Television and social behavior*. Volume I: *Media content and control*, eds. G. A. Comstock and E. A. Rubinstein. Rockville, Md., National Institute of Mental Health.

———. 1972-73. Teacher image and the hidden curriculum. *American Scholar* 42.

Gerson, W. M. 1966. Mass media socialization behavior: Negro-White differences. *Social Forces* 45.

Gieber, W. 1956. Across the desk: a study of 16 telegraph editors. *Journalism Quarterly* 33.

———. 1964. News is what newspapermen make it. In *People, society and mass communication*, eds. L. A. Dexter and D. M. White. New York, Free Press.

Gilbert, R. E. 1967. The influence of television on American politics. Ph.D. dissertation, University of Massachusetts.

Glaser, W. A. 1965. Television and voting turnout. *Public Opinion Quarterly* 29.

Glessing, R. J. 1970. *Underground press in America*. Bloomington, Ind., Indiana University Press.

Goldhamer, H. and A. Marshall. 1953. *Psychosis and civilization—conditional expectancy of mental disease*. Glencoe, Ill., Free Press.

Goldstein, P. 1973. Information systems and the role of law: some prospects. *Stanford Law Review* 25.

Goodman, J. 1972. "Fairness" today (censorship tomorrow?). Address at the University of Southern California.

Gotschalk, D. W. 1947. *Art and social order*. Chicago, University of Chicago Press.

Goulden, J. D. 1965. *The Curtis caper*. New York, Putnam.

Graber, D. 1971. The press as an opinion resource during the 1968 presidential campaign. *Public Opinion Quarterly* 35.

Greeley, B. 1972. The world's richest TV station. *More* 2.

Green, E. J. 1973. The communication crisis. *Management Forum* 2.

Gregg, P. M. and A. S. Banks. 1971. Dimensions of political systems. In *Macro-quantitative analysis*, eds. J. V. Gillespie and B. A. Nesvold. Beverly Hills, Calif., Sage.

Grotta, G. L. 1970. Changes in the ownership of daily newspapers and selected performance characteristics, 1950-1968: an investigation of some economic implications of concentration of ownership. Ph.D. dissertation, Southern Illinois University.

————. 1971. Consolidation of newspapers. *Journalism Quarterly* 48.

Grupp, F. W., Jr. 1969. The magazine reading habits of political activists. *Public Opinion Quarterly* 33.

Guillaumin, C. 1971. The popular press and ethnic pluralism. *International Social Science Journal* 23.

Gurevitch, M. 1969. L'attente du public: l'example de la télévision Israelienne. *Communication* 14.

Haisman, S. F. 1970. Television's world view: one month of network international news. Ph.D. dissertation, University of Iowa.

Hall, B. (ed.). 1964. *Tell me, Josephine*. New York, Simon and Schuster.

Hall, E. T. 1959. *The silent language*. New York, Doubleday.

Hallie, P. 1972. *The paradox of cruelty*. Middletown, Conn., Wesleyan University Press.

Halloran, J. D. and P. Croll. 1972. Television programs in Great Britain: content and control. In *Television and social behavior*, Volume I: *Media content and control*, eds. G. A. Comstock and E. A. Rubinstein. Rockville, Md., National Institute of Mental Health.

Harney, R. F. and V. A. Stone. 1969. Television and newspaper front page coverage of major news story. *Journal of Broadcasting* 13.

Henderson, G. 1973. Introduction. In *Public diplomacy and political change*, ed. G. Henderson. New York, Praeger.

Hersh, S. 1972. *Cover-up*. New York, Random House.

Herzog, H. 1941. Professor Quiz: a gratification study. In *Radio research, 1941*, eds. P. F. Lazarsfeld and F. N. Stanton. New York, Duell, Sloan and Pearce.

————. 1944. What do we really know about day-time serial listeners? In *Radio research, 1942-43*, eds. P. F. Lazarsfeld and F. N. Stanton. New York, Duell, Sloan and Pearce.

Heussenstamm, F. K. 1971. Activism in adolescence: an analysis of the high school underground press. *Adolescence* 23.

Higbee, A. L. 1970. A survey of the attitudes of selected radio and television broadcast executives toward the educational background and experience desirable for broadcast employees. Ph.D. dissertation, Michigan State University.

Hill, R. B., *et al.* 1969. Coverage of minority group affairs in the New York news media and the black evaluation. Bureau of Applied Social Research, Columbia University.

Himmelweit, H., A. N. Oppenheim, and P. Vince. 1958. *Television and the child*. New York, Oxford University Press.

Hirsch, P. M. 1971. Sociological approaches to the pop music phenomenon. *American Behavioral Scientist* 14.

————. 1972. Processing fads and fashions: an organization-set analysis of cultural industry systems. *American Journal of Sociology* 77.

Hitler, A. 1944. *Mein kampf*. Munich, Franz Eher Nachf.

Hoffman, F. J., C. Allen, and C. F. Ulrich. 1946. *The little magazine: a history and a bibliography*. Princeton, N.J., Princeton University Press.

Hoffman, E. P. 1967. Ideological administration in the Soviet Union, 1959-63. Ph.D. dissertation, Indiana University.

Hollander, N. 1971. Adolescents and the war: the sources of socialization. *Journalism Quarterly* 48.

Hooper, M. 1969. Party and newspaper endorsement as predictors of voter choice. *Journalism Quarterly* 46.

Horton, D. and R. Wohl. 1956. Mass communication and para-social interaction. *Psychiatry* 19.

Hovland, C. I., I. L. Janis, and H. H. Kelley. 1953. *Communication and persuasion*. New Haven, Conn., Yale University Press.

The Hutchins report: a twenty-year view. 1967. *Columbia Journalism Review* 6.

Hvistendahl, J. K. 1970. Publisher's power: functional or dysfunctional? *Journalism Quarterly* 47.

Hyman, H. 1959. *Political socialization*. New York, Macmillan and Free Press.

————. 1963. Mass media and political socialization: the role of patterns of communication. In *Communications and political development*, ed. L. W. Pye. Princeton, N.J., Princeton University Press.

————, and E. Singer (eds.). 1968. *Readings in reference group theory and research*. New York, Macmillan and Free Press.

Information or noise? . . . an environmental approach. 1974. A report of the Stockholm symposium of the Secretariat for future Studies. *Intermedia* (International Broadcast Institute) No. 5.

Inkeles, A. 1950. *Public Opinion in the Soviet Union*. Cambridge, Mass., Harvard University Press.

Innis, H. 1950. *Empire and communication*. Oxford, Clarendon Press.

————. 1951. *The bias of communication*. Toronto, Toronto University Press.

Isaacs, H. R. 1958. *Scratches on our minds*. New York, John Day.

Isaacs, N. E. 1970. Why we lack a national press council. *Columbia Journalism Review* 9.

————. 1972. Beyond "Caldwell." *Columbia Journalism Review* 11.

Ivey, A. E. and J. C. Hurst. 1971. Communication as adaptation. *Journal of Communication* 21.

Jacobs, F. 1972. *The mad world of William Gaines*. Secaucus, N.J., Lyle Stuart.

Janowitz, M. 1952. *The community press in an urban setting*. Glencoe, Ill., Free Press.

Japan Computer Usage Development Institute. 1972. The plan for information society—a national goal toward year 2000.

Jarrell, R. 1960. A sad heart at the supermarket. *Daedalus* 89.

Jarvie, I. C. 1970. *Movies and society*. New York, Basic Books.

Jennings, R. M. 1968. Dramatic license in political broadcasts. *Journal of Broadcasting* 12.

Jessup, J. K. 1969. *The ideas of Henry Luce*. New York, Atheneum.

Johnson, J. S. 1970. Radio music—the gatekeepers. Ph.D. dissertation, Michigan State University.

Johnson, N. 1973, April 20. (An interview). *Media Industry Newsletter* 26.

Johnson, P. B., D. O. Sears, and J. B. McConahay. 1971. Black invisibility, the press, and the Los Angeles riot. *American Journal of Sociology* 76.

Johnstone, J. W. C. 1961. Social structure and patterns of mass media consumption. Ph.D. dissertation, University of Chicago.

————, E. J. Slawski, and W. W. Bowman. 1972-73. The professional values of American newsmen. *Public Opinion Quarterly* 36.

Julian, J. 1966. Compliance patterns and communication blocks in complex organizations. *American Sociological Review* 31.

Karp, R. 1972. Newspaper food pages: credibility for sale. *Columbia Journalism Review* 10.

Kato, H. 1973. *Japanese communication research abstracts*. Honolulu and Kyoto, East-West Communication Institute in cooperation with Communication Design Institute.

Katz, D. 1967. The practice and potential of survey methods in psychological research. In *Survey research in the social sciences*, ed. C. Y. Glock. New York, Russell Sage.

Katz, E. and P. F. Lazarsfeld. 1955. *Personal influence*. New York, Free Press.

————, and D. Foulkes. 1962. On the use of mass media as "escape." *Public Opinion Quarterly* 26.

————. 1971. Platforms and windows: broadcasting's role in election campaigns. *Journalism Quarterly* 48.

————, M. Gurevitch, and H. Haas. 1973. On the use of mass media for important things. *American Sociological Review* 38.

Katzman, N. 1972. Television soap operas: what's been going on anyway? *Public Opinion Quarterly* 36.

————. 1973. The impact of communication technology: some theoretical premises and their implications. Unpublished report for the Institute for Communication Research, Stanford University.

Kaufman, H. and M. Couzens. 1973. *Administrative feedback: monitoring subordinates' behavior*. Washington, D.C., Brookings Institute.

Kecskemeti, P. 1950. Totalitarian communication as a means of control. *Public Opinion Quarterly* 14.

Keesing, F. M. and M. M. Keesing. 1956. *Elite communication in Samoa*. Stanford, Calif., Stanford University Press.

Kelber, H. and C. Schlesinger. 1967. *Union printers and controlled automation*. New York, Free Press.

Kelley, H. H. 1958. Salience of membership and resistance to change of group anchored attitudes. *Human Relations* 8.

Kendrick, A. 1969. *Prime time: the life of Edward R. Murrow*. Boston, Little, Brown.

Klapper, J. T. 1960. *The effects of mass communication*. Glencoe, Ill., Free Press.

————. 1963. Mass communication research: an old road resurveyed. *Public Opinion Quarterly* 27.

Kletter, R. and A. Rucker. 1972. Cable television: sample program costs. Unpublished report for the Institute for Communication Research, Stanford University.

Klimek, D. and C. Kubasik. 1970. Press criticism in the Wroclaw dailies. *Zeszyty Prasoznawcze* 11.

Kline, F. G., K. Kent, and D. Davis. 1971. Problems in causal analysis of aggregate data with applications to political instability. In *Macroquantitative analysis*, eds. J. V. Gillespie and B. A. Nesvold. Beverly Hills, Calif., Sage.

Kornhauser, W. 1959. *The politics of mass society*. New York: Free Press.

Kracauer, S. 1949. National types as Hollywood presents them. *Public Opinion Quarterly* 13.

Kreiling, A. L. 1973. The making of racial identities in the Black press. Ph.D. dissertation, University of Illinois.

Kris, E. and H. Speier. 1944. *German radio propaganda*. New York, Oxford University Press.

Krisher, B. 1972. What public TV can be. *Columbia Journalism Review* 11.

Kroeber, A. L. and C. Kluckhohn. 1952. *Culture: a critical review of concepts and definitions*. Cambridge, Mass., Peabody Museum.

Kruglak, R. E. 1955. *The foreign correspondents: a study of the men and women reporting for the American information media in Western Europe*. Geneva, E. Droz.

Kuhn, R. S. 1962. The structure of scientific revolutions. In *International encyclopedia of unified science*. 2nd Ed., enlarged. Chicago, University of Chicago Press.

Lago, A. M. and D. P. Osborne. 1971. *A quantitative analysis of the price effects of joint mass communication media ownership*. Bethesda, Md., Resource Management Corporation (for National Association of Broadcasters).

Lamberton, D. M. 1971. *Economics of information and knowledge*. Harmondsworth, England, Penguin.

Land, H. W. Associates Inc. 1968. *Television and the wired city*. Washington, D.C., National Association of Broadcasters.

Lang, K. and G. E. Lang. 1953. The unique perspective of television and its effect. *American Sociological Review* 18.

———. 1961. *Collective dynamics*. New York, Crowell.

Lange, D., R. Baker, and S. Ball. 1969. *Mass media and violence*. Volume XI of the report to the National Commission on the causes and prevention of violence. Washington, D.C., U.S. Government Printing Office.

Larsen, O. N. 1964. Social effects of mass communication. In *Handbook of modern sociology*, ed. R. E. Faris. Chicago, Rand McNally.

Lasswell, H. D. 1927. *Propaganda technique in the world war*. London, Kegan Paul.

———. 1936. *Politics: who gets what, when, how*. New York, McGraw-Hill.

———, and D. Blumenstock. 1939. *World revolutionary propaganda*. New York, Knopf.

———. 1948. The structure and function of communications in society. In *The communication of ideas*, ed. L. Bryson. New York, Harper.

———, N. Leites, *et al*. 1949. *Language of politics*. New York, George Stewart.

————, and A. Kaplan. 1950. *Power and society*. New Haven, Conn., Yale University Press.

————, and D. Lerner. 1951. *The policy sciences*. Stanford, Calif., Stanford University Press.

Lazarsfeld, P. F. 1940. *Radio and the printed page*. New York, Duell, Sloan and Pearce.

————, and F. N. Stanton (eds.). 1942. *Radio research, 1941*. New York, Duell, Sloan and Pearce.

————, and F. N. Stanton (eds.). 1944. *Radio research, 1942-43*. New York, Duell, Sloan and Pearce.

————, B. Berelson, and H. Gaudet. 1944. *The people's choice*. New York, Duell, Sloan and Pearce.

————, and F. N. Stanton (eds.). 1949. *Communications research, 1948-49*. New York, Harper.

————. 1963. Afterword. In Gary Steiner, *The people look at television*. New York, Knopf.

Leab, D. J. 1970. *A union of individuals: the foundation of the American Newspaper Guild, 1933-36*. New York, Columbia University Press.

Leamer, L. 1972. *The paper revolutionaries: the rise of the underground press*. New York, Simon and Schuster.

Lee, A. M. 1947. *The daily newspaper in America*. New York, Macmillan.

Lemert, J. B. and K. J. Nestvold. 1970. Television news and status conferral. *Journal of Broadcasting* 14.

Lerner, D. 1951. *Propaganda in war and crisis*. New York, George Stewart.

————. 1957. Communication systems and social systems. *Behavioral Science* 2.

————. 1958. *The passing of traditional society*. New York, Free Press.

————. 1963. Toward a communication theory of modernization. In *Communications and political development*, ed., L. W. Pye. Princeton, N.J., Princeton University Press.

————, and W. Schramm (eds.). 1967. *Communication and change in the developing countries*. Honolulu, East-West Center Press.

Levin, H. J. 1960. *Broadcast regulation and joint ownership of media*. New York, New York University Press.

———. 1971. *The policy on joint ownership of newspapers and television stations: some assumptions, objectives and effects*. New York, Center for Policy Research.

Lewis, J. D. 1969-70. Programmer's choice: eight factors in program decision-making. *Journal of Broadcasting* 14.

Lewis, R. 1972. *Outlaws of America: the underground press and its content*. Harmondsworth, England, Penguin.

Lichty, L. W. and J. M. Ripley. 1967. Size and composition of broadcasting stations' staffs. *Journal of Broadcasting* 11.

Lindstrom, C. E. 1960. *The fading American newspaper*. New York, Double-day.

Lippmann, W. 1922. *Public opinion*. New York, Harcourt, Brace.

———.1956. *The public philosophy*. New York, Mentor.

———, and C. Merz. 1920. A test of the news. *The New Republic* (August 4).

Lipset, S. M., M. Trow, and J. Coleman. 1956. *Union democracy*. New York, Free Press.

Littlewood, T. B. 1972. What's wrong with statehouse coverage. *Columbia Journalism Review* 10.

Litwin, G. II. and W. H. Wroth. July, 1969. The effects of common ownership on media content and influence. Washington, D.C., National Association of Broadcasters.

Liu, H. C. 1973. Media use, academic performance, and social-demographic background. Ph.D. dissertation, University of Minnesota.

Locher, J. S. 1970. Changing media and presidential campaigns: 1900, 1928, 1948, 1956. Ph.D. dissertation, University of Pennsylvania.

Lois, G. 1972. *George, be careful*. New York, Saturday Review Press.

Love, R. L. 1969. Television and the death of a president: network decisions covering collective events. Ph.D. dissertation, Columbia University.

Lowe, C. K. 1970. *Image making and integrity: an historical survey and analysis of the priorities and value systems of image makers and image viewers in American society*. Ohio, Ohio State University Press.

Lowenthal, L. 1944. Biographies in popular magazines. In *Radio research, 1942-43*, ed. P. F. Lazarsfeld and F. N. Stanton. New York, Duell, Sloan and Pearce.

Lundberg, D. and O. Hulten. 1968. *Individen och massmedia*. Stockholm, EFI.

Lundberg, F. 1936. *Imperial Hearst, a social biography*. Westport, Conn., Greenwood.

Lyons, E. 1960. *David Sarnoff*. New York, Harper and Row.

Lyons, L. M. 1971. *Newspaper story: one hundred years of the Boston Globe*. Boston, Harvard University Press.

Maccoby, E. E. 1954. Why do children watch TV? *Public Opinion Quarterly* 18.

————, and W. Wilson. 1957. Identification and observational learning from films. *Journal of Abnormal & Social Psychology* 55.

————. 1964. Effects of the mass media. In *Review of child development research*, Vol. I, eds. M. L. Hoffman and L. W. Hoffman. New York, Russell Sage.

MacDonald, D., Jr. 1957. A theory of mass culture. In *Mass culture: the popular arts in America*, eds. B. Rosenberg and D. M. White. Glencoe, Ill., Free Press.

MacDougald, D., Jr. 1942. The popular music industry. In *Radio research, 1941*, eds. P. F. Lazarsfeld and F. N. Stanton. New York, Duell, Sloan and Pearce.

Machlup, F. 1962. *The production and distribution of knowledge in the United States*. Princeton, N.J., Princeton University Press.

MacNeil, R. 1968. *The people machine: the influence of television on American politics*. New York, Harper and Row.

MacRae, D., Jr. 1970. Some political choices in the development of communications technology. In *The information utility and social choice*, eds. H. Sackman and N. Nie. Montvale, N.J., AFIPS Press.

Madden, T. J. 1971. Editor authoritarianism and its effect on news display. *Journalism Quarterly* 48.

Makal, M. 1954. *A village in Anatolia*. London, Vallentine, Mitchell.

Mandelbaum, S. J. 1972. *Community and communications*. New York, Norton.

Marvick, D. 1970. Some potential effects of the information utility on citizen participation. In *The Information utility and social choice*, eds. H. Sackman and N. Nie. Montvale, N.J., AFIPS Press.

Maslow, A. H. 1954. *Motivation and personality*. New York, Harper.

Matson, F. W. and A. Montagu. 1967. *The human dialogue: perspectives on communication*. New York, Free Press.

Mayer, M. 1972. *About television*. New York, Harper and Row.

McCamy, J. L. 1964. *Conduct of the new diplomacy*. New York, Harper and Row.

McCartney, J. 1970-71. Can the media cover guerrilla wars? *Columbia Journalism Review* 9.

————. 1971. What should be secret? *Columbia Journalism Review* 10.

McClelland, D. 1961. *The achieving society*. New York, Van Nostrand.

McCombs, M. E. 1967. Editorial endorsements. *Journalism Quarterly* 44.

————, and D. L. Shaw. 1972. The agenda-setting function of the mass media. *Public Opinion Quarterly* 36.

————. August, 1972. Mass media in the marketplace. *Journalism Monographs*.

McCrone, D. J. and C. F. Cnudde. 1967. Toward a communications theory of democratic political development. *American Political Science Review* 61.

McDaniel, D. O. 1970. Television newsfilm: a study in audience perception. Ph.D. dissertation, Ohio University.

McDougall, W. 1960. *An introduction to social psychology*. New York, Barnes and Noble.

McGinnis, J. 1968. *The selling of the president*. New York, Trident.

McIntyre, R. L. 1971. Managerial roles in public television and academic subjects applicable to role fulfillment. Ph.D. dissertation, Ohio State University.

McLeod, J. M. and G. J. O'Keefe, Jr. 1972. The socialization perspective and communication behaviour. In *Current perspectives in mass communication research*, eds. F. G. Kline and P. J. Tichenor. Beverly Hills, Calif., Sage.

McLuhan, M. 1962. *The Gutenberg galaxy*. Toronto, University of Toronto Press.

_____. 1964. *Understanding media*. New York, McGraw-Hill.

McPhee, W., P. Ennis, and R. Meyersohn. July, 1953. *The disc jockey*. Bureau of Applied Social Research, Columbia University.

McQuail, D. 1969. *Towards a sociology of mass communications*. London, Collier-Macmillan.

_____. 1969. Uncertainty about the audience and the organization of mass communications. *Sociological Review Monograph* 13.

_____, J. G. Blumler, and J. R. Brown. 1972. The television audience: a revised perspective. In *Sociology of mass communication*, ed. D. McQuail. Harmondsworth, England, Penguin.

McWilliams, C. 1970. Is muckraking coming back? *Columbia Journalism Review* 9.

Meier, R. L. 1962. *A communications theory of urban growth*. Cambridge, Mass., MIT Press.

Melody, W. 1973. *Children's TV: the economics of exploitation*. New Haven, Conn., Yale University Press.

Mendelsohn, H. 1964. Listening to radio. In *People, society and mass communications*, eds. L. A. Dexter and D. M. White. Glencoe, Ill., Free Press.

Menzel, H. 1971. Quasi-mass communication: a neglected area. *Public Opinion Quarterly* 35.

Merritt, R. and S. Rokkan (eds.). 1966. *Comparing nations*. New Haven, Conn., Yale University Press.

Merton, R. K. 1946. *Mass persuasion: the social psychology of a war bond drive*. New York, Harper.

_____. 1957. *Social theory and social structure*. Glencoe, Ill., Free Press.

Metzker, I. 1972. *The Bintel brief: sixty years of letters from the lower East Side to the Jewish Daily Forward*. New York, Ballantine.

Miller, J. G. 1956. Living systems: basic concepts. *Behavioral Science* 10.

Miller, M. and R. Evans. 1964. *Only you Dick Daring!* New York, William Sloane.

Mintz, M. and J. S. Cohen. 1971. *America, Inc.: who owns and operates the U.S.* New York, Dial.

Montagu, A. 1967. Communication, evolution, and education. In *The human dialogue: perspectives on communication*, eds. F. W. Matson and A. Montagu. New York, Free Press.

Mott, F. L. 1962. *American journalism: a history of newspapers in the United States through 260 years, 1690-1960*. New York, Macmillan.

Moznette, J. and G. Rarick. 1968. Which are more readable: editorials or news stories? *Journalism Quarterly* 45.

Muecke, M. M. 1967. Ownership forms of regional magazines. *Journalism Quarterly* 44.

Murphy, L. B. 1937. *Social behavior and child personality: an exploratory study of the roots of sympathy*. New York, Columbia University Press.

Murray, G. 1972. *The press and the public: the story of the British Press Council*. Carbondale, Ill., Southern Illinois University Press.

National Commission on the Causes and Prevention of Violence. 1969. Violence and the media. *Report of the National Commission. . . .*

Nesvold, B. A. 1971. Scalogram analysis of political violence. In *Macroquantitative analysis*, eds. J. V. Gillespie and B. A. Nesvold. Beverly Hills, Calif., Sage.

Neurath, O. n.d. *International picture language*. Psyche Miniatures, General Series No. 83.

Nie, N. H. 1970. Future developments in mass communication and citizen participation. In *The information utility and social choice*, eds. H. Sackman and N. Nie. Montvale, N.J., AFIPS Press.

Nilsson, S. 1971. Publikens upplevelse av TV-program. Stockholm, Sveriges Radio (duplicated paper).

Nimmo, D. C. 1964. *Newsgathering in Washington*. New York, Atherton.

Nixon, R. B. 1968. Trends in U.S. newspaper ownership: concentration with competition. *Gazette* 14.

————, and H. Tae-youl. 1971. Concentration of press ownership: a comparison of 32 countries. *Journalism Quarterly* 48.

Nordenstreng, K. 1970. Comments on "gratifications research" in broadcasting. *Public Opinion Quarterly* 34.

Northcott, B. February 16, 1973. Rite and ring. *New Statesman*.

Ogilvy, D. 1963. *Confessions of an advertising man*. New York, Atheneum.

O'Loughlin, E. T. 1970. *Hearst and his enemies*. New York, Arno.

Olson, M., Jr. 1965. *The logic of collective action*. Cambridge, Mass., Harvard University Press.

Orwell, G. 1949. *Nineteen eighty-four*. New York, Harcourt, Brace.

Paletz, D. L. and R. Dunn. 1969. Press coverage of civil disorders. *Public Opinion Quarterly* 33.

Park, R. E. 1922. *The immigrant press and its control*. New York, Harper.

————. 1925. The natural history of the newspaper. In *The city*, eds. R. E. Park and E. W. Burgess. Chicago, University of Chicago Press.

Parker, E. B. and W. J. Paisley. 1966. Research for psychologists at the interface of the scientist and his information system. *American Psychologist* 21.

————. 1970a. Behavioral research in the development of a computer-based information system. In *Communication among scientists and engineers*, ed. C. E. Nelson and D. K. Pollock. Boston, D. C. Heath.

————. 1970b. Information utilities and mass communication. In *The information utility and social choice*, eds. H. Sackman and N. Nie. Montvale, N.J. AFIPS Press.

————, and D. A. Dunn. 1972. Information technology: its social potential. *Science* 176.

————. 1973a. Information and society. In *Annual review of information science and technology*, ed. C. A. Cuadra. Washington, D.C., American Society for Information Science.

————. 1973b. Information and society. *Report to the National Commission on Libraries and Information Science*. Bethesda, Md., ERIC Reproduction Service.

————. 1973c. Technological change and the mass media. In *Handbook of communication*, eds. I. de S. Pool, W. Schramm, *et al.* Chicago, Rand McNally.

————. 1973d. Technology assessment or institutional change? In *Communications technology and social policy*, eds. G. Gerbner, L. P. Gross and W. H. Melody. New York, Wiley.

Parsons, T. and R. F. Bales. 1955. *Family socialization and interaction process.* New York, Free Press.

Pearce, A. 1968. NBC news division: a study of the costs, the revenues, and the benefits of broadcast news. Ph.D. dissertation, Indiana University.

The people's comic book. 1973. Garden City, N.Y., Anchor.

Peters, C. and T. Branch (eds.). 1972. *Blowing the whistle.* New York, Praeger.

Pierce, R. N. 1969. Public opinion and press opinion in four Latin American cities. *Journalism Quarterly* 46.

Pietila, A. 1971. Swedish editor's views on government support of the press. *Journalism Quarterly* 48.

Pietila, V. 1969. Immediate versus delayed reward in newspaper reading. *Acta Sociologica* 12.

Pool, I. de S. 1963. The mass media and politics in the modernization process. In *Communications and political development*, ed. L. W. Pye. Princeton, N.J., Princeton University Press.

———. 1972. Newsmen and statesmen. Paper prepared for the Workshop on Government and the media of the Aspen Program on Communications and Society, Aspen, Colorado.

Posner, R. A. 1972. The appropriate scope of regulation in the cable television industry. *Bell Journal of Economics and Management Science* 3.

Powdermaker, H. 1950. *Hollywood: the dream factory.* Boston, Little, Brown.

———. 1962. *Copper town: changing Africa.* New York, Harper and Row.

Powers, R. and J. Oppenheim. 1972. Is TV too profitable? *Columbia Journalism Review* 11.

Price, J. L. 1968. *Organizational effectiveness.* Homewood, Ill., R. D. Irwin.

Rarick, G. and B. Hartman. 1966. The effects of competition on one daily newspaper's content. *Journalism Quarterly* 43.

Raskin, A. H. 1963. The New York newspaper strikes. *Columbia Journalism Review* 2.

———. May 8, 1965a. The great Manhattan newspaper duel. *Saturday Review.*

———. October 11, 1965b. The newspaper problem: major labor issues in industry still unresolved. *New York Times.*

Reeves, R. 1972. Newark's fallen giant: euthanasia or murder. *Columbia Journalism Review* 11.

Report from Washington. Washington, D.C., Common Cause.

Rhea, J. W. 1970. An investigation of relationships among specified variables in the management of television stations. Ph.D. dissertation, Ohio University.

Riesman, D., N. Glazer, and R. Denney. 1950. *The lonely crowd*. New Haven, Conn., Yale University Press.

Riley, J. W., Jr. and M. W. Riley. 1959. Mass communication and the social system. In *Sociology today*, eds. R. K. Merton, L. Broom, and L. S. Cottrell, Jr. New York, Basic Books.

Riley, M. W. and J. W. Riley, Jr. 1951. A sociological approach to communication research. *Public Opinion Quarterly* 15.

Rivers, W. L. 1965. *The opinionmakers*. Boston, Beacon.

————, and W. Schramm. 1969. *Responsibility in mass communication*. Rev. Ed. New York, Harper and Row.

————. 1970. *The Adversaries*. Boston, Beacon.

————, W. Blankenburg, K. Starch, E. Reeves. 1972. *Back talk: press councils in America*. New York, Canfield.

Roberts, D. F. 1973. Communication and children: a developmental approach. In *Handbook of Communication*, eds. I. de S. Pool, W. Schramm, *et al.* Chicago, Rand McNally.

Robinson, G. J. 1968. TANJUG: Yugoslavia's multi-faceted national news agency. Ph.D. dissertation, University of Illinois.

Robinson, J. P. 1972a. Toward defining the functions of television. In *Television and social behavior*, Vol. 4, *Television in day-to-day life*, eds. E. A. Rubinstein, G. A. Comstock, and J. P. Murray. Rockville, Md., National Institute of Mental Health.

————. 1972b. Mass communication and information diffusion. In F. G. Kline and P. J. Tichenor, eds., *Current perspectives in mass communication research*. Beverly Hills, Calif., Sage.

Robinson, M. J. 1972. Public affairs television and the growth of political malaise. Ph.D. dissertation, Ohio State University.

Rogers, E. M. 1972. *The communication of innovations*. New York, Free Press.

Rogers, R. 1970. Education and political involvement in USSR elite newspaper reading. *Journalism Quarterly* 47.

Rosario, F. Z. 1973. A researcher's guide to social-psychological-communication variables in family planning research. *Papers of the East-West Communication Institute*, Honolulu.

Rose, E. D. and D. Fuchs. 1968. Reagan vs. Brown. *Journal of Broadcasting* 12.

Rosengren, K. E. 1974. Uses and gratifications: a paradigm outlined. In *Audience gratifications and mass media functions*, eds., E. Katz and J. G. Blumler. Beverly Hills, Calif., Sage.·

————, and S. Windahl. 1972. Mass media consumption as a functional alternative. In *Sociology of mass communication*, ed. D. McQuail. Harmondsworth, England, Penguin.

Roshwalb, I. and L. Resnicoff. 1971. The impact of endorsements and published polls on the 1970 New York senatorial election. *Public Opinion Quarterly* 35.

Rosse, J. N., B. M. Owen, and D. L. Grey. 1970. Economic issues in the joint ownership of newspaper and television media. Comments in Docket no. 18110, FCC Hearings, Washington, D.C.

Rosten, L. C. 1937. *The Washington correspondents*. New York, Harcourt, Brace.

————. 1941. *Hollywood: the movie colony, the movie makers*. New York, Harcourt, Brace.

Rubin, D. M. 1972. Reporting the corporate state. Ph.D. dissertation, Stanford University.

Rucker, B. 1968. *The first freedom*. Carbondale, Ill., Southern Illinois University Press.

Russell, B. 1951. *Autobiography, 1872-1914*. Vol. I. Boston, Little, Brown.

Sachsman, D. B. 1973. Public relations influence on environmental coverage. Ph.D. dissertation, Stanford University.

Sackman, H. and N. Nie (eds.). 1970. *The information utility and social choice*. Montvale, N.J., AFIPS Press.

————, and B. W. Boehm (eds.). 1972. *Planning community information utilities*. Montvale, N.J., AFIPS Press.

Sagasti, H. E. de. 1972. Social implications of adult literacy. Ph.D. dissertation, University of Pennsylvania.

Samstag, N. 1966. *How business is bamboozled by the ad boys*. New York, Heineman.

Sapir, E. 1930. Communication. In *Encyclopedia of the social sciences* 4., eds. R. A. Seligman and A. Johnson. New York, Macmillan.

Scheler, M. 1972. *Ressentiment*. New York, Schocken Books.

Schneider, M. 1973. Information resources and personal communication. *USIA Communicator* 1.

Schramm, W. (ed.). 1948. *Mass communication*. Urbana, Ill., University of Illinois Press.

————. 1949. The nature of news. *Journalism Quarterly* 26.

————, J. Lyle, and E. B. Parker. 1961. *Television in the lives of our children*. Stanford, Calif., Stanford University Press.

————. 1963. Role of communication in the nation-state. In *Communications and political development*, ed. L. W. Pye. Princeton, N.J., Princeton University Press.

Seldes, G. 1938. *Lords of the press*. New York, Messner.

Shafer, B. and R. Larson. 1972. Did TV create the "social issue"? *Columbia Journalism Review* 11.

Sheatsley, P. B. and J. J. Feldman. 1965. A national survey of public reactions and behavior. In *The Kennedy assassination and the American public*, eds. B. S. Greenberg and E. B. Parker. Stanford, Calif., Stanford University Press.

Sherkovin, Y. A. 1969. Some socio-psychological problems of propaganda influence. *Voprosy Psikhologii* 4.

Shils, E. A. and M. Janowitz. 1948. Cohesion and disintegration in the Wehrmacht in World War II. *Public Opinion Quarterly* 12.

Shinar, D. 1972. Structure and content of television broadcasting in Israel. In *Television and social behavior*, Volume I: *Media content and control*, eds. G. A. Comstock and E. A. Rubinstein. Rockville, Md., National Institute of Mental Health.

Siebert, F. S., T. Peterson, and W. Schramm. 1956. *Four theories of the press*. Urbana, Ill., University of Illinois Press.

Siegel, R. S. 1965. Television and the reactions of school children to the assassination. In *The Kennedy assassination and the American public*, eds. B. S. Greenberg and E. B. Parker. Stanford, Calif., Stanford University Press.

Siegelman, L. 1973. Reporting the news: an organizational analysis. *American Journal of Sociology* 79.

Simon, H. A. 1955. The effect of television upon voting behavior in Iowa. *American Political Science Review* 49.

——. 1965. *Administrative behavior*. New York, Free Press.

Sinclair, U. 1919. *The brass check*. Pasadena, Calif. The Author.

Sloan Commission. 1971. *On the cable; the television of abundance*. New York, McGraw-Hill.

Smelser, N. J. 1962. *Theory of collective behavior*. New York, Free Press.

Smith, A. 1969. *The theory of moral sentiments*. New Rochelle, N.Y., Arlington House.

Smith, A. L., Jr. 1972. Life in wartime Germany. *Public Opinion Quarterly* 36.

Smith, W. A. 1972. A description of the organization production process, and production environment of a dramatic television series. Ph.D. dissertation, University of Southern California.

Snider, P. B. 1967. Mr. Gates' revisited: a 1966 version of the 1949 case. *Journalism Quarterly* 44.

Snow, P. G. 1971. A scalogram analysis of political development. In *Macro-quantitative analysis*, eds. J. V. Gillespie and B. A. Nesvold. Beverly Hills, Calif., Sage.

Special Canadian Senate Committee. 1971. Canada's media report. *Columbia Journalism Review* 10.

Speier, H. 1951. Psychological warfare reconsidered. In *The policy sciences*, eds. H. D. Lasswell and D. Lerner. Stanford, Calif., Stanford University Press.

——. 1957. *German rearmament and atomic war*. Evanston, Ill., Row, Peterson.

Spence, M. 1972. Market signalling: the informational structure of job markets and related phenomena. Discussion paper no. 4, Public Policy Program, February 1972, at John F. Kennedy School of Government, Harvard University, Cambridge, Mass.

Stamm, K. R. 1972. Environment and communication. In *Current perspectives in mass communication research*, eds., F. G. Kline and P. J. Tichenor. Beverly Hills, Calif., Sage.

Stein, A. H. and L. K. Friedrich. 1972. Television content and young children's behavior. In *Television and social behavior*, Vol. II, *Television and social learning*, eds. J. P. Murray, G. A. Comstock and E. A. Rubinstein. Rockville, Md., National Institute of Mental Health.

Stephenson, W. 1967. *The play theory of mass communications*. Chicago, University of Chicago Press.

Sterling, C. H. 1969. Newspaper ownership of broadcast stations, 1920-1968. *Journalism Quarterly* 46.

Stern, J. D. 1962. *Memoirs of a maverick publisher*. New York, Simon and Schuster.

Stern, M. P. 1969. Palmer Hoyt and the Denver Post: a field study of organizational change in the mass media of communication. Ph.D. dissertation, University of Dever.

Stillman, D. 1970-71. Tonkin. *Columbia Journlaism Review* 9.

Stone, G. C. January 22, 1972. Research on going daily. *Editor and Publisher* 105.

Strasser, J. 1971. Cable TV: stringing us along. *Pacific Research and World Empire Telegram*. Palo Alto, Calif., Pacific Study Center.

Strauss, A. 1956. *The social psychology of George Herbert Mead*. Chicago, University of Chicago Press.

Suchman, E. 1942. An invitation to music. In *Radio Research, 1941.*, eds. P. F. Lazarsfeld and F. N. Stanton. New York, Duell, Sloan and Pearce.

Surgeon General's Scientific Advisory Committee on Television and Social Behavior. 1972. *Television and growing up: the impact of televised violence*. Washington, D.C., Government Printing Office.

Swanberg, W. A. 1961. *Citizen Hearst*. New York, Scribner.

————. 1972. *Henry Luce*. New York, Scribner.

Swanson, W. A. 1964. *The thin gold watch*. New York, Macmillan.

Swayne, E. E. 1969. The last families: a study of metropolitan newspaper ownership, 1950-1967. Ph.D. dissertation, Northwestern University.

Szalai, A., *et al.* 1972. *The United Nations and the news media*. New York, UNITAR.

Talese, G. 1969. *The kingdom and the power*. New York, World.

Tannenbaum, P. H. 1963. Communication of science information. *Science* 140.

Tanter, R. 1967. Toward a theory of political development. *Midwest Journal of Political science* 11.

Television today: the end of communication and the death of community. 1969. Washington, D.C., Institute for Policy Studies.

Thoeny, A. R. 1968. Press treatment of crisis and noncrisis international politics. Ph.D. dissertation, University of Wisconsin.

Tichenor, P. J., G. A. Donohue and C. N. Olien. 1970. Mass media flow and differential growth in knowledge. *Public Opinion Quarterly* 34.

Tocqueville, A. de. 1956. *Democracy in America*, ed. R. D. Heffner. New York, New American Library.

Toogood, A. F. 1969. Canadian broadcasting. Ph.D. dissertation, Ohio State University.

Tooley, R. V. 1949. *Maps and map makers*. London, B. T. Batsford.

————, and C. Bricker. 1958. *Landmarks of mapmaking, an illustrated survey of maps and mapmakers*. Brussels, Amsterdam Elsevier.

Torsvik, P. 1967. The 1965 election campaign in TV and radio. *Tidskrift for Samfunnsforskning* 8.

Tuchman, G. 1969. News, the newsman's reality. Ph.D. dissertation, Brandeis University.

————. 1973. Making news by doing work: routinizing the unexpected. *American Journal of Sociology* 79.

Tuchman, S. and T. E. Coffin. 1971. The influence of election night broadcasts on television in a close election. *Public Opinion Quarterly* 35.

Tunstall, J. 1964. *The Westminster lobby correspondents*. London, Chapman and Hall.

————. 1971. *Journalists at work*. London, Constable.

UNESCO. 1969. Mass communication and society. Paris.

————. 1970. Mass media in society: the need of research. Reports and papers on mass communication, #59. Paris.

————. 1971. Proposals for an international programme of communication research. Paris.

————. 1972. Report of the meeting of experts on communication policies and planning. Paris.

Ungar, S. J. 1972. *The papers and the papers, an account of the legal and political battle over the Pentagon Papers*. New York, Dutton.

Urwin, K. April 25, 1973. Blessed are the television poor. *The Guardian*.

U.S. Congress. 1972. *Report of the Subcommittee on Priorities and Economy in Government of the Joint Economic Committee Congress of the United States*. American productivity: key to economic strength and national survival. Washington, D.C., Government Printing Office.

Van Horn, G. A. 1966. Analysis of AP news on trunk and Wisconsin state wires. *Journalism Quarterly* 29.

Veblen, E. P. 1969. Newspaper impact in election campaigns: the case of two New England states. Ph.D. dissertation, Yale University.

Vincent, C. S. 1951. Trends in infant care ideas. *Child Development* 22.

Voos, H. 1967. Organizational communication; a bibliography. New Brunswick, N.J., Rutgers University Press.

Wade, D. Feb. 17, 1973. *The Times*. London.

Wade, S. and W. Schramm. 1969. The mass media as sources of public affairs, science, and health knowledge. *Public Opinion Quarterly* 33.

Waples, D., B. Berelson, and F. R. Bradshaw. 1940. *What reading does to people*. Chicago, University of Chicago Press.

Warner, M. 1969a. Decision-making in American TV political news. *Sociological Review Monograph* 13.

————. 1969b. American television's power elite. *New Society* 13.

————. 1971. Organizational context and control of policy in the television newsroom: a participant observation study. *British Journal of Sociology* 22.

Warner, W. L. and W. E. Henry. 1948. The radio daytime serial: a symbolic analysis. *Genetic Psychology Monograph* 37.

Wassermann, J. 1924. *Caspar Hauser oder die Trägheit des Herzens*. Berlin, Germany, Fischer Verlag.

Weaver, P. 1968. The metropolitan newspaper as a political institution. Ph.D. dissertation, Harvard University.

Wedell, E. G. 1969. The objectives of the controllers. *Sociological Review Monograph* 13.

Weiss, W. 1969. Effects of the mass media of communication. In *The handbook of social psychology*, Vol. 5, eds. G. Lindzey and E. Aronson. Reading, Mass., Addison Wesley.

————. 1971. Mass communication. *Annual Review of Psychology* 22.

Westley, B. H. and M. S. MacLean, Jr. 1957. A conceptual model for communications research. *Journalism Quarterly* 34.

White, D. M. 1964. "The Gatekeeper." In *People, society, and mass communication*, eds. L. A. Dexter and D. M. White. New York, Free Press.

White, T. H. 1961. *The view from the 40th floor*. New York, New American Library.

Wicker, T. 1971. The greening of the press. *Columbia Journalism Review* 10.

Wiebe, G. 1969. Two psychological factors in mass audience behavior. *Public Opinion Quarterly* 33.

Wilde, W. A. 1969. Official news: decision-making in a metropolitan newspaper. Ph.D. dissertation, Northwestern University.

Wilensky, H. C. 1967. *Organizational intelligence*. New York, Basic Books.

Wilhoit, G. C. and K. S. Sherrill. 1968. Wire service visibility of U.S. senators. *Journalism Quarterly* 45.

Wilhoit, G. C. 1969. Political symbol shifts in crisis news. *Midwest Journal of Political Science* 13.

Wilkins, C. K. 1971. Attitudes and predictive ability of managers of AM radio stations in small, single-station markets. Ph.D. dissertation, University of Utah.

Will, G. F. (ed.) 1972. *Press, politics and popular government*. Washington, D.C., American Enterprise Institute.

Lord Windlesham. 1969. Television: some problems of creativity and control. *Sociological Review Monagraph* 13.

Winick, C. 1961. Censor and sensibility: a content analysis of the television censor's comments. *Journal of Broadcasting* 5.

Wise, K. L. 1967. The war news system. Ph.D. dissertation, American University.

Wise, T. A. 1968. Coup d'état at Interpublic: Marion Harper, Jr. *Fortune Magazine* 77.

Witcover, J. 1970-71. Where Washington reporting failed. *Columbia Journalism Review* 9.

―――――. 1972a. Washington's uncovered power centers. *Columbia Journalism Review* 10.

―――――. 1972b. William Loeb and the New Hampshire primary. *Columbia Journalism Review* 11.

Wolf, F. 1971. Some determinants of public affairs programming on commercial television in the United States. Ph.D. dissertation, Columbia University.

Wolfe, B. N., Jr. 1970. Communication habits as predictors of commercial success among United States farm broadcasters. Ph.D. dissertation, Michigan State University.

Wolfe, K. M. and M. Fiske. 1949. Why children read comics. In *Communication research, 1948-49*, eds. P. F. Lazarsfeld and F. N. Stanton. New York, Harper.

Woods, J. H. 1962. The employee publication. In *Public Relations Handbook* (2nd ed.), ed. Philip Lesly. Englewood Cliffs, N.J., Prentice-Hall.

Wright, C. 1959. *Mass communication: a sociological perspective*. New York, Random House.

―――――. 1960. Functional analysis and mass communication. *Public Opinion Quarterly* 24.

Yu, F. T. C. 1964. *Mass persuasion in Communist China*. New York, Praeger.

―――――, and J. Luter. 1964. The foreign correspondent and his work. *Columbia Journalism Review* 3.

Zierold, N. J. 1969. *The moguls*. New York, Coward-McCann.

Zigler, E., and I. L. Child. 1969. Socialization. In *Handbook of Social Psychology*, Vol. III, eds. G. Lindzey and E. Aronson. Reading, Mass., Addison-Wesley.

ABOUT THE EDITORS AND CONTRIBUTORS

W. PHILLIPS DAVISON has been Professor of Journalism and Sociology at Columbia University since 1965, and for eight years was Editor of the *Public Opinion Quarterly*. He is a trustee of the Institute for International Social Research and Chairman of the Board of Trustees of the Bureau of Social Science Research, both of Washington, D.C.

Among his publications on public opinion and mass communication, are *International Political Communication* (Praeger, 1965) and *Mass Communication and Conflict Resolution* (Praeger, 1974).

Professor Davison previously taught at Princeton University, American University, and the Massachusetts Institute of Technology, and has been a member of the research staff of the Rand Corporation and the Council on Foreign Relations.

FREDERICK T. C. YU is a professor at the Graduate School of Journalism of Columbia University and was associate dean of the school from 1970 to 1973. He has taught at the University of Iowa, University of Southern California, University of Montana, and the Chinese University of Hong Kong. He has also been on the editorial staff of the Springfield (Ohio) *News-Sun* and the *Washington Post*.

Professor Yu is the author of *Mass Persuasion in Communist China* and editor of *Behavioral Sciences and the Mass Media*.

He did his undergraduate work at the University of Nanking in China, received his M.A. and Ph.D. from the University of Iowa, and was a Ford Foundation postdoctoral fellow at the M.I.T. Center for International Studies.

BEN H. BAGDIKIAN is National Correspondent of the *Columbia Journalism Review*, and former Assistant Managing Editor of the *Washington Post*.

JAY G. BLUMLER is Reader in Mass Communication and Director of the Centre for Television Research, University of Leeds.

DAVIS B. BOBROW is Professor of Political Science and Director of the Quigley Center of International Studies, University of Minnesota.

LEO BOGART is Executive Vice President and General Manager of the Newspaper Advertising Bureau of the American Newspaper Publishers Association.

FORREST CHISMAN is the Executive Assistant, The John and Mary R. Markle Foundation.

MICHAEL GUREVITCH is Senior Research Fellow, Centre for Television Research, University of Leeds, and Associate Director (on leave) of the Communications Institute, Hebrew University of Jerusalem.

HERBERT H. HYMAN is Professor of Sociology at Wesleyan University.

ELIHU KATZ is Professor of Sociology and Director of the Communications Institute, Hebrew University of Jerusalem.

DANIEL LERNER is Ford Professor of Sociology and International Communication at the Massachusetts Institute of Technology.

EDWIN B. PARKER is Professor of Communication at Stanford University.

ADMINISTRATION OF THE FREEDOM OF INFORMATION ACT:
An Evaluation of Government Information Programs
Under the Act, 1967-72
House Subcommittee on Foreign
Operations and Government Information
foreword by Representative William S. Moorhead

ASPEN NOTEBOOK ON GOVERNMENT AND THE MEDIA
Sponsored by the Aspen Program
on Communications and Society
edited by William L. Rivers
and Michael J. Nyhan

MASS COMMUNICATION AND CONFLICT RESOLUTION:
The Role of the Information Media in the Advancement of
International Understanding
W. Phillips Davison

SURVEILLANCE AND ESPIONAGE IN A FREE SOCIETY:
A Report by the Planning Group on Intelligence and
Security to the Policy Council of the Democratic
National Committee
edited by Richard H. Blum
foreword by Senator Adlai Stevenson III

THE USES OF COMMUNICATION IN DECISION-MAKING:
A Comparative Study of Yugoslavia and the United States
Alex S. Edelstein